SPEECH COMMUNICATION: An Interpersonal Approach

under the advisory editorship of J. Jeffery Auer

HARPER & ROW, PUBLISHERS / NEW YORK EVANSTON SAN FRANCISCO LONDON

ERNEST G. BORMANN
University of Minnesota

NANCY C. BORMANN
Normandale State Junior College

speech
communication
AN INTERPERSONAL APPROACH

contents

preface

The first course in speech communication has been undergoing an important change which reflects a growing student demand for pertinent information as well as skills related to life experiences. A decade ago, most courses emphasized public speaking or the fundamentals of speech. Today the trend is toward an interpersonal approach to speech communication in the first course. This new approach emphasizes the study and practice of the less formal and more common communication patterns that characterize contemporary society. The interpersonal approach is also based upon the results of behavioral research in communication. The objective of a good course in interpersonal communication is to provide an educational experience that will be of lifelong daily use to the student.

Many excellent books on interpersonal communication reflect a growing interest in the new approach. Most of them, however, are written at a level of complexity and in a style more suitable for upper-division and graduate students than for freshmen and sophomores—or so our beginning students found. We wrote *Speech Communication: An Interpersonal Approach* to meet the current need for a brief, clear, readable book for the beginning student of speech communication. We have kept in mind that, for many students, the first course will be the only college-level course they will take in the vital area of speech communication, and we have worked to keep the level of presentation practical.

In our approach to interpersonal communication we have incorporated theories and research results from many different disciplines as the core of the book. In these pages the reader will find information from nonverbal communication research, psycholinguistics, small group communication, persuasion and attitude studies, and humanistic psychology. We have not, however, ignored the still-useful tradition that comes from the study of rhetoric and public speaking in regard to such matters as the use of evidence, the organization of messages, and the delivery of public speeches.

Speech Communication: An Interpersonal Approach is organized as a teaching aid to help structure a student's learning experiences. Theoretical material is alternated logically with practical application, since teachers often organize a course that emphasizes learning by doing. The practical applications also appear in a logical progression. We deal first with two-person communication, then with small groups, and finally with speaking to larger audiences on formal occasions.

The book begins with an overview of modern communication theory, including a basic model of the process and a consideration of the nature of verbal and nonverbal communication. A unique feature of this general communication theory is the detailed treatment of the nature of dialects and the social effects of minority- and ethnic- group uses of language from a psycholinguistic perspective. The basic theory is then applied to two-person communication with special emphasis upon trust, protective and defensive communication, and self-disclosure. A chapter on informative speaking and three chapters on persuasion, which present a thorough and complete analysis of these topics from the perspective of the latest research developments, precede two chapters which apply this theory to small-group communication. Two theoretical chapters follow—on listening and audience analysis—and the final application deals with public-speaking occasions as special communication events common to our culture. A unique consideration of the multimedia presentation as a new communication form is included in the last chapter.

The teachers working with us in our effort to tailor this book to the needs of the first course have been instructors in urban community colleges with a great diversity of ethnic- and minority-group enrollments on the one hand, and in private religious colleges with homogeneous student populations on the other. They teach in schools all over the country. We have put the emphasis of this book where we found their needs overlapping. Above all, they advised us to stress solid information that the student can use throughout life. Cut the jargon. Keep it practical. Write a book the student will be able to read and understand. We have tried to follow this advice.

ERNEST G. BORMANN
NANCY C. BORMANN

acknowledgments

For their assistance in the preparation of *Speech Communication: An Interpersonal Approach,* we want to thank most particularly our colleagues at the University of Minnesota, Minneapolis, and at Normandale State Junior College in Bloomington, Minnesota. The teaching associates in the first course at the University of Minnesota were most helpful. Special thanks go to Mrs. Linda Putnam of Normandale, who read and criticized several drafts of the manuscript most helpfully. We are also grateful to Dr. Hazel Heiman of the University of North Dakota, and to John Breitlow of St. Teresa's College in Winona, Minnesota, both of whom read portions of the manuscript. These teachers have each directed large programs of first-course instruction, and they gave us the benefit of their experience and suggestions.

Professor J. Jeffery Auer, Indiana University, under whose auspices this book was written, gave us his fine editorial help throughout, and we thank him especially.

SPEECH COMMUNICATION: An Interpersonal Approach

1 the role of communication in the modern world

THE GROWING IMPORTANCE OF THE SPOKEN WORD

Prior to the invention of the printing press, man lived in a largely speech-oriented world. Only a few could read or write. Speech communication helped get most of the work of the world done. Religious observances were spoken or sung. Culture was oral. With the invention of the printing press and increasing literacy in Western Europe and North America, written messages became much more important. Marshall McLuhan has argued with considerable wit that printing after Gutenberg became one of the most important shaping forces in society. The alphabet, reading, writing, and the print media, according to McLuhan, taught people to break things into parts, to specialize in narrow ways, and to be detached from the stuff of experience.

Since World War II, however, the technology that emphasizes the spoken word has grown with great rapidity. The invention of the telephone and the radio had led the way; after the war, the development and acceptance of television, communication satellites, and worldwide electronic communication followed in rapid succession. Written records are time-consuming to prepare, to retrieve, and to store. We found ourselves, after the war, almost buried under a blizzard of paper memos, forms, reports, abstracts, prospectuses, and letters. The reaction soon set in, encouraged by the development of ways to talk together across distances, such as the efficient telephone systems that allow conference calls among several people in different cities so that business meetings can be held immediately, without the difficulties of letter writing. Many observers, McLuhan being perhaps the most popular, found the growing importance of speech communication profoundly significant.

Television, information-retrieval systems, and all the technology of spoken communication create a new way of thinking and give us new perceptions of the entire world. Events around the globe pour in upon everyone's living room. A natural disaster in Pakistan is as close as a tornado in a neighboring state. The typical American is washed in oral messages for several hours every day. We live in the age of information, which is to say, we live in an age of communication in which the basic quality of life and of consciousness is largely a function of communication skills. A brilliant atomic physicist from Chile who lived for a year in the United States while studying at Oak Ridge, Tennessee, once remarked that because of his lack of skill in speaking English, he had lived an intellectually poor life during his stay here. In Chile he led a life of rich cultural complexity; he experienced and discussed classical music, the fine arts, politics, philosophy, and religion. In the United States, his limited language ability caused him to lead an inner life largely confined to the "give-me-a-cup-of-coffee" level of existence. What he could not talk about, he could not fully experience.

We live in an age in which we sometimes get messages from someone standing in front of us giving a speech, but we also get messages while being hammered by rock music while we watch light shows and look at images projected on a screen. Perhaps most effective of all modern persuasion devices is the television commercial—using music, slogans, dance, drama, still pictures, moving pictures, animated cartoons, poetry, and argument—all orchestrated into a tight, smooth sales pitch, crammed into 60 seconds or less.

The communication events of today are frequently aimed at mass audiences; messages are brief and polished, and usually have to compete for our attention with hundreds of other messages. This fight for attention leads communicators to use every avenue of the senses to reach us, hold our attention, and persuade us to buy a particular car, adopt a new hemline, or vote for a certain candidate.

Much occurs, however, on the motion picture screen, on the television set, and over the radio waves, that is unintentional; yet we take it in even as we pay attention to other things. Are the long-haired characters the good guys or the bad guys? Are the hippies the heroes or the villains? Are the drug users we see in the movies or on TV cool and admirable or sad and bewildered? Do you gradually get the impression that the mayor is a fool as you watch him answer reporters on a news show? Do you begin to wonder if marines are great guys or if the cops are the good guys? Much of what we believe and much of how we act derives from those sometimes unintended impressions gained from radio, television, and film—impressions which are reinforced when we talk with our family and friends.

Talking and listening are among the most important things we do; yet we do them so easily and naturally, for the most part, that we often think there is nothing difficult about communicating effectively. Actually, sometimes the hardest thing we have to do is to talk to someone or to a group of people. Usually those moments when we cannot talk easily are the very times we want most to talk smoothly, clearly, interestingly, and convincingly. Why do we feel tense or excited when we try to communicate with some people? Tension comes when much is at stake, when we feel failure will be unpleasant, perhaps even punishing, to us and success will be pleasant and rewarding. The body alerts itself for verbal battle or for flight.

A good way to understand how vital speech communication is to you personally is to sit down for a few minutes and recall your own feelings over the last couple of days. Did you get churned up in an argument with a friend, with a date, with your wife or husband? Did you feel nervous and excited in a class because you wanted to say something but were afraid of what others would think of you? Were you ill at ease at a party where you did not know anybody? Did you turn your face away and avoid having to talk to somebody because you felt that particular conversation might be uncomfortable?

Before we get any further into the ways we are all involved in communication, you should realize two things: If you are shy and find it difficult to talk to people, you are not necessarily a poor communicator; if you talk easily with anybody and everybody, you are not necessarily a good communicator. The shy person can be compassionate and understanding and convey more with a quiet, "Yes, I understand," than the person who talks on and on. Both extremes of people need to work toward the goal of give-and-take communication.

THE SOCIAL IMPORTANCE OF COMMUNICATION

Man is a social animal. Loneliness is punishing and friendships are rewarding. We all have to get along with people every day. If we live in a family, we have to get along with parents, brothers, sisters, other relatives, and most importantly, when married, with husbands and wives and children.

Most young men and women are anxious to be able to talk easily and well with other young people, to make friends, enjoy dates, and come to know prospective mates. With so much evidence around us that communication problems cause unhappiness, even divorce, most of us are eager to do a better job of communicating than, perhaps, our parents or grandparents. If you were fortunate enough to grow up in an atmosphere of free and open and supportive communication, you will have less trouble talking with others than someone who was raised in a family that did not discuss family problems, family skeletons, or socially or politically sensitive matters. Unfortunately, much that passes for communication within the family is repetitive chatter that covers up thoughts and feelings rather than shares them.

Most of us are drawn to people outside the family, particularly to others in our peer group, people our own general age and stage in life, those with similar interests, people with whom we feel we have a lot in common. Sometimes, though, we find ourselves drawn to people who are quite different from us, people who strike us as being unusual, novel, and exciting, perhaps largely because they do differ from us. Communicating with people who are quite different from us poses additional problems of insight and understanding and requires a higher level of communicating ability.

Much of the misunderstanding that plagues us in our social relationships, both with those who are close to us and who are much like us and with those who are quite different from us, comes from bad habits of communication. If we look at our communication habits honestly and objectively and make conscious, supervised efforts to improve ourselves, we can form better habits.

THE ECONOMIC IMPORTANCE OF COMMUNICATION

Most college students have already come in contact with the communication difficulties and special needs every person finds when he moves outside the home and school and into the world of work. Suddenly you present yourself as a person and as a commodity at the same time; you are a particular person, but you are trying to sell your skills to somebody who needs those skills. You have, in other words, your first job interview.

Face to face with a prospective employer, we all become acutely aware of the importance of basic communication skills in getting and holding a job. But while the job interview may be a particularly graphic example of the importance of communication in business, industry, government, education, and the professions, every work situation demands a wide variety of speaking abilities.

Every job in today's complex urban culture brings us in contact with other people. Often we must cooperate with others as part of a team working to reach some objective. We have to get along comfortably with other people as we work together. We often must be able to explain things to others so they can carry out their part of a job or join with us if the job requires coordinated efforts.

People in management positions discover that most of what they do in their jobs is communication. After all, a supervisor seldom moves a subordinate around physically. Management requires the ability to organize, coordinate, delegate duties and responsibilities, and integrate the efforts of the group. A manager must also gain the willing cooperation of the workers. All managerial tasks require the ability to communicate clearly and persuasively with subordinates.

No matter what sort of job one has, many decisions are made in a meeting of several people. Much important work is thus done in small group discussions, and the ability to communicate effectively in group meetings is basic to success on the job. Much research has been done about how groups work, and this book will give you tested and proven advice about how to work more effectively in group situations.

We need communication skills to live successfully and happily and to work effectively; we need them also to help us move through what is popularly called the maze of governmental red tape with which all of us come in contact at one time or another. Government agencies related to city, county, state, and nation have an important dollars-and-cents effect upon us. We have to learn how to talk with people responsible for income tax problems, housing, licensing, and social welfare; we may have to help our parents fill out intricate Medicare forms.

Frequently we find ourselves in positions where we must meet the public either as part of a service industry or in some sales capacity. Meeting the public requires skill in opening conversations and giving clear directions or providing information quickly and in an interesting fashion. To be a successful salesman, you need a high level of speaking ability. Selling requires the ability to meet people and to explain ideas clearly. Selling also requires skill in the use of techniques of persuasion. Persuasion is one of the most challenging, interesting, and exciting dimensions of interpersonal communication, and we have devoted Chapters 8–10 to it.

Communication ability is vital in a final economic sense when we spend the money we have earned on the job. Wherever we go, we are encouraged to buy something. Billboards, television and radio commercials, newspaper and magazine ads tell us how to spend our money. Persuasive messages are everywhere. We need to know about persuasion not only to be more influential in our own lives, but also to be able to spot a phony ad, an illogical argument, or an appeal to our emotions rather than to our logical consideration.

When we buy something really important, such as an automobile or a house, or even when we make a sizable purchase such as a refrigerator, color television set, or boat, we find ourselves involved in an important communication event. Skillful persuaders try to sell us their particular product. If a person does not listen carefully and critically, a salesman will give him, in addition to the information he needs in order to compare products, much additional suggestion aimed at persuading him to buy the salesman's product. Salesmen sometimes seem to work at keeping the customer from making careful comparisons with other similar products on the market. As we stand there, knowing we are listening to a hard sell, we nonetheless want the basic information about his product, and we try to sift facts from suggestion. Most of us find it far easier to turn off a television commercial than to resist the efforts of a face-to-face salesman.

As you learn more about communication techniques, particularly about persuasion, you will become much more aware of the techniques used to make you consume this or that particular product or idea.

COMMUNICATION AND INDIVIDUAL FULFILLMENT

Man has a basic urge to symbolize—to communicate—but more than that, to generate words and images for the pure joy of playing with language and with ideas. Even when we are resting, our minds think up symbols. When people find themselves thrown together by accident or for purely social reasons, they feel the urge to talk to one another. Idle chit-chat can be playful and great fun. A rich fantasy life can make a lonely existence bearable. Word play and small talk provide pleasant moments for all of us, and such communication should not be considered trivial, for the same tendency reaches into such important and fulfilling activities as theater, painting, the writing of fiction, and sculpture. Religion, too, is deeply symbolic and an expression of man's basic need to share his most intense experiences.

Most people gain satisfaction from creating something, from discovering a new idea or product or way to do something, from writing a poem or a good letter, from concocting a new recipe, or even from finding a new way to get from one place to another. If we are lucky enough to have a job that allows us to be creative, to figure out solutions to important and difficult problems, we gain much satisfaction from this and find our work rewarding. If we cannot get achievement rewards from our work, we say it is dull, routine, and boring, and our lives are not enriched by our work even if our pocketbooks are sufficiently filled. People with uncreative jobs usually seek individual fulfillment in other activities related to hobbies, volunteer work for the public welfare, or social contacts that enable them to feel important as individuals, not just cogs in a machine.

We talk to people to be creative as well as to get some job done or to make social contacts. Often we do not know the outcome of our communication. We try out ideas in a tentative way with people who have similar interests and abilities. We "brainstorm" or "kick ideas around" or try out wild and far-out notions on close friends. Playing with words and ideas in a nonthreatening communication situation not only helps us do creative things and solve problems, but the act of communication itself becomes fun.

Finally, some of the highest and most satisfying moments for a human being come when two people transcend their self-centeredness and reach a high level of understanding. One of the warmest rewards in life is to really know another, to achieve what the theologian Martin Buber called the I-thou relationship. In the search for identity and fulfillment, the ability to communicate at the highest levels is a basic requirement.

Maybe you can remember a time when feelings or thoughts welled up inside you to the point where you felt you had to share them with somebody else. Artur Rubinstein, classical pianist and world citizen, was in his forties when he met and married his wife, Aniela; Rubinstein had traveled the world over from the time he was a boy, giving concerts in major cities and for heads of government. He had been wined and dined in the best restaurants in the world, had met and talked with many of the world's leading figures in politics and the arts; yet after he had been married a short while, he literally began his career all over again. Everything was new now that he had someone to share it with, he felt, and he gave no public concerts for 2 years while he worked diligently, relearning many of the pieces he had played for years, determined to be absolutely the best pianist he could be, for Aniela. He wanted to share the best of himself, and he has continued to do so for another 40 years.

Most people look for a deep personal relationship with one or two people in their lives, and building it is as much a creative act as the painting of a picture or the building of a highway. Communication can be an act of creativeness in a relationship.

COMMUNICATION AND CITIZENSHIP

Huey Long, a colorful southern politician in the 1930s, gained a large following during the Depression with his slogan, "Every Man a King." In a very real sense, every citizen is a ruler in a representative democracy such as the one in the United States. The basic assumption of our government is that with freedom of speech, of press, and of assembly, all points of view will be given an opportunity to be heard and the people, once they have heard the competing positions debated, will have the wisdom to choose the best policy and the best representatives.

The leaders in a democracy must be skilled debaters and persuasive speakers. Democracy has always encouraged the study and practice of real communication. Our earliest and still some of our most sophisticated ideas about communication were first developed in the Greek states several thousand years ago; they received their greatest development in the democracy of Athens, and were further refined in Rome during the days when the Roman senate was a power. Totalitarian governments discourage the study of communication skills by all citizens and try to keep such skills in the hands of those working for the power structure. Controlled communication can be a powerful propagandistic tool. Open communication in which everyone is expected to participate is doubtless one of the best methods we, as private citizens, have to maintain a free and open society.

Every citizen must be skilled in debate and discussion of public issues to be a participant in the democratic processes. Informal discussions in the home or on the job about various candidates and political programs are important to intelligent voting. A citizen in a democracy has to be more responsible, more politically knowledgeable and active, than a citizen in any other form of society. Citizens have to become as wary of political candidates and campaign techniques as consumers are of sales pitches; *as* wary? far more so.

We should be aware that candidates often hire ghostwriters to help them prepare messages for the public. At best the ghostwriter helps the candidate frame his ideas in more effective language; at worst the ghostwriter provides both ideas and language and may fool the public into thinking a poor candidate is a good one. Some candidates have teams of ghostwriters, and several persons contribute to the preparation of a single speech. Most politicians running for important public office now use the latest persuasive techniques developed by advertising agencies and public-relations firms to produce their television programs. How can a person know for whom he is voting under such circumstances? Are the policies the candidate's or did they spring from other brains? Will the candidate be able to cope with the pressures of office? Will he be able to deal with the problems he must face? If we have been conned by human merchandising, our elected officials may be inadequate for effective government.

Fortunately television not only encourages a candidate to use advertising agencies, short commercial-type announcements, and ghostwriters, but also forces politicians to appear on shows such as "Meet the Press" and "Face the Nation." On such programs, skilled newsmen and political analysts ask probing questions, and the candidate cannot rely on other people to answer for him. Indeed, on the better public-affairs programs, the issues receive a fuller airing and more intensive probing than is the case with the typical political address or rally speech delivered in person by a candidate before an audience. As these probing question sessions continue, the public soon gets to know the genuine articles from the phonies. Television gives us the best tool yet to take the measures of political candidates and policies. The cold fish eventually comes across as a cold fish, and an involved, concerned, effective human being projects his personality as well. You cannot fool the public long if what it sees is an unedited close-up of a person working in an unrehearsed communication event.

To be a citizen in a democracy, therefore, a person needs to know how to analyze political persuasion, how to test the validity of an argument, the truthfulness of evidence, and the wisdom of policy. All citizens also need to have basic communication skills to support the positions in which they believe and to bring their points of view into public discussion. The Greek philosopher Aristotle wrote one of the ancient world's most famous books on communication. In his *Rhetoric,* Aristotle argued that the truth has a basic advantage over error and if truth fails to win out in public debate, it is because the defenders of the truth are inept, lacking in persuasive skill. He therefore urged the development of communication skills to assure that truth would always have able defenders. To avoid a horrible world such as the one George Orwell envisioned in *1984,* where all our thinking is done for us, we would do well to remember Aristotle's 2300-year-old advice. It is still valid.

MULTIMEDIA COMMUNICATION

Today the old emphasis on reading and writing as the basic avenues for effective communication is outdated. The most important messages tend to use all the resources of film, drama, dance, music, poetry, speech, and technology to make their point. As we have said earlier, the television commercial is a prime example. Brief persuasive messages costing thousands of dollars per minute to plan and produce are broadcast over television every hour. Many talented people and much money have combined over the years to develop the necessary technology to produce effective messages. The same tendency is reflected in the use by business, government, and the professions of the *presentation,* in which important messages are developed using visual aids, videotape recorders, films, music, and all the modern communication technology.

Although teachers have not been in the forefront of the multimedia revolution, more and more instructors are using modern technology in developing new ways of teaching. In the early 1970s a popular television program for preschool children, "Sesame Street," proved the popularity and effectiveness of teaching basic information by means of a great variety of visual approaches together with music and dramatic presentations.

Communication in the world of tomorrow will continue the trend toward greater use of multimedia and technology. The electronic music and light shows of today's entertainment and the artistry of today's television commercial are but clues to the information culture and speech communication of the future.

GROUP LEARNING

The search for identity, community, and fulfillment through communication has resulted in the growth of learning and human-potential groups. The group-dynamics movement developed in the 1960s into the T-group or sensitivity-group approach. The main source of group dynamics has been the National Training Laboratory at Bethel, Maine. Sensitivity groups are training devices to make participants aware of the importance and the dynamics of groups and to make individuals more sensitive to how they come across in a communication situation. Sensitivity groups have been used to train management personnel, to improve organizational communication, and to institute individual and organizational change. Business and industrial training programs, church groups, educational organizations, and charitable institutions all have sponsored sensitivity programs in attempts to bridge the various communication gaps between generations, religions, and economic and racial groups, and to increase individual potential.

Somewhat analogous to the sensitivity approach but centered more on the West Coast at such places as the Esalen Institute and the Western Behavioral Sciences Laboratory is the human-potential movement which utilizes encounter groups. The encounter group is an intensive emotional experience in group communication. The professional trainer or facilitator who organizes and supervises the encounter group usually stresses authentic, sincere communication. The facilitator often uses nonverbal techniques which encourage the participants to touch fingers, feel faces, and hug one another.

The search for authenticity of communication through group techniques, no matter what its origin or the details of its practice, reflects the needs of contemporary society for new and better communication skills. The philosophy underlying the group search for solutions (sometimes referred to as group grope) emphasizes the fight against fragmentation, isolation, alienation, and loneliness. Man is once again battling to conquer his environment, but this time instead of the wilderness, he is trying to deal with an urban social scene.

From time to time we all feel misinterpreted. We feel that people do not understand us or do not take into consideration the reasons for our reactions and statements. Sensitivity and encounter groups probe these actions and reactions, statements and responses, always trying to help the individual become more aware of how he affects others as well as how he allows others to affect him. At best, sensitivity and encounter groups can lead people toward increased awareness of their own needs and the needs of others. At worst, they can be punishing, painful experiences, similar to a "truth" session in junior high school when your "best friends" tell you all your faults "for your own sake."

Obviously, the mysticism, the drama, and the possibility of an intensely exciting and rewarding experience of genuine group feeling or belonging, of sharing and brotherhood, of acceptance, even if only temporary, make sensitivity and encounter groups appealing. You should be aware, however, of the possible dangers of participating in such groups; what starts out as a lark or a whim to get in on something exciting may turn out to be a valuable growth experience or it may turn out to be a painful, destructive exercise producing few new insights. A long talk with the leader of any sensitivity or encounter group with which you plan to involve yourself would be worth your time. You must be completely aware of what you are getting into.

The fact that such groups as those described above are so common—in churches and organizations, in businesses, and in schools and universities—says much about our society at this stage in its development. We need contact. We need communication. We need interplay and interaction with other human beings. The more our lives become surrounded by the unfamiliar and the uncaring, the more we need the strengths of good relationships with a few—at least one—other persons.

THE BASIC COURSE
IN SPEECH COMMUNICATION

The search for a solution to the needs of the future is evident also in the growth of the discipline of speech communication in our high schools, colleges, and universities. More and more schools are developing programs in research and teaching of communication theory and skills relevant to the world of the future.

The first course in interpersonal communication is designed to help you understand that everyone needs to communicate. If you become aware of how similar other peoples' needs in this area are to your own, you can grow into greater maturity in your communication with others.

To some degree, we all appreciate positive communication from others and are upset by negative communication. Marriages fail because, where it counts, one partner is not able to fulfill the ego needs of the other. Communication within marriage and the family is now a big part of most family-education courses. When young people talk of forming a meaningful relationship with someone, they have a good idea of what this means and of what is needed to achieve and sustain such a relationship.

As to more formal communication, preachers, priests, and rabbis still deliver sermons. Politicians still give rally speeches. Formal occasions still require formal addresses. Teachers still lecture to inform. The speech to inspire, to inform, or to persuade is still an important form of communication, and as students of interpersonal communication we need to study public speaking. But the public speech is only one of the ways in which people communicate, and it is becoming a less important way. The increasing use of small groups to achieve religious conversion and mystical experience, and the use of small groups by Students for a Democratic Society, Gay Liberation, Women's Liberation, and Black Power movements to convert to political radicalism, testify that the persuasive revival speech is but one form of persuasive communication.

The heavy reliance on political persuasion via television since 1948 and the increasing importance of interviews, conferences, business meetings, rap sessions, discussions, and public-affairs question-and-answer shows indicate that the student of modern communication preparing for the future needs a much broader introduction to communication theory and practice than is provided by a course in public or platform speaking only.

This book, therefore, discusses communication attitudes, theories, and skills in relation to interviews, conferences, and group communications, as well as the preparation of materials and the performance skills needed for public speaking. We will also give you tools for becoming a more knowledgeable consumer of communication, especially that directed at you by the mass media. The emphasis will be upon theory and techniques so you can understand communication well enough both to improve your own abilities and to listen critically to others. This book should help you to participate more effectively in your personal life and work, to be a more aware consumer, and to be a more capable citizen.

Since each instructor tells you how important the subject he teaches is, you may naturally say, "Sure, from where *you* stand, but not from where *I* stand." Or, as the talk-show people on television sometimes say to one another when too much manufactured enthusiasm has been called for, "Who cares?" We have spent many hours trying to help people who have considered their formal education long over, who have risen to positions of importance in

the key ideas

We live in an age of information, which is to say, we live in an age of communication.

Television creates a new way of thinking and gives us a new perception of the world.

The fight for our attention leads professional communicators to use every avenue of the senses to reach us.

Much of what we believe comes from unintended impressions gained from radio, television, and film.

Sometimes the hardest thing we have to do is to talk to someone.

If you talk easily with anybody and everybody you are not necessarily a good communicator.

Much that passes for communication within the family is repetitive chatter that covers up thoughts and feelings.

Management is largely communication.

The ability to communicate effectively in group meetings is basic to success on most jobs.

Man has a basic urge to symbolize.

We often talk just for the fun of it.

---

their businesses and professions; these same people now have information others need, and they do not have the skills to give out this information effectively. They have been promoted to positions in management and they are having trouble communicating with people. Time and time again they say to us, "If only I had had some training in communication years ago." In the world of the future an understanding of, and an ability to communicate with, the spoken word will be essential to any person's individual quality of life. We can give you only a glimpse of the complexities that the in-depth study of communication includes, problems that have long fascinated serious students of modern culture. Our purpose

in chapter 1

The highest and most satisfying moments of human communication come when we transcend ourselves to reach a high level of understanding.

Democracy has always encouraged the study and practice of real communication.

A citizen in a democracy has to be more responsible, more politically knowledgeable, and more skillful in communicating than a citizen in any other form of society.

On the better public-affairs television programs political issues get a fuller airing than in the typical rally speech.

Television gives more of us the best tool yet to measure a political candidate and his policies.

If the truth loses in public debate, the fault lies with its defenders.

Today's important messages use all the resources of film, drama, dance, music, poetry, and speech to make their points.

The search for real communication through group methods reflects society's need for better communication skills.

The more our lives become surrounded by the unfamiliar and uncaring, the more we need authentic communication with a few people significant to us.

The thorough study of communication raises problems that have long fascinated serious students of modern culture.

---

in this book, and in this course, is to give you an appreciation of the importance of communication in your life and in the world today.

SUGGESTED PROJECTS

1 / Think of some person you know who, in your judgment, communicates exceptionally well with others. Pick a personal acquaintance, not a public figure. What qualities does this person have that contribute to his or her skill in communication? What sorts of

things does this person do that others seldom do? After providing a thorough description of this "unusually good communicator," compare yourself with this person. Be frank and candid. Make a list of the qualities you already possess that help you as a communicator; make another list of the things you should work on to improve your ability. Do you feel you have any habits that you particularly need to work on and change in order to improve your ability to communicate?

2 / This project is designed to help class members become better acquainted with one another. First think of some appropriate method of name identification. (We take a wide roll of white adding-machine tape, cut it into pieces long enough to be taped or pinned from shoulder to shoulder, and print the student's name on each piece in huge letters that can be read across the room.) The instructor divides the class into pairs. The pairs are given 5 minutes during which one person interviews the other and takes notes so that he or she can tell the class about the other person for 2 or 3 minutes. The student who has been described to the class then has a few moments to add to or amend the comments of the introductory speech given by the interviewer if he wants to. If time permits, the students in each pair may then switch roles.

3 / Estimate how much time in a typical day you spend reading, writing, speaking, and listening. Keep a personal log of these communication experiences for one 24-hour period. Further, classify your communication within this period as to its type— social conversation, business communication, school-related communication, communication related to self-fulfillment, and multi-media communication. Keep the log with you and record your communication each hour; be accurate and complete. Afterwards, make a percentage scale approximation of your typical daily communication interaction. What percentage of your day do you spend reading, writing, speaking, and listening? Were you aware of any times during the 24-hour period when you consciously avoided a communication situation? If so, be specific as to what and why.

SUGGESTED READINGS

Bormann, Ernest G., William S. Howell, Ralph G. Nichols, and George L. Shapiro. *Interpersonal Communication in the Modern Organization.* Englewood Cliffs, N.J.: Prentice-Hall, 1969. "The Spoken Word in the Modern World," pp. 3–18; "Epilogue," pp. 296–306.

Brooks, Keith (ed.). *The Communicative Arts and Sciences of Speech*. Columbus, Ohio: Charles E. Merrill, 1967.

McLuhan, Marshall, and Quentin Fiore. *The Medium Is the Message: An Inventory of Effects*. New York: Bantam Books, 1967.

Reid, Ronald F. (ed.). *An Introduction to the Field of Speech*. Glenview, Ill.: Scott, Foresman, 1965.

2 the process of communication

When people talk together we call what happens a communication event. We have difficulty studying communication events because so much is going on when people talk with one another that we have trouble keeping track of everything. This may seem to be an overstatement, but it is not. Communication events have the characteristics of a dynamic process. By *process*, we mean a series of give-and-take moves by which some end is reached. By *dynamic,* we mean the process contains forces that push and pull the parts and set them in motion.

To understand a process, we need to know the parts that make it up, how these parts fit together and move, and the nature and source of the forces that power the action and reaction.

THE PARTS OF A COMMUNICATION EVENT

We will use the letters *S M C R* as a key to remember the parts of a communication event. Figure 1 presents the basic elements of the process. The *S* stands for *source*. The source is the person or group who decides to communicate with some other person or persons. If you meet someone in the hall and say, "Good morning," you are the source of the communication.

The *M* stands for *message*. In our example the message is the words *good* and *morning,* plus the way you gesture and emphasize the words to indicate, "I really mean it is a pleasant morning" or "I am glad to see you again" or "I am saying these words because I always say these words even if the day is lousy and I feel terrible."

The *C* stands for *channel* or channels through which the message moves. Television messages come through channels. Each person can receive messages by way of his senses—sight, smell, taste, hearing, and touch. Thus, a message may travel through several channels at the same time, as is the case with television, where a viewer both sees the picture and hears the sound. You are most likely to hear, see, or read a message, since the most popular communication channels are through the eye or the ear. But we could make up a language that used the sense of touch. If we were on a secret mission and it was dark and we did not wish to be heard, we could plan some signals such as a touch on the shoulder to mean, "Be careful"; a grab of the arm to mean, "Stop"; and a push on the side to mean, "Change direction." Of course, before we have a chance to see, feel, hear, touch, or smell a message, it may be sent through a radio or television channel, over a telephone wire, or by some other device. But when you say, "Good morning," in the hall to someone, the sound and light waves between you and the other person carry the message, and the listener sees you smile and nod and hears you say the words.

The final letter R means *receiver*. The listener or viewer is the receiver of the message. When you greet someone in the hall you are the *source;* the words and the way you say them are the *message;* the message goes through the *channels* of sound (hearing) and light (sight) to the *receiver*.

Now that you know the S M C R way of looking at communication events you can examine different situations and decide whether they are complete examples of the process of communication. For example, if John telephones Mary for a date, is that communication? Is there a source? A message? Channels? A receiver? All the parts are there: John is the source, what John says is the message, the channels are the telephone and hearing, and Mary is the receiver. Take another example: The national committee of a political party buys time on a television network and runs a short political announcement on nationwide TV. Is this an example of communication? Again all the parts are there: The national committee is the source; the television waves, television set, sight, and hearing are the channels; and the people at home who see and hear the announcement are the receivers. One more example and then you can think up some other situations and see if they are communication events. A candidate for student-body president is talking from the auditorium stage to an assembly, urging the audience to vote for a platform to improve the school. The candidate is the source, the message is what he says and the way he says it, the channels are the light waves (sight) and sound waves (hearing), and students in the auditorium are the receivers.

The S M C R key to the study of communication covers

figure 1 elements of the

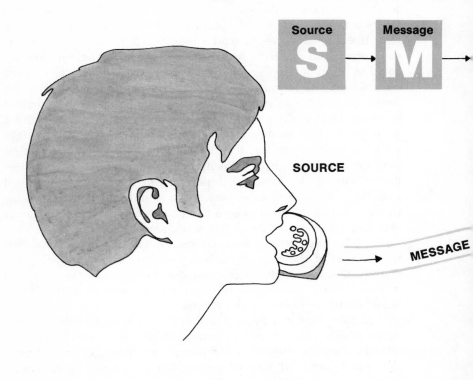

every sort of communication. We have seen the four basic parts in a telephone call, a television message, and a public speech. If we learn how the spark plug works to cause the gas to explode in an engine cylinder, we know a lot about many different car engines. In the same way, if we learn about the source of messages, we know a good deal about many different kinds of communications. We can say the same for what we learn about messages, channels, and receivers.

A PROCESS MODEL OF COMMUNICATION

To illustrate the way people talk to one another, we will use the basic situation of a two-person conversation. Our approach is to

communication event

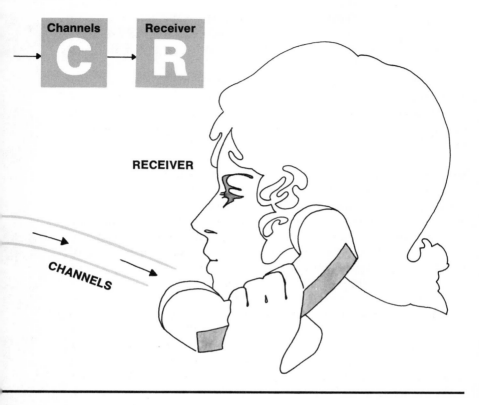

describe an ideal communication event which contains all the possible parts operating under good conditions. Our description of idealized conditions results in a *model* of the event. A good communication model contains all the main parts of a typical conversation in standard form, in their usual places, functioning at peak efficiency.

Assume a situation in which one person wishes to talk to another. The first person arranges for a conference with the second. The person who calls the conference has something he wishes to discuss, and he tells the listener about it. If the listener understands the message, the first person has succeeded in communicating with the second.

Can we locate the $S M C R$ parts in the process of communication in our model of the two-person conference? The source is the individual who makes the appointment. The message consists of the words, gestures, and vocal melody the source uses in talking with the listener. The channels in this instance are sight and hearing. The receiver is the individual called in for the conference.

Our model of a communication event perhaps seems relatively cut and dried. Actually, what happens when two people talk with one another is very complicated. Probably the two people in our hypothetical conference spent some minutes passing the time of day before the source began to talk about his business.

Perhaps the person who requested the appointment was a worker who wanted to talk to the boss about a raise, or he may have been the boss who wanted to talk to the worker about improving his performance on the job. In either case, the fact that one was boss and the other worker would affect the communication. We could develop a long list of things that affect the two people.

Probably the first message failed to achieve a meeting of minds, and the participants had to try, again and again, to come to an understanding satisfactory to both.

Because of the unpredictability of human beings we must describe many possible choices and behaviors to explain adequately the process of human communication. We will begin our explanation with a simplified situation and then move to the more complex. We start with the simplified situation in which the receiver is completely predictable. We are referring to the process by which a man talks to a machine.

Assume that we want to talk to a computer. The first step is to decide what we want the machine to do. We then plan a message to reach our goal, put the message into symbols the computer can understand, and taking care that each sentence is in the correct form and that no information is left out, we punch the message onto cards and feed it into the computer. The computer reads the cards until it comes to a sentence with a mistake in it. Perhaps we forgot to put in a comma where we should have. The computer stops and its typewriter prints out a sentence that tells us we have made a mistake. We then go back to the card that caused the trouble, check the sentence, discover the mistake, put in the comma, and replace the card in the computer. Now the computer understands; it keeps on in this way, either understanding completely or stopping and asking for a correction or for new information. Thus we work together with the machine to achieve understanding.

Remember that we defined process as a series of give-and-take moves by which some end is reached. The linking between man and machine is a communication process. Note that when we talk to the computer we start the communication and continue it until the computer fails to understand a part of the message. The back-and-forth part of the process is clear because the machine prints out an error statement indicating that it fails to understand. Although we start the process, and the machine is helping us reach the goal, we still have to talk the machine's language and follow the rules of the machine's thinking if we are to succeed.

When the computer indicates it does not understand a message, it feeds back information to the programmer to clear up the misunderstanding. *Feedback* consists of information about the errors in the message that enables the man to clear up the machine's lack of understanding.

Feedback is an important idea in a general communication theory. We can explain feedback in much the same way we used $S\ M\ C\ R$ to refer to the parts of the communication event. We will use the letters $A\ G\ P$ as the key to the process of feedback. The A refers to an *actor* (a person or thing) that does something to reach a *goal* (G). The P indicates the *perceptor* built into the actor to provide information on how he is doing so he can correct mistaken attempts to reach his goal. We will examine some simple events in which feedback is important and then show how it works in communication.

Let us say you see a pencil on the desk and decide to pick it up. You stretch your hand out for the pencil, and as you watch your hand you see that you are going to overreach the pencil so you tighten certain muscles in your arm and shoulder and slow down the movement. You keep watching your hand and now see that you have slowed down too much and your hand will fall short. Again you adjust the push you give your hand until your fingers land on target and you pick up the pencil. One action loops back and causes another.

Does the situation of picking up the pencil contain the necessary parts for a feedback loop? You are the *actor* (person or thing) with the *goal* (picking up the pencil), and you sense (the *perceptor*) through your eyes information about how your arm is moving in comparison with where it ought to be if you are to reach your goal. Using the information you get from watching the path of your hand, you change your reach to hit directly on target. The situation illustrates all the parts, $A\ G\ P$, of feedback as presented in Figure 2.

To return to the person talking with a computer, notice

figure 2 the concept of feedback (AGP)

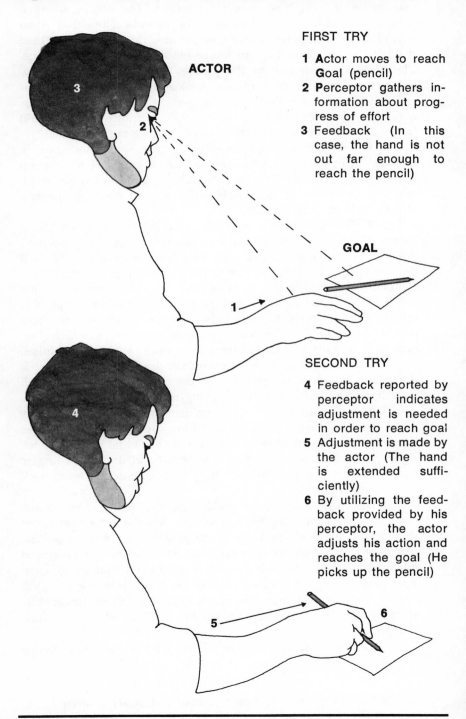

FIRST TRY

1 **A**ctor moves to reach **G**oal (pencil)
2 **P**erceptor gathers information about progress of effort
3 Feedback (In this case, the hand is not out far enough to reach the pencil)

ACTOR

GOAL

SECOND TRY

4 Feedback reported by perceptor indicates adjustment is needed in order to reach goal
5 Adjustment is made by the actor (The hand is extended sufficiently)
6 By utilizing the feedback provided by his perceptor, the actor adjusts his action and reaches the goal (He picks up the pencil)

how the person (A) has a goal (G) to have the computer programed to solve a problem or process data. The person sends the
computer messages and the computer sends back information
when it fails to understand. Thus the programmer can perceive
(P) the actual level of understanding in the machine and check it
against what is needed to reach the goal.

One important feature of the feedback loop is that only
one person or thing has the goal. The pencil does not have a goal;
the computer does not set up a different goal and fight the programmer over what they ought to do as a team. (You know, of
course, about some dramas based on the idea that our machines
begin to have goals of their own and start to take over the world,
but up to now such stories remain science fiction.) In this simplified situation, feedback is information that enables the source
to modify his message so the receiver understands it and the goal
can be reached.

When people communicate with one another, the process
is similar, but is highly complicated by the fact that when another
person is the potential receiver we cannot predict his behavior as
completely as we can the response of a machine. The message
source begins a communication event with another person much
as a programmer begins talking with a computer. The message
source has some end he wishes to reach, and keeping in mind the
receiver's ability to use language and his way of thinking, the
source plans a message to reach his goal and speaks to the receiver.

The largest difference between person-to-machine and person-to-person communication is the machine's willingness to be
bossed around to achieve the programmer's objective and a person's tendency to resist being the receiver of messages.

In our model of a communication event, represented by
Figure 3, an important element is the fact that the message source
has an end in view and sends out messages to achieve that goal.
The communication process is a step-by-step, give-and-take interaction between source and receiver by which the source reaches
the desired goal. The idea of feedback includes the notion that the
source receives information so he can correct his attempts to
reach his goal. The programmer gets error statements from the
computer so he can rephrase his program until the computer
understands it. The computer is willing to take the programmer's
directives and accepts the programmer's goal without question.
When the target for the message is another human being, the
receiver often is not willing to be controlled and does not accept
the objective of the source.

figure 3 a model of the

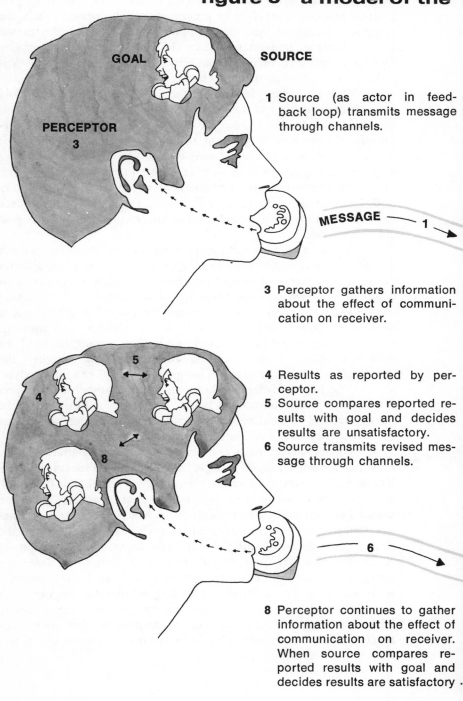

GOAL

PERCEPTOR
3

SOURCE

1 Source (as actor in feed-back loop) transmits message through channels.

MESSAGE —— 1 →

3 Perceptor gathers information about the effect of communication on receiver.

4 Results as reported by perceptor.
5 Source compares reported results with goal and decides results are unsatisfactory.
6 Source transmits revised message through channels.

6

8 Perceptor continues to gather information about the effect of communication on receiver. When source compares reported results with goal and decides results are satisfactory .

process of communication

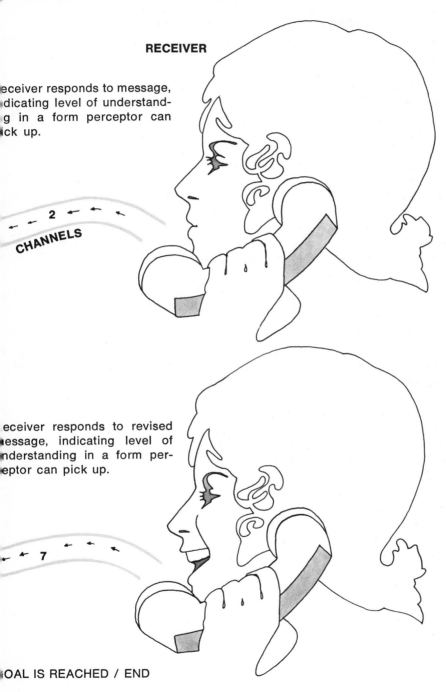

RECEIVER

eceiver responds to message,
dicating level of understand-
g in a form perceptor can
ck up.

2

CHANNELS

eceiver responds to revised
essage, indicating level of
nderstanding in a form per-
eptor can pick up.

7

OAL IS REACHED / END

What often happens in the conversation between people is that after a first attempt by one person to be the source of messages in a communication event, the other person tries to be the source also. When both try to be the source, neither gives the other feedback. The result is a battle over who will control the situation and whose ends will be achieved by the talk.

Even when a person willingly accepts the listener's role and tries to achieve understanding, the response of a human being is much more complex than that of a machine. A person who listens to a message must, like the machine, receive the sentences in the right form, made up of words he understands. If you understand computer language you can always tell when somebody has made a mistake in writing a sentence because the machine accepts only messages put in precisely the right form. A message for a computer is like an arithmetic or geometry problem in that you can tell whether the message can be understood simply by checking its form. But people can understand messages whether or not they are expressed in proper grammar. Of course we cannot put together just any bunch of English words and expect people to understand them. Within limits, our grammar must be correct to be understood. We are not talking about the difference between "it don't make no difference," and "it doesn't make any difference." The question of what is proper grammar is an important one, and we will discuss it in Chapter 3. Our point here is that, in order to be understood, we have to put our ideas into the right form according to some basic rules of American English.

Even when communication does not at first appear to make sense, people will try to find out the meaning of grunts, one-word exclamations, unstructured poetry, and ideas expressed in improper grammar. In that respect, people are much different from computers, and while the difference is helpful because it enables people to talk about complicated ideas and complex feelings, it is a disadvantage because while the computer never proceeds until it understands completely, people often plunge deeper and deeper into misunderstandings.

Like the computer, human beings *can* feed back error statements and thus indicate when they do not understand the message. As a matter of fact, people ought to be much better than a machine at giving feedback because they can explain in greater detail exactly what they do not understand. In practice, however, people are often much worse than a machine at providing a speaker with feedback. People often hear only a few words of a message and then get the idea that they know what it is all about without listening to the rest. ("I know, I know, I've heard it a hundred times," says the teenager as he starts out with the family car.) People often hear what they expect to hear instead of what a speaker is saying. If a teacher assigns a difficult term paper, the student may not hear the assignment. Finally, and most important, people tend not to ask questions even when they do not understand because they are afraid a question may make them appear stupid, or they feel that if they keep quiet, at least nobody will know how little they understand. We are all guilty of bad communication habits at one time or another.

A model of a general theory of communication is useful to the student of communicative interaction (see Figure 4). Remember that we are trying to picture a dynamic process, and a moving picture would do a better job. Without this moving picture, you must add your imagination. The parts of the process are put into the model but they are actually parts in motion; as you look at the picture, imagine them in a give-and-take, step-by-step way.

Notice that the model in Figure 4 has two new terms to indicate the last important ideas about communication that we need to complete the picture. Between the source and the message we have placed the word *encode* and between the message and the receiver we have placed the word *decode*. We know that special codes or code words are used by soldiers or spies in wartime to keep secrets. Breakfast food companies often use decoder rings or other secret code devices as prizes to get children to buy their products. When a spy decodes a secret message, he discovers what it means. The other term, encode, is not as widely used, but it means putting the ideas into a code and is the opposite of decode.

Look again at Figure 4. Before a source can communicate with a receiver, he must make a message out of something that can be sensed by the receiver. People who wish to communicate must make some link to establish contact. (Some people believe that contact can be made without going through the senses and they try to communicate with the spirit world or with others by means of extrasensory perception or ESP.) When a person makes a message he encodes his ideas into a form the receiver can take in. Breaking the code, understanding the message, is the decoding process.

THE NATURE OF A CODE

To encode and decode messages we must have a *code* which can bridge the gap between source and receiver. You may think first

figure 4 complete

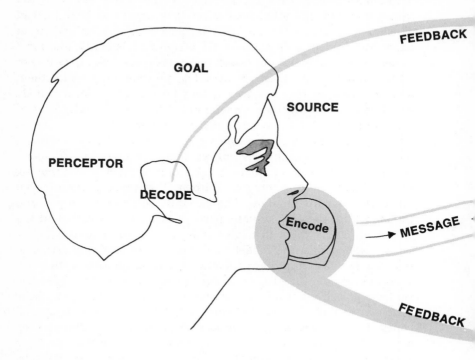

of such things as the Morse code or a secret code such as the one you can make by giving each letter in the alphabet a number and then writing notes in numbers to those who know the code. The important thing about a code is that the people who use it must know all its parts and how they fit together into sentences. If a person has a private code it is useful only to talk to himself. Sometimes people make up a secret code and use it to write their personal diaries. (Our communication model is useful in studying the situation where a person talks to himself. Simply make the source and the receiver the same person.)

Usually we know the code and can spend our efforts on trying to use it. Sometimes, though, we have to stop in the middle of a conversation and check to be sure that everybody is using the

communication event

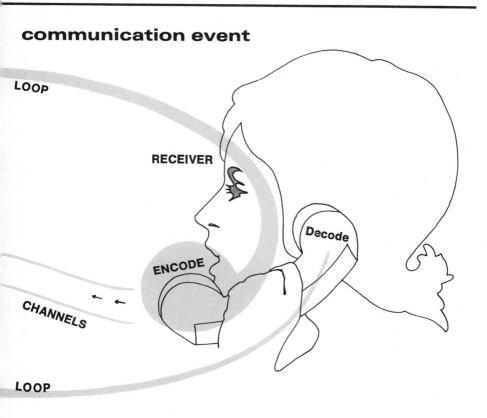

LOOP

RECEIVER

Decode

ENCODE

CHANNELS

LOOP

same code. Have you ever talked with someone from another country who speaks a different language? Perhaps the other person speaks some English, but from time to time wishes to say something and does not know the right English word. He may then ask for the right word by pointing or gesturing, or he may use other English words he does know to solicit your help. Even if both people are speaking English as natives, they may have to stop and make sure that they are using words that mean the same things to both of them.

We have mentioned one important code for those of us who live in the United States—English. All other languages are codes as well. But there are many other kinds of codes in addition to the natural languages like English, French, and German. Some, like the Morse code, use dots and dashes to represent letters and are simply added onto a language such as English. Other codes are not composed of words at all. For example, the American Indian tribes developed a sign language in which certain hand movements meant certain ideas. Although each tribe had its own language and often a member of one tribe could not talk with someone from a different tribe using language, all the tribes knew the sign language, and though it was somewhat limited, they could communicate with one another using the sign code.

We might say that nature communicates with man. A scientist who makes a new discovery breaks nature's code. For example, scientists say that the hereditary genes, which pass on from parents to children the things like eye color, nose shape, talent, and ability, do so by means of a code. We can look upon the code as information, and some scientists like Norbert Wiener, a computer specialist and mathematician, argue that some day people may become messages and when a fast reading device is invented the information contained in a person's body can be sent by radio or telephone across the country where a receiver can build up the body again from suitable materials. Wiener's point is that *we* are primarily information and not the physical materials —water and other chemicals—that compose us at a given time.

Nature's code enables man to "read" that when we see lightning, we will soon hear thunder. Nature's codes cannot be changed. We find that we cannot change the code from lightning means thunder to seeing a rainbow means thunder. Lightning is always connected with thunder in the very nature of things.

Man-made codes, such as the English language, have no natural connection, and so parts of the code can be made to stand for different things and ideas. For example, if several of us decide to make a code in which the letters of the alphabet are numbered from 1 to 26, starting with A as 1, B as 2, and so on, we can write messages in our code; at a later time we can agree, that since an outsider has broken our code, we will turn the numbers around and have 26 stand for A, 25 for B, and so on. There is nothing in the way the world works to make us assign numbers to the letters in a certain way.

The English language has certain words that stand for certain things. Thus the word *dog* stands for an animal of a certain kind. There is nothing about the animal that makes the word *dog* the one and only word that can stand for it. Other languages use other words: German, *Hundt;* French, *chien.* When we talk in a language, we must learn how the language is used, what the words mean, and how they can be put together in a sentence. For several people to talk to one another, they must all understand the words they use to mean pretty much the same things. When a person has in mind a furry, four-legged, domesticated animal that barks and eats meat, and he encodes a message that has the word *dog* in it, the listener who hears the word *dog* should not decode it to mean a two-legged bird that cackles and is good to eat southern-fried.

Among the important codes used in interpersonal communication are several that use not words but gestures, such as the Indian sign language, or changes in the voice pattern. For example, when a person looks at another, smiles, and nods his head up and down, this behavior may be part of a code and mean agreement. Shaking the head from side to side, looking the other person in the eye, frowning, moving away, looking at the ground, and other such gestures may be part of a nonverbal code. Everybody who knows the code understands what these actions mean.

Another important code that is added onto speech is like the melody that enhances a poem set to music. The code includes the way the voice changes pitch, the rate of speech, the changes in loudness, and the pauses that separate words and clumps of words. Thus two people who speak the same body and vocal codes can say a great deal to one another by the way one draws out the sound "ooo" and at the same time smiles, and holds up his right hand in front of his shoulder and forms a circle with his thumb and forefinger.

When we speak to other people we punctuate our comments with pauses and changes in the rate of speech, loudness, and pitch. By proper use of vocal punctuation we can make the same sentence mean several different things. Take the sentence, "Youth today is revolting." Can you read the sentence aloud so it means two different things? Try the sentence, "Woman without her man is a beast." Can you read it first so woman is the beast and then so man is the beast?

We will call the body codes and the vocal melodies *nonverbal* communication. While we can think of many other languages, and some of these are fun to play with, your concern in the book will be with speech communication that uses some dialect of American English as the verbal code and uses the nonverbal codes common in North America.

One final point about nonverbal communication and our model of the communication process will be complete. Many gestures and voice changes are not part of a code. A person may shift his eyes, jerk his head, and move his shoulders as he speaks, and other people in the same culture may still not know what all the body movements mean. For example, when Joe talks he makes a lot of movements that nobody else makes and these do not mean anything to anyone who does not know Joe well enough to have learned that when Joe gets red in the face, moves his head from side to side, and starts to stammer, he will soon begin to hit somebody or kick or throw something. Gestures that are nearly always made when a person is angry, afraid, sad, or happy are like those natural signs of lightning always followed by thunder. We do not know if certain gestures always accompany anger, fear, sadness, or happiness as thunder always accompanies lightning. We do know that some groups of people expect certain nonverbal communications at certain times because actors can convey feelings and ideas to an audience by the way they pantomime on television, in films, and on stage.

For the most part we must study the people we often talk with to try to find the nonverbal cues that indicate their feelings and attitudes. When Father meets you at the door with anger written all over his face, he does not even have to ask, "Why are you so late?" But when we talk with strangers, the best we can hope to do is learn the nonverbal codes, that is, the gestures everybody knows mean something in the same way all people who speak English understand the word *dog* to mean a certain kind of animal. A tight face puts us down; an open face helps us relax and invites communication.

THE GOALS OF COMMUNICATION

We have been assuming that the goal or purpose of a message source is to achieve a meeting of minds: The source wants to achieve understanding with the receiver. The purpose of feedback is, thus, to give the message source information on how well the listener understands the message so the source can make further efforts, if need be, to achieve understanding. People who talk to one another do not always have as their goal the meeting of minds. Sometimes people want to confuse their listeners; sometimes they want to make their listeners angry or sad, to entertain them, or just to make contact with them. Sometimes people encode messages for the pure joy of using a code. Some people talk to themselves or to imaginary listeners. (Most of us spend some time in this sort of fantasizing, using our imaginations to rehearse for the future or to relive the past; this is quite normal.) The goals for which people start talking to people are thus much more varied than the reasons people start talking to computers. When a person programs a computer, he wants the computer to understand the program, for if the machine does not, some other goals outside the communication event will be frustrated.

We must now understand that a person talking to another human being may well have goals outside the communication event, just as the person programing a computer may be doing so in order to have the machine keep records, solve a mathematical problem, or make a prediction about the outcome of an election. The source of a message in interpersonal communication may wish to be elected to office, to get someone to marry him, or to become part of a group. A speaker seeking office may feel that an angry listener will be more likely to vote for him, so his real goal within the context of the communication is to get the listener angry about something which he, the speaker, will point out as something bad that he, if elected, will correct. Our communication model assumes no hidden goals. The source and the receiver assume the goal to be the same.

SUGGESTED PROJECTS

1 / You may keep the pairs set up in Project 2, Chapter 1, for this project, or you may pair up with another member of the class. Either way, make an appointment to have a coke or coffee with the other person during your free time outside class. Talk with each other for a good hour and learn as much about each other as you can. Then, separately, write a short paper in which you discuss how well the communication model in Chapter 2 explains what happened during your conversation. Did the two of you alternate playing the roles of source and receiver? What was the nature of feedback during your talk? Were there important things happening that the model could not explain? How would you change the model to make it more satisfactory as a basic tool for studying communication?

2 / The class is divided into groups of five or six. Each group creates a *code* suitable for communicating among themselves. This code may be a verbal one, a nonverbal one, or it may combine both verbal and nonverbal symbols. Each group has a few minutes for members to communicate with one another, using their code, in front of the class. The class then has 10 minutes to try to "break" the code. After all the groups have finished, there is a general

the key ideas

THE *S M C R* key to the process of communication covers every sort of communication event.

A good communication model contains all the main parts of a typical conversation in standard form and working in the usual way.

The first attempt at communication usually fails.

A process is a series of give-and-take moves by which some end is reached.

Feedback consists of information about the errors in a message that helps the source clear up misunderstandings.

One important feature of the feedback loop is that only one person or thing has the goal.

People tend to resist being the receivers of messages unless they trust the source or think they stand to gain from working to achieve understanding.

People have greater potential to provide feedback than machines but often fail to do so.

People often hear what they expect to hear instead of what is being said.

People who wish to communicate must make some link to establish contact.

class discussion of the nature of codes and how they work in the communication process.

3 / This is an exercise in feedback. Each student prepares a 5-minute oral message. After 1 minute of the presentation, the instructor announces "Feedback begins." Class members may then call out "What do you mean?" whenever they genuinely do not understand what the speaker is saying. A timekeeper keeps a record of how long it takes to make ideas clear whenever the audience has an opportunity for unlimited verbal feedback.

SUGGESTED READINGS

Berlo, David K. *The Process of Communication*. New York: Holt, Rinehart and Winston, 1960.

in chapter 2

When a person makes a message, he encodes it into a form the listener can take in.

American English is a code.

Codes such as the English language have no natural connection with the objects of the world.

Among important codes for communication are several which use gestures.

Another important code that adds meaning to speech is like the melody that enhances a poem set to music.

By proper use of vocal punctuation we can make the same sentence mean several different things.

Body codes and vocal melodies are nonverbal communication.

Many gestures and voice changes are not part of a code but are simply personal characteristics of the speaker.

People sometimes talk to confuse their listeners.

A person talking to another may have a goal outside the communication event and use the communication as a way to achieve the larger object.

Howell, William S., and Ernest G. Bormann. *Presentational Speaking for Business and the Professions*. New York: Harper & Row, 1971. "The Dynamics of Face-to-Face Communication," pp. 38–61.

Miller, Gerald R. *Speech Communication: A Behavioral Approach*. Indianapolis: Bobbs-Merrill, 1966.

Murray, Elwood, Gerald M. Phillips, and J. David Truby. *Speech: Science-Art*. Indianapolis: Bobbs-Merrill, 1969. "A Structure To View the World," pp. 36–62.

3 how words communicate

In Chapter 2 we discussed the encoding and decoding links in the communication process in terms of a wide range of codes. In this chapter we will talk about the verbal code of American English. We will examine such questions as: Is there *a* right way to speak English? Should you learn *better* pronunciation? Should you improve your articulation? Correct your grammar? Can you move from the lower class to the middle class, or from the upper middle class to the upper class, by changing the way you speak?

If you do not speak black English, can you communicate with black Americans? Are Chinese students, black students from big-city ghettos, American Indians, and Puerto Rican students culturally deprived because their dialects are inferior to white-middle-class speech? Why does the sentence, "There ain't no such word as *ain't*," strike some people as funny?

All these questions are important to every person living in the United States today because they have to do with life style, economic success, feelings of racial and cultural pride, and educational and social opportunity. Before we try to answer the questions, however, we must look at some basic features of language to lay the groundwork for our responses.

THE NATURE OF VERBAL CODES

Messages contain two basic kinds of verbal symbols. The first kind of message symbol is a *form* word. When workers put in a sidewalk or build concrete steps, they first prepare the ground and build forms into which they will pour the mixture of concrete. The forms hold the concrete in a certain way, shaping it, making sure that the end result is, say, a sidewalk, and not curbing. Form words in messages are like the forms used by cement workers. The form words structure questions, statements, and commands into their characteristic shape. Some typical form words are *what, when, where, how, is, the, a, if . . . then, or, but.*

Messages require the proper form in order to communicate. Here are some typical form words in place to shape a message: "If the _____ is _____, then the _____ is also _____." "What is the _____ for the _____?" Notice that the first example is in the right form to make an assertion or statement, and the second is shaped to ask a question. We can tell that the form is right simply by looking at the shape of sentences. We do not need to look at the world of objects, things, and events to check the proper form for messages in a verbal code. When a mother tells her child, "Stop that!" even a very young child knows he is not being asked a question.

The second kind of message symbol is a *content* word. Content words consist of *names* for things and words that stand for properties and relationships. We commonly think of names as words that stand for important things such as human beings like *Mary* or *John,* families of humans like *the Smiths* or *the McCoys,* or classes of things like *dogs* or *cats;* but we also name less important things. When we talk of *carrots* or speak of one from a bunch as *a carrot,* we are also using names. When we name some thing, person, or event, we point to it and call the receiver's attention to the thing so we can go on to discuss it in greater detail.

If after we have named something and called the listener's attention to it, we want to say something further about it, we can use either *property* or *relation* words to comment about the thing already named. Property words indicate something that belongs to the object we are talking about. Some typical property words are those that stand for colors, such as *red, blue, orange;* those that stand for shape such as *square* or *round;* or those that stand for how things feel such as *rough* or *smooth.* We thus add the properties or qualities that further define the thing we have named. If we name a thing, for instance, "that carrot" and go on to shape a proper sentence that connects several property words to the thing, we could say, "That carrot is orange and hot." Every language has rules about the proper form to use when saying something about a thing that is named. Conventional English would not allow a person who wished to say that the thing named *carrot* was orange and hot to do so with a sentence formed as follows: "That hot is orange and carrot."

Relation terms indicate how two or more things fit together

or stand in terms of one another. Some typical relation words that can be used with two name words are *taller* and *above*. Thus, a person could say, "John is taller than Harry." Again the form of the sentence is important in English. If you want to say that the thing named *John* is taller than the thing named *Harry,* you must not say, "Harry is taller than John." Relation words may need more than two names to complete them. For example, the relation term *between* requires three names to properly form a sentence in English: "John sits between Paul and Harry."

To examine language use, we will divide the process into three features. The Romans had a god of the doorways, of beginnings, and of the rising and setting sun, who was called Janus and was represented by a statue with one head having two faces looking in opposite directions. If we were to represent language similarly, we might create a statue having one head with three faces. One face would symbolize the spirit of work, language as an aid to understanding the world, a giver of information, a servant to solve problems, and a teacher; the second face should be well-formed, beautiful, and pleasing, because it follows the formal rules of language; and the third face should be the spirit of enchantment, mystery, magic, confusion, language as a snare and a delusion, language as power.

The three faces of language are all related, but we can gain a greater understanding of the total process by viewing it from the three sides. We often use the term *denotative meaning* as a key to the first aspect of language. When we say a word denotes something we mean that the word points to, notes, stands for, or indicates the thing. Thus we can say that the word *chicken* denotes a certain kind of fowl that is a certain general size, is feathered, cackles, and lays our breakfast eggs.

The denotative meanings of a language are the way the words are plugged into the worlds of the source and the receiver. The words of any language are not related to the objects of our experience by any law of nature or because of any necessary connection. Thunder and lightning, as things that happen, are connected by a law of nature, and we cannot keep the thunder from following the lightning even if we wished to do so. The word *dog,* however, is not connected by any law of nature to the animal that barks, is friendly to his master, and likes bones. Our decision to use a given word to stand for some object, person, or event is up to us. If the language is to work as a code for communication, however, we must decide which words stand for which objects, and we must agree about it and come to share the *common* code or understanding.

Of course we cannot change the denotative meaning of words willy-nilly if we speak American English because if we did, we would confuse people. Naturally language is continually changing, and we do change the denotative meanings of some words over time. We have inherited the tradition of using certain words for certain objects, however, and we learn these rules when we learn the vocabulary of our language. We all come to have a number of common denotative meanings for words in a language we use to talk with one another. If a waiter gives us fried dog when we order fried chicken, he has violated our rules for the denotative meaning of *chicken*, to say nothing of our sensibilities.

The first aspect of language thus refers to those common meanings, shared by all people who use the language, about what objects, things, people, or events the words of the language denote. A common dictionary is a list of rules connecting words with denotative meanings, and we can read, write, and understand dictionaries because we share the same understanding of how words relate to things. We must point out the difference between the denotative meanings which are common to a number of people and the individual responses we all have to words. Although we may all know what animal is meant by the term *dog*, we may respond to that word in different ways because of our past experience. One of you reading about the notion of *fried dog* may respond differently from another one of you, but both of you will have a clear idea of what the words stand for or denote.

The second feature of language has to do with the rules by which the sounds and words can be put together to make sensible statements, ask meaningful questions, or give orders or suggestions for action. The second aspect of language relates only to the way sounds are arranged to make words and the way words are fitted together to make sentences. If you know the rules for using the language, you can check a chain of sounds and decide whether it is a meaningful sentence without looking at the world to check the denotative meaning of the sentence to see if it is true or false. Thus if you know the rules of forming good English sentences, you know that the string of words, "chicken minus over divided between chicken apple car," is not a good sentence. You would likewise know that "hetrologue minus over divided between hetrologue aardvark hieroglyph" is not a good sentence even if you did not know the denotative meanings of *hetrologue, aardvark,* and *hieroglyph.* These sentences simply do not make any sense to us.

The first two features of language are closely related, and before a person can say something that is true or false about the world he must encode a message in a form that makes sense to both source and receiver. Both source and receiver must also share a common denotative meaning for the content words. A less obvious connection between form and content of messages is the fact that a source can say the same thing about the world in a denotative sense using a number of different expressions. For example, the same basic proposition about an individual animal and a car in a certain relation can be stated by the following good sentences:

Look at that dog running after the car.

Look, that dog is running after the car.

Look at that car with the dog running after it.

We will call the one common denotative meaning of a group of sentences their *deeper* meaning and the various ways of putting the basic ideas the *surface* forms. Any English-speaking person hearing any one of the three *surface* form sentences about the dog-car event knows the *deeper* meaning of all three sentences, which is what actually happened and what all three sentences report.

An interesting and important area of language study deals with the way the surface forms are related to the deep structures. One result of studying the connection between deep and surface forms of expressions is a set of rules or a grammar to guide a person in moving from one form to another. These rules show how to *transform* a surface form into its deep structure. The technical name for the set of rules is *transformational grammar*. Scholars of transformational grammar have found some important things. For example, their study of deeper forms of several languages reveals many common features. Finding out how languages are alike helps us understand how languages in general allow man to organize his world. Discovering similarities between two languages also helps with the problem of translating a message from one language to another (from code to code) and reveals what meanings remain and what meanings are lost in the translation process. An expert in transformational grammar can use the same procedure to study differences and similarities among the dialects of a language as well as differences and similarities between languages. Within American English, for example, scholars have studied the similarities and differences between white upper-middle-class dialects and black urban-ghetto dialects. Such studies give us a basis for deciding whether the black English dialects are more or are less able than the white dialects to express denotative meanings about the world and whether the language rules of any particular dialect are simpler or more complex than those of another dialect.

The third feature of language has to do with the total response of the people involved in the verbal communication. Response to language is both individual and cultural. Sometimes we respond to a word or an expression because of our personal experience. According to the first feature of language the word *chicken* refers to a certain kind of fowl. Both speaker and listener usually understand the denotative meaning for the word to be the same kind of fowl. If the receiver has a violent dislike of fried chicken because of past experience, however, his response to the word will be emotional as well as reasonable. He may not only picture a chicken in his mind but he may feel a shudder of revulsion go through his entire body when he hears the word. Another person using the same dialect and in the same situation might feel a warm pleasant glow when he pictures the same fowl as the favorite pet chicken he had when he was a little boy.

Sometimes a number of people share a common response to language because they share a common situation. Consider the example of two grade-school boys arguing during recess. A circle of other children is soon ringed around them. The two boys become angry and one yells at the other, "You're chicken!" The sentence is in the proper form for American English and thus is a good sentence in terms of the second aspect of language. Few of the children watching the argument, however, think that the first boy is saying to the second that he is really a fowl capable of laying eggs and cackling. The first feature of language, denotative meaning, is pushed into the background by the situation. The sentence expresses the source's emotional feeling and attitude; he breaks out with a cry of anger and frustration and he might have expressed his feelings almost as well with a grunt or a shout as with the sentence. The other boy interprets the sentence in a similarly emotional fashion. The context and the culture which suggests that in a conflict the word *chicken* is a taunt and an insult come into play to form the response to the word. Every student of public speaking learns the importance of analyzing the effect of the situation and the occasion on the response of the audience. The speaker finds that an expression which is appropriate and gains him the desired response on one occasion may well be all wrong on another.

Some words and statements are closely tied to the structure of society and tend to arouse a common reaction from entire groups of people. Look at the following examples:

Winston tastes good like a cigarette should.

He played it as he should.

Whom did you wish to see?

It is I.

It don't neither.

Dese cigarettes are better'n dose.

Andy, he be with us.

Ya'll come back soon, heah?

I hain't seen 'im.

You probably found some of the examples odd and somehow not right, and others seemed quite right and comfortable. You might decide that some of the expressions were incorrect or bad grammar or show-off ways of talking that only affected people would use, or people speaking with a southern dialect or an urban-ghetto dialect. Your response to the expressions reflects your response to the people and the culture, the way of life, of those who speak the various dialects. Do you like the southern geographic region? Do you feel it is an area of pleasant, cultured, and gracious life? Do you feel the South is a closed society, racist and bigoted? All these feelings come into play when you hear a person speak in a southern dialect. Some critics of political speaking argued that President Lyndon Johnson's Texas drawl damaged the effect of his television talks to the nation because many opinion leaders, particularly those from the intellectual center of Boston, responded emotionally and negatively to the Texas dialect. Your response to an expression in black English likewise reflects your attitude toward race relations and your feelings about black culture. Whoever you are, wherever you live, you have to accept the fact that *you* speak a dialect. To someone from a different heritage and environment, the way you speak is strange.

The third feature of language reflects geographic regions, social classes, and economic, ethnic, religious, and racial differences. People in different geographic regions have developed different styles of speaking; working-class members use different forms of expression, different vocal inflections, different rules to form sentences, according to the second aspect of language, than do upper-middle-class people. People who live in the black urban ghettos of the North develop some unique patterns of speech, as do bilingual members such as the Mexican-American and Puerto Rican ghetto dwellers.

All the different ways of talking within the United States make up a single complicated system in which people move around from place to place, from one social and economic class to another. We must add to the system the effect of the mass media—film, television, and radio—which transmit a steady flow of messages in a standard dialect. Even within the same geographic regions, such as the southeastern United States, the lower class speaks differently from the upper middle class; the black worker speaks differently from the white worker. In practice, however, since all classes within a region talk with one another and all are exposed to radio, television, and film, the various expressions and ways of speaking rub off on one another. Thus you probably shift back and forth in your style of speaking depending upon how formal the situation is and on the people with whom you happen to be speaking at the time.

We will call the various different ways of speaking American English within the United States *dialects*. A *dialect* of American English is a variety of that language which is different from other varieties in terms of all three faces of language. A dialect differs from other dialects in vocabulary. Some words are commonly used in one dialect and not in another. The same word can denote different things in one dialect than in other dialects. For example, some dialects use the word *man* frequently as a word of emphasis, not merely to refer to a human male. A dialect may use a word to mean something quite different from the usual meaning associated with the same word in another dialect. The words *bread, grass,* and *trip* come to mind in this regard. A given dialect differs from others in the way the various sounds are made and in the way they fit together to form words, as well as in the way the words fit together into sentences. Those people who first learned to speak in a given dialect tend to have a common set of emotional responses to it. People who do not know the dialect or who learn it later in life often have a different set of responses to the dialect than do native speakers. Because the third face of language is a reflection of, a support for, and a factor in changes of class structure, race relations, and economic privilege, people respond with deep and profound emotions to dialects and the changing of speech habits. Often a comment intended to correct a dialect is taken as a personal insult or a slur on a class, race, or region.

Some people we know went to live in Paris for a year. The parents decided to send their two young sons to a private boys' school so that the two Americans could learn a little French that year. What the parents had not counted on was that their boys were subjected to taunts, teasing, and finally fights and beatings by the French boys who called them "so stupid . . . they can't even talk!" The American boys did, indeed, learn French that year, first to defend themselves and later to excel in the classroom. We might like to think this is a rather barbaric, isolated instance of language snobbery, and of course it involved two entirely different languages, not merely two different dialects within the same language. But if you have ever tasted the bitterness that can accompany dialect put-downs—being laughed at or misunderstood for speaking as you were taught to as a child—you can understand how belittling a dialect can cause conflict and misunderstanding.

Hawaii has a rich, diverse culture composed of many races. For years, speech teachers in Hawaii tried to change the pidgin and other native dialects of students to conform to a standard white middle-class dialect. Recently the entire program was re-evaluated and changed so that the students are allowed to use their native dialects and learn skills using them. In Brooklyn for many years, people who were studying to become teachers and who spoke native Brooklynese were retrained to speak with a standard American dialect. In Washington, D.C., a program to teach black children from the city's ghettos a standard white middle-class dialect came under heavy fire and was finally discontinued because enough people felt the program was racist and demeaning to black culture and to the students' pride in being black. Nevertheless, even within native dialects, most students need to learn to improve their communication skills. Some people are simply better able to communicate within their native dialect than are others, and most of us could improve our ability to communicate effectively with persons whose native dialect is different from ours.

If you wish to improve your ability in verbal communication, you must carefully study all three features of language. The first feature requires that you know how the language works to talk about the world and the way content words can be defined and sentences can say things that are true and false about facts. Chapter 7, "How To Inform," will deal in detail with these matters of definition and description of facts.

The second feature requires that you know the way words are formed to communicate a deep structure best for a given receiver or audience. Usually you can say the same thing in a number of different ways. The skillful communicator is good at picking a surface expression to convey his denotative meaning in the best way for a given situation and listener.

The third feature requires that you know how language is tied to personal experiences with words, dialects, and expressions. The student of interpersonal communication needs to be aware that a given individual, because of his uniquely personal experience with words, responds to some terms or expressions in an unusual or surprising way. He needs to know how the situation often affects the way people use and respond to terms and expressions. Finally, he needs to know how dialects affect his own plans to improve his speech and how dialects are related to the responses of various members of social, economic, geographic, and racial groups. In Chapter 8, "How To Persuade: The Persuasive Power of Personality," and Chapter 9, "How To Persuade: The Persuasive Power of Suggestion," we will examine in detail the third feature of language in use as it relates to individual responses and the influence of context on reactions to language. In the rest of this chapter we will examine the nature of dialects.

DIALECTS

What is a *dialect*? The differences that make one group's way of speaking a dialect in comparison with another's are part and parcel of the entire language. Dialect differences include the way people say the individual sounds, such as the /r/ sound or the /aw/ sound. Differences include the way people say larger units, such as the word *pin* (denoting a small, slender, sharp thing useful for sticking pieces of cloth together) and the word *pen* (an enclosure useful for keeping babies confined in a small area). Differences also include the way people say clusters of words, such as "Charlie Aunt she be with us" and "Ya'll come back soon, heah?"

In order for a person to say a sound, a word, or a cluster of sounds in running speech, he must know the rules for what sounds are to be said and in what order. He must also have the ability to form the sounds asked for by the rules. The rules of *pronunciation* relate to standards of what sounds to say, in what sequence, in order to speak the language. *Articulation* refers to a speaker's skill in physically forming the sounds of a given language dialect. A person might be unable to say certain sounds required to speak a language and would thus have a problem of articulation. This is particularly true when a person tries to learn some foreign languages, for certain sounds common in one language may never appear in another. Americans learning German as a second language often have trouble saying the guttural sound peculiar to German that is represented by the letters *ch* as in the word *Ich*. People whose native language is Japanese have trouble saying the American English /l/ sound.

Native speakers may misarticulate sounds in their own language. A person may lisp because he distorts the /s/ sound. Some speakers of American English cannot form the /r/ sound in certain words and say *wabbit* for *rabbit*. A speaker can know the standard way of pronouncing a word in his dialect but be unable to form all the sounds in the proper order with the right stress, and thus not say the word properly because of an articulation disorder. Young children often have articulation problems as they begin to speak. On the other hand, a person may be able to make all the sounds of a dialect but mispronounce a word because he does not know the standard way of saying it.

Articulation difficulties can be helped by increasing skill in saying the basic sounds of the language. Just as a basketball player can improve basic skills by practice under guidance, so a speaker can improve his articulation, no matter what dialect he may be speaking. We are all well advised to become skillful at articulation because to articulate clearly is to be more intelligible. The question of what standards of pronunciation we should follow is more complicated.

In some countries there is an arbitrary universal standard language. In France, the standards of language usage, including pronunciation, are decided by a group of experts. In Germany, one dialect has come to be considered the dialect for proper speech and it is taught in the schools. Educated Germans can speak high German in addition to whatever dialect they may speak at home or with their friends in more relaxed conversation. In the United States, the standards of usage are much less clear-cut. Dictionaries provide some guidance in pronunciation and are particularly useful if you are learning to say a new word. But what does a person do when a word is pronounced differently in different dialects? Perhaps his parents say a word one way, his friends on the block say it another way, and his teacher at school says the same word still a third way. Does he choose one way or another or keep various pronunciations for use at different times?

What is the right way to pronounce a word? The dictionary usually suggests a *preferred* pronunciation of a word and then it may list a second or third choice. Editors of dictionaries are careful not to say that the pronunciation they list as preferred is the right way to say a word. The editors of dictionaries do not make laws about correct pronunciation; rather, they discover the preferred pronunciation by surveying expert opinion and observing usage among those people the editors feel use the language well. In short, the editors take a poll of well-informed people and report the results in the dictionary. The "Preface" of *The Random House Dictionary of the English Language,* for example, characterizes the pronunciation standards in that work as being "acceptable" to "cultivated speakers."[1]

Editors often consult people who are engaged in broadcasting, journalism, lecturing, and writing when they are deciding about the pronunciation of a word. The dictionary's poll is thus weighted in the direction of certain groups of people, and certain dialect patterns tend to be emphasized. The dictionary's pronunciation standards tend to be accepted by the public as prestigious dialect and those who use the standard speech tend to be stereotyped as educated and cultured.

In the United States the standard is often called *general American speech.* Most radio and television announcers and actors learn and use the general American dialect. No matter what an announcer's native dialect may be, he tries to develop general American speech in order to find employment in any region of the country or to take part in a program or film planned for the entire country. Actors talented in mimicry not only learn to speak in the general American dialect, but also study many American dialects to use in playing as wide a variety of roles as possible. A skillful actor can tell an audience much about a character's geographic origins and social and economic background by a judicious use of dialect variations as he creates a role.

The influence of the prestigious general American dialect is felt all over the country. For example, at one time the dialects along the East Coast from north to south were divided according to whether people said the sound /r/. In the last few years, the sounding of the /r/ has been standard for broadcasters and the result is that the prestigious pronunciation of /r/ at the end of words has changed in the old r-less dialects. Most young speakers shift from sounding the final /r/ (hear) to dropping it (heah),

[1] New York, Random House, 1967, p. vi.

depending upon whether they are speaking carefully and formally or just talking casually with friends.

THE BEST WAY TO SPEAK

Should one standard dialect of American English be the prestigious way of speaking? The general opinion of experts in the study of language is that no one dialect should be singled out as better than all others. The test for judging speech ought to be how well the dialect communicates meaning effectively, easily, and appropriately to the situation in which it is used.

The fact is, however, that despite the efforts of experts in language usage, many people continue to view some ways of speaking as better than others and to take speech as an index of a person's education, sophistication, intelligence, and social position. Labov, an expert in the way various social and cultural groups use language, notes that "for decades, educational leaders have asked teachers to regard the child's nonstandard language as 'another' way of speaking, to recognize it as simply 'different' from school language rather than condemning it as sloppy or illogical."[2] Nonetheless, many people, including many teachers, unfortunately continue to view language as a clue to social and individual worth.

Many citizens of the United States have believed the American dream that the son or daughter of working-class parents could move into the middle or upper middle class, and that the grandson or granddaughter could become a member of the upper classes. Large numbers of Americans have fulfilled the dream and have moved up in wealth and social status. In the happy absence of a hereditary nobility and the influence of family that accompanies inherited social position, one of the few clues to social-class background remaining in the United States is the way a person speaks. After all, wealth can allow a person to get professional advice on hair style, dress, and home decorating, but speech is somewhat more difficult to change. While pronunciations vary among the well-educated, cultivated, and upper classes in the United States, grammar tends to be more uniform. Thus one

---

[2] William Labov, *The Study of Nonstandard English,* Champaign, Ill., National Council of Teachers of English, 1970, p. 28. In the discussion of psycholinguistics which follows we are indebted to Labov's work, particularly as it is summarized in this excellent little monograph.

authority asserts that "grammar is the surest linguistic index of a speaker's education and general culture."[3]

When people believe that a better way of speaking, or the use of a prestigious standard of speech, is the only way for educated people to speak, some damaging things can happen. One of the developments that followed the awareness of the racial problems in the United States during the 1950s and 1960s was an intensive investigation of the teaching of black children. Investigators discovered that black children often did not learn to read and write at the same rate as nonblack children. Some scholars decided that the difficulty was largely a result of the cultural deprivation of the black children. In their view, the black urban-ghetto child was deprived in his early years of the cultural advantages of the white middle-class child, particularly in regard to language development. Proponents of the deprivation view argued that black children spoke a dialect that was impoverished, illogical, and inadequate to meet the demands of schooling.[4] The remedy, they felt, was to improve the child's speech by teaching him standard English.

Another group of scholars emphasized the growing sense of black pride and awareness that developed during the same decades. These scholars argued that black nonstandard English was "a system of rules, different from the standard but not necessarily inferior as a means of communication"[5] and that the black child should be taught that his speech was different from other dialects but not inferior. Typical of the controversies resulting from these two views is the one that arose in Washington, D.C., where a committee of speech therapists in the teachers union argued with the school board that teachers should stop trying to correct the dialect that inner-city blacks spoke at home. The committee called itself Speech Therapists for Human Dignity and argued that the speech-improvement program was another way of robbing black people of their pride. The school board finally directed that the program of dialect change be dropped and told the speech therapists to spend their time correcting speech disorders such as lisps and stuttering. The supervisor of the program, however, opposed ending it and argued against the dialect theory, asserting

[3] I. McDavid Raven, Jr., "Usage, Dialects, and Functional Varieties," *The New Random House Dictionary of American English*, p. xxii.

[4] See Labov, *op. cit.*, pp. 46–50, for a summary and refutation of the deprivation theory. For further discussion of the cultural deprivation notion, see Fred M. Hechinger, ed., *Pre-School Education Today*, Garden City, N.Y., Doubleday, 1966.

[5] Labov, *op. cit.*, p. 14.

that the theory was grossly insulting to inner-city children.[6] The argument against using nonstandard black English in the classroom is that it insults black people by suggesting they cannot acquire the language other Americans use and that continued use of the black dialect will ultimately hold back black children from learning and success. Black as well as white educators are still divided about whether to attempt to change in any way the dialect spoken by children in the big-city ghettos as well as in the Deep South.

The interest in black English soon led to a concern for the speech dialects of bilingual students such as Mexican-Americans (Chicanos) and Puerto Rican Americans. Many of the same issues were raised in regard to Chicano dialects and Puerto Rican dialects as were discussed in regard to black English. In general, the social and cultural implications of the third feature of language came strongly to bear in these discussions. Students who are personally involved in this problem now have strong feelings about it. Countless Americans who now speak standard American English, but whose parents or grandparents or great-grandparents spoke another language before emigrating to the United States, cannot understand why "people make such a fuss about it; we learned it; why don't they?" These people still regard the United States as a melting pot, and they are eager to blend into the general population. Now minority-group members often believe they must build a strong pride and identity as a group so they will be considered equals in American culture. We appear to be on the way toward developing a democracy of differences.

However you view yourself and where you fit in your own culture, you will make certain decisions about the way you speak, just as you make decisions about other people because of the way they speak. If your native dialect is not general American you may decide you would like to develop that prestigious dialect at least for more formal speaking situations; in that case you will have to work on modifying your natural dialect. You may, on the other hand, decide that your life is going to be spent among people who speak your dialect and that there is no good reason for you to modify the dialect you speak right now. Except in the case of actors or politicians practicing the "just plain folks" appeal when they speak, most dialect changes are from nonstandard to standard, from working class to middle class, from upper middle class

---

[6] Discussed in Orlando L. Taylor, "Some Sociolinguistic Concepts of Black Language," *Today's Speech*, XIX (1971), 19–20. This entire issue of *Today's Speech* is devoted to black communication.

to upper class. In other words, dialect modification is often part of the upward mobility in American culture the sociologists talk about.

If you speak an inner-city black dialect, a dialect of the Deep South, or Brooklynese, or if English is your second language, the question of what you want to do about the way you speak is of great importance to you. If you speak a dialect of white working-class or lower-middle-class American English, you must face the same problem of whether to work at changing the way you speak. In the final analysis, of course, the decision is an individual one which each reader must make for himself or herself, but your decision should be made on the basis of an understanding of the way dialects are actually used in the United States and of the way in which they reflect social distinctions, class differences, and economic positions.

LANGUAGE IN USE

If English is our first language, all of us have learned a basic dialect before we get to high school. Generally we become native speakers of the given dialect sometime between the ages of 4 and 13. Children do not speak like their parents so much as they speak like the other children in their generation. The neighborhood gang is more influential in setting speaking norms than are parents. A good picture of an individual's dialect comes from his speech in the fourth and fifth grades when the 10-year-old conforms most strongly to the peer-group pressures.

When a person learns a native dialect, he learns three kinds of things about the way to speak in the code. He first learns automatic and basic responses that become habitual. These basic rules are never violated except by accident, and without them, we could not speak with one another at all. An example of this first kind of rule concerns when a person can change "she is" to "she's." The rule allows the form "she's here" but does not allow "here she's." People who speak the language know the first kind of deep basic rule and teachers do not have to teach it. If teachers had to teach the first kind of rule they would have a difficult time improving the student's approach.

The second kind of rule a person learns when speaking a language can be, and generally is, taught in school. Most speakers know that the second kind exists, and they know that it can be violated without destroying the possibility of communication.

These are rules about common usage. We are taught not to say "it don't," because it is ungrammatical. The reason is not that people will fail to understand, "It don't make no difference to me how I talk," but rather that if you speak in this way, you appear ignorant and uneducated. Rules of this second sort have social implications and are related to social class and status. Recall the notion that grammatical errors are the surest index to a person's lack of education and culture. Whether they ought to be is not the point; they often *are* taken to be important clues to the kind of person you are. People are even sometimes labeled "dumb" if they use poor grammar, which is often an unfair and illogical judgment. Violations of this second sort of rule are rare enough to stand out; they can be reported and discussed, and teachers can advise students to change their usage when it deviates from what is considered correct. The more common violations of grammatical rules occur during those times when language is in the process of change, especially at the beginning or toward the end of the period of change. Some time back, for example, people did not know whether to pronounce the word *aunt* as "ant" or "awnt." Nowadays most people say "ant" so the question of which to say is no longer very important.

Violations of the second sort of rule occur in about 1–5 percent of the instances covered by the rule in the speech of native speakers of a dialect. Violations are thus unusual enough to become the focus of class and status differences.

The third type of rule deals with the same language features as the first and second, but native speakers violate it more often than they do the second. Because the usage is so inconsistent, the rule is seldom enforced in school and is much less likely to be used as a clue to education, social status, culture, and background. Even with rules that are often broken, consistently extreme violations make a difference in the receiver's response to the speech. For example, the sound /th/ can be articulated (especially in isolation) in several ways without drawing much attention to it; however, should a person consistently, or when the same sound appears several times in rapid sequence, say /d/ for /th/ as in "dese folks speak better den dose folks do," he might be thought uneducated. People also articulate the sound /s/ in a wide variety of ways without drawing undue attention to their speech, but extreme distortions of the /s/ sound are noticeable as a lisp or a funny way of talking.

In general if a person learns a second or third sort of language rule after the age of 13 or 14 (the first type of rule is learned by that time), he will never follow the latter rule as regularly as he follows the first kind of rule. If you practice critical listening to your own speech and find yourself breaking rules of the second sort from time to time, you will have to make a special effort if you want to conform consistently. When a person is tired or distracted or highly involved and emotional about something, the newly learned rules give way to the native vernacular speech learned in the earlier years. The more consistent and regular speech of a dialect group is the basic way of talking learned before age 13.

Dialects may contain within them variations reflecting social classes among the people who speak essentially the same dialect. Thus we can talk in general terms of certain people in every dialect group whose speech is effective and prestigious because of their skill in communication and because of their status. Status in a dialect community may be based on a number of things including wealth, education, skills, or natural leadership. Scholars refer to the speech of the élite within the dialect group as the *cultivated* usage of the dialect.[7] The community also contains members with little formal education, little experience from travel, little status from natural leadership or skills. Scholars refer to the speech of the lower-status members of the community as *folk* usage of the dialect. Between the cultivated and folk usages is a *common* usage which characterizes much of the speech in the dialect. How different the cultivated usage may be from the folk usage differs from dialect group to dialect group, depending upon the structure of the community. The point is that one person may speak black English with great skill and sophistication, while another person may speak black English with little skill and much less effectiveness. Almost all people could learn to speak their native dialects more effectively than they do, and no student should assume that because he learns his dialect is as good as any other dialect, his speech is necessarily as good as it could be *within the rules that govern that dialect.*

Just as there are different levels of usage within a dialect group, so there are different styles of speech within the communication of an individual. Every speaker shows variations in speech style depending upon the relations between source and receiver and the power, status, and solidarity ties between them. Speakers also vary styles depending upon the wider social context in which they operate, such as school, job, neighborhood, church or syna-

---

[7] See, for example, Arthur J. Bronstein, "The Pronunciation of English," *The New Random House Dictionary of American English,* pp. xxiii–xxiv.

gogue, and depending upon the topic and occasion. Ability to shift styles varies considerably from person to person. Children, for example, may have a narrow range of speech style because they lack experience. Old men may show a narrow range simply because they no longer care about power and status and manners.

Studies of the way people talk in a variety of situations reveal that casual speech can be distinguished from careful speech in terms of the way people use their dialects. A person tends to monitor his speech carefully in formal or important situations such as a job interview, a first meeting with someone he wants to impress, or a formal public speech. Casual speech is the way a person talks when at ease and relaxed with people he can trust and with whom he is willing to be natural and off guard. Studies of casual and careful speech indicate that lower-class speakers tend to model their careful speech upon the standards of the upper classes. The speech of the upper class is not completely different from that of the lower class. Rather, the same differences in usage exist between careful and casual speech in all social classes. The careful speech of the lower class is more like the upper-class speech, and the upper-class casual speech relaxes into the patterns of the lower class. In general, however, the lower social classes have more deviations from careful upper-class speech in both casual and careful speech.

Other style variations come about from rhetorical reasons we mentioned before. There is a long tradition in the United States for persuaders to adopt the dialect of the audience, at least in part, to show they are "just like" the people to whom they are speaking. Politicians sprinkle ungrammatical expressions or use variations in dialect when they are speaking out among the voters, informally, during election campaigns. The same politicians, however, are careful to confine themselves to correct or even formal grammar on certain state or solemn occasions. The leaders of the Black Power and other black nationalist movements rarely use nonstandard black English in their public speeches. Their grammar then is essentially standard. Often, however, they use fragments of black English when talking to all-black audiences.

IMPROVING VERBAL COMMUNICATION

Should you change your way of speaking if you use a dialect that is not the same as the standard general American speech of radio, television, and film? Should you change your grammar to that which is commonly used by educated and cultured people of all dialects? You now have an understanding of some basic facts about language and dialects to help you make that decision for yourself.

You should keep the following points in mind as you decide whether you need to change or improve your own language:

1 / More middle-class speakers have skills primarily related to school language, but working-class speakers also have a wide range of verbal skills including many not mastered by middle-class speakers; and in the urban ghetto, speakers communicate in ways that demand ingenuity, originality, and complex language behaviors.

2 / Black English and other nonstandard dialects are not deficient uses of standard English. They are logical outgrowths of the linguistic history of the people who speak them.

3 / Because of the social, economic, and geographic anchoring of speech, people tend to make stereotyped judgments on the basis of the way you talk. Television announcers, school teachers, office managers, and so forth are stereotyped as having excellent speech with regard to their use of grammar, their articulation and pronunciation. A man who uses such nonstandard terms as "dem," "dese," "dose," and "dat" and double-negative expressions such as "don't never do dat to me agin," is stereotyped as a tough guy, one who probably fights a lot. Upper-middle-class and upper-class speakers are stereotyped as using correct grammar, pronunciations, and articulation.

4 / The more style changes you have at your command, the better you can communicate in a wide range of situations for a larger number of different receivers.

5 / Your instructor can help make you aware of any differences between your dialect and the standard grammar and pronunciation. Simply becoming aware of differences will not teach you to use the standard dialect. Certainly what you learn in the classroom will not become an unconscious verbal habit according to the first kind of rule. Probably the best you can hope for is a control such as that typical in the second kind of rule, when a person learns to use standard grammar at least in more formal speaking situations. Your casual speech will tend to remain much what it has always been.

6 / The most important consideration is for you to decide what you plan to do with your life. Do you plan to adopt a life style that requires talking with many different kinds of people? Do you plan to move from one part of the country to another? Do you expect to work with people from different social classes? From

We appear to be on the way toward developing a democracy of differences.

Message structure is a necessary part of communication.

We do not need to look at the world of objects, things, and events to check the structure of a message.

After we have named something, we can use either property or relation words to comment about it.

The denotative meanings of language relate to the description of the world.

We make the decision to use a given word to stand for some object, person, or event.

A common dictionary is a list of rules connecting words with their denotative meanings.

Response to language is both individual and cultural.

Every experienced public speaker learns that a word or an expression that gains him the desired response on one occasion may well be wrong on another.

Some words and statements are closely tied to the structure of society and arouse a common reaction, positive or negative, from entire groups of people.

Whoever you are, wherever you live, you speak a dialect.

You will shift back and forth in your style of speaking depending on the formality of the situation and on the people to whom you are talking.

Often a comment intended to correct speech is taken as a personal insult or a slur on a class, a race, an ethnic group, or a region of the country.

Belittling a dialect can cause emotional responses, conflict, and misunderstanding.

Even within their native dialects most people need to improve their communication skills.

Most people can learn to speak their native dialect more effectively than they do.

A person who is unable to say certain sounds used in a language has an articulation problem.

in chapter 3

The more clearly we articulate the sounds of a language, the easier it is for a listener to decide what words we are saying.

Editors of American dictionaries do not make laws about the right way to pronounce words; rather, they survey the way educated and cultured people pronounce words and decide what pronunciations are preferred.

Most radio and television announcers and actors learn to use the general American dialect in their work.

The influence of the prestigious general American dialect is felt all over the country.

When people believe that a better way of speaking is the only way for educated people to speak, some damaging results may follow.

One of the few clues to social background remaining in the United States is the way a person speaks.

No dialect should be singled out as better than all others.

Dialect modification is only part of the upward mobility in American culture.

All of us have learned a basic dialect before we get to high school.

Children speak more like their friends than like their parents.

Some rules of language use are so basic that they are hardly ever violated and we seldom are aware of their existence.

Some rules of language are violated often enough so people become aware of them and they tend to become markers of social class and status.

Levels of usage within a dialect group vary from cultivated, to common, to folk.

Casual speech is different from formal speech in most individuals.

A person is often stereotyped on the basis of his dialect.

Persuasive speakers often use the dialect of the audience in an attempt to identify with their listeners.

If a person wants to be an effective communicator in a mobile society, he is well advised to develop the ability to shift styles within his native dialect and to use other dialects in careful speech.

different ethnic backgrounds? Do you plan to work at a job in which your native dialect is basic and sufficient? Do you plan a career that would require you to use standard general American dialect and standard school grammar, and do you speak this way now? In general, you should consider that life in the complex, shifting, urban, multiracial culture of the future in the United States will put increasing demands upon college-educated people to be able to shift styles of speech and dialect over a wide range.

SUGGESTED PROJECTS

1 / The instructor makes a short tape recording of all of the students' voices. No names are on this tape, only voices. This exercise can be done by the class as a whole, but it is more effective when several machines can be used in smaller groups, members of each group recording only their own voices. The students listen to the voices and try to make a description, oral or written, of the various dialects and ethnic, religious, geographic, and national influences heard in each one's speech. At the end of the hour, the class discusses these dialect variations and further discusses the stereotypes that are sometimes associated with these various dialects.

2 / Each student listens to his own voice recording and describes his own dialect and verbal skill. Depending on time, the instructor and/or other class members help make an analysis of individual voices. Each student then writes a short paper analyzing his future career hopes and where and how he desires to live. Then he discusses the adequacies and inadequacies of his verbal communication, at this particular stage in his life, for his chosen career and life style.

3 / Find a newspaper article that reports some dramatic news event involving interesting people. Rewrite the news story in two ways: First, emphasize the denotative factual description of the event. Try to keep the names, the relational terms, and the property terms as neutral as possible. Second, slant the message to create an emotional response to the event. Use words likely to arouse positive or negative responses in a reader. If time permits, tape record the two versions for playback to the class in order to point out the differences in an oral presentation.

SUGGESTED READINGS

"Black Language, Literature, Rhetoric, and Communication," *Today's Speech*, XIX (1971).

Clark, Margaret L., Ella A. Erway, and Lee Beltzer. *The Learning Encounter: The Classroom as a Communications Workshop.* New York: Random House, 1971. "A Dialect for Meaning," pp. 157–183.

Labov, William. *The Study of Nonstandard English.* Champaign, Ill.: National Council of Teachers of English, 1970.

Lieblich, Malcolm. "Be Proud of Your Brooklyn Accent," *Today's Speech,* XVII (1969), 50–54.

Shuy, Roger W. *Discovering American Dialects.* Champaign, Ill.: National Council of Teachers of English, 1967.

4 how to improve nonverbal communication through vocal emphasis

Nonverbal communication consists of the body language and the vocal melodies that accompany a speaker's words. In this chapter we shall concentrate on the way a speaker makes the sounds of a language to communicate meanings beyond those conveyed by the three faces of language discussed in Chapter 3.

We should never underestimate the importance of nonverbal communication. One expert, Ray L. Birdwhistell, estimates that the words in a message carry about 35 percent of the social meaning in a situation, and the nonverbal elements convey 65 percent. Another expert, Albert Mehrabian, makes the same point, suggesting that the total impact of a message is a result of about 7 percent verbal, 38 percent vocal, and 55 percent facial elements. Of course, we have no way to measure exactly how much effect our use of vocal emphasis has upon our communication. We use such percentages, simply to emphasize the importance of nonverbal communication.

The technical name for the nonverbal features of communication related to voice and the articulation of sounds is *paralinguistics. Para,* a prefix borrowed from the Greek language, in this instance means *beyond.* Linguistics refers to language. The term *paralinguistics* thus means "beyond language," or that part of the talk that goes beyond the words.

Most dialects have some unique vocal patterns. People whose native language is Spanish, for instance, often speak English with a pattern of pitch inflection and a rate of speech similar to the one used in Spanish. Natives of India often speak English with a characteristic pattern of vocal emphasis. Ghetto blacks have some characteristic vocal patterns unique to their dialect—

for instance, an extreme rise in pitch. People speaking a general American dialect seldom use a high pitch except in times of emergency when under great emotional stress. Speakers of black English, however, use a high pitch more often.

You should be aware of the nonverbal features of a dialect as you study your own voice and analyze its strengths and weaknesses. However, our emphasis in this chapter is on the way you can use your voice to increase your ability to communicate specific meanings on specific occasions. We are primarily interested in how to punctuate and emphasize your messages by the way you say the words of running speech.

EMPHASIS

In encoding a message, a skillful speaker uses the nonverbal elements of pitch, loudness, rate, and pauses to add information both about his attitude toward the receiver and the message and about the content of the message.

Generally a part of the message is emphasized by separating it from the context with pauses. This can also be done by varying the rate of speech, the pitch, and the loudness, or by both separating it and varying the vocal elements. When you speak in a monotone (poor Johnny-one-note) at the same steady rate and at the same level of loudness, you lose much of the nonverbal potential of speech communication. You might almost as well communicate in writing. A good speaker has considerable range of pitch flexibility, loudness variations, and speeds of speech. If you wish to improve your nonverbal communication skills, therefore, you must drill your voice in the fundamentals of flexibility.

In working to improve your voice, you should try to find the unique variations of time, pitch, and loudness which best communicate your interpretation of a message. An oft-told anecdote about Mark Twain illustrates the importance of fitting the vocal emphasis to the meaning of the words. According to legend, Mark Twain was mightily put out on one occasion and, unaware that his wife was nearby, he cut loose with a string of swear words. He was surprised to hear the same words next pronounced by his wife, who hoped to shame him by her recitation. He listened appreciatively and then said, "My dear, you have the words but you haven't got the tune." The tune, in any case, should be appropriate to the meaning of the words, and simply singing the same tune over and over again, even though the tune has considerable flexibility of pitch, time, and loudness, does not communicate the ideas as effectively as it should. The key to the successful use of emphasis and flexibility is: *Get your meaning across.*

HOW WE TALK

Speech is an overlaid function, in that the lungs, the muscles with which we breathe, the voice box, the windpipe, the mouth, nose, teeth, lips, and tongue—all the parts of the body used to produce speech—have other, more basic, life functions.

Because producing sounds that others can understand and interpret is a somewhat unnatural process, it must be learned. All this means that an expressive voice is the result of natural talent, good vocal equipment, and training.

To understand better the natural functions of the organs used to produce voice and to use the vocal mechanism most efficiently—to train your voice to be pleasant, expressive, and capable of sustained speech for long periods of time without becoming strained, hoarse, or harsh—you must understand how the voice mechanism works to produce a sound wave and how the sound wave is modified to articulate sounds.

A channel of considerable importance in our *S M C R* model of communication is hearing. The gap between source and receiver is bridged by sound waves which impinge upon the receiver's ear and, through his sense of hearing, gain access to his meaning bank. The meaning bank is the storehouse of meanings, or words, the listener has in his brain.

The energy source for human speech is provided by the breathing mechanism. Air is sucked into the lungs by the action of certain muscles of the chest and rib cage and by the tightening and pulling down of a large, flat muscle that divides the body into two major cavities. The large muscle which forms the floor of the area which houses the ribs, and the ceiling of the cavity that contains many of the digestive organs, is called the *diaphragm.* When the diaphragm is tensed, it flattens down, pulling the bottom of the lungs down with it and thus creating a partial vacuum in the lungs. When a person takes in a breath of air, at the same time the diaphragm tenses, the muscles of the upper chest pull the ribs upward and outward. When the ribs move upward, they expand the chest cavity both from side to side and from front to back. Take a deep breath and notice the way your ribs lift up and your chest cavity grows larger as a result.

As a person breathes out, the muscles of the chest relax and gravity pulls the rib cage down. The muscles across the stomach tighten up, pushing in on the organs below the diaphragm, and they, in turn, push up on the relaxing diaphragm. Contracting the chest cavity squeezes the lungs and forces the air out through the windpipe (trachea) past the voice box (larynx, also called the Adam's apple in males). The vibrating mechanism in the production of the human voice is the voice box at the top of the windpipe designed by nature to prevent foreign particles from reaching the lungs. The voice box contains a valve which is open while we breathe but closes when we swallow, to keep food from going into the lungs. When we swallow something the wrong way, the valve has malfunctioned, and the coughing fit that follows is an attempt to remove the foreign particles that have gotten past the valve. When the valve is closed and the muscles used in breathing out air are tensed, air pressure builds up and the valve begins to vibrate and form a sound wave much as a trumpeter creates a tone for his instrument by vibrating his lips.

The vibrating sound wave now moves up into the throat and out the nose and mouth. As the voice moves through the throat, nose, and mouth, the sound is amplified and made larger and fuller. The shape of a musical instrument such as a trumpet affects the way the tone sounds. To understand the way in which the trumpet itself changes the quality of a sound wave, we must understand the concept of *resonance.* One dictionary synonym for resonance is *re*sound. The word refers to the increase of certain parts, the resounding or amplification of elements, of the complex sound wave as it travels through a horn. The lyric for an old song went something like, "the music goes round and round . . . and it comes out here." In the process of going round and round, the sound wave changes because some parts of it are resounded and become stronger, and other parts are not resounded and are damped out or made weaker as they fail to be amplified. When you speak, the tone is amplified or dampened by the natural resonant frequencies of the upper throat (pharnyx), the mouth, and the nose, all hooked together into a resonating system similar to that of a musical instrument.

The quality of your voice—whether it is pleasant, nasal, weak, thin, flat, rich, full, clear—is largely dependent upon the resonance given to the sound wave as it passes through your upper throat, your mouth, and your nose. Some of the quality is thus beyond your control. You cannot greatly change your throat, mouth, and nose (except by surgery). One cannot make a trumpet sound like a bassoon. However, within the range of the sounds produced by a trumpet, a good musician can certainly make much more pleasant tones than a bad musician. In the same way you can learn to play your particular horn (your own vocal equipment) better than you now do, in all likelihood. Most of us are lazy about speaking. Talking seems so natural, we seldom stop to think about it.

We sometimes say that an exceptional player has really made his trumpet talk, but we are speaking metaphorically because a trumpet cannot produce connected and intelligible speech. In order to talk, we must do more than produce a sound wave in the voice box and change its quality by resonating it through the throat, mouth, and nose. Speech requires that we encode messages. *Articulation* is the moving and adjusting of the speech organs to make the speech sounds that form a code for a group of people. The technical word for the basic units of sound for a language code is *phoneme*. The written symbols which stand for the basic units of sound in a language are part of what is called the *international phonetic alphabet*. The English alphabet is a written code and should not be confused with the oral code of English because we require more phonemes to speak English than we require letters to write English. Consider the two common pronunciations of the word *tomato*. The letter *a* as written remains the same, but the broad *a* sound in toe-*mah*-toe is not the same as the *a* sound in toe-*may*-toe. We have many more sounds in our everyday speech than we have letters. Take the sounds in the following English words: bait, bat, bought, bet, beet, bit, boat, boot, but, bite, and bout. Each vowel in these 11 words is phonetically different, and yet we encode these sounds when writing the words with just five letters *a, e, i, o,* and *u.*

The articulatory mechanism of speech consists of the vocal cords, the soft palate, the tongue, the lips, and the teeth. Make the sounds /s/ /t/ or /b/ or any of the vowels and notice how active your tongue is and how many changes you make in the position of your jaw and lips. Exaggerate slightly to emphasize these differences.

Proper articulation is a matter of being intelligible—of being able to make all the sounds of a dialect. *Pronunciation* is a matter of being able to use well-made sounds in words in the generally accepted way for a particular dialect. One might articulate the sounds properly and still mispronounce a word.

The phonemes (sounds) can be divided into two main categories. (Phoneticians point to other important distinctions, but for our purposes, one major difference needs to be stressed.) Most speech sounds can be classified as either vowels or consonants. All vowels require a sound wave of a regular frequency. The tone of the voice and its musical characteristics are, therefore, a function of the way we say the vowels. Because the vowels are phonated, that is, because the vocal folds are always in vibration to produce them, they contain more sound energy than many of the consonants. The vowels also carry your voice quality. If a person has a pleasant musical voice, it is because of the way he forms his vowel sounds and the way he utilizes his resonators. If a person's voice is breathy, nasal-sounding, weak, harsh, or in any other way distinctive, the vowels are largely responsible. That means that if you want to improve your voice *quality*, you should work on improving the way you make the vowel sounds. You have doubtless all heard the old line, "How now brown cow." It is a senseless sentence, the repeated saying of which makes much sense. Now to the other speech sounds, consonants.

Consonants tend to come in pairs and to be distinguished by the presence or absence of sound produced by the vocal cords. For example, the difference between /t/ and /d/ is that while the tongue, lips, and teeth are in the same position for both sounds, when one says /d/, he adds a sound produced by the vocal cords. The same is true of /s/ and /z/, /f/ and /v/, and a number of other consonants. Consonants thus may or may not have a regular tone associated with them, but they all have a plosive, noisy, clicking, hissing, or whistling quality. Most consonants are short and cannot be drawn out the way vowels can. Because of their shortness and the noisiness of most of them, consonants do not carry the musical or voice-quality features that the vowels do. Their main function is to distinguish among the various parts of an oral code such as the English language. The differences among words such as bit, hit, sit, and bit, bill, big, is in the consonants that surround a common vowel.

The consonants often contain less sound energy than the vowels. One of the weakest sounds in English, for example, is the unphonated stop plosive /t/. Try saying just the little sound /t/ without adding a vowel such as "eee" to it. Do not say "tee," say only the first sound /t/. Because the consonants generally have less energy in them, the listener cannot easily hear them. As a result, the receiver cannot decode the words; if the consonants are not heard the message is lost. Often we can overhear a conversation without understanding it because all we can distinguish are the vowels, and we hear something like "oh, ee, awww, ooo." On the other hand, we can use the same vowel and if the consonants are clear, we can understand the words even though the conversation sounds strange and stilted. For example, say the following sentence using the same vowel every time, "Mu futhur dumunds thut u gu tu culludg."

The lesson to be learned from the nature of consonants is clear. If you want to be understood, in the most basic sense of the receiver's getting the words you are saying, you must articulate the consonants clearly. The technical term for decoding the verbal content of a speech message is *intelligibility*. If the message is intelligible, the receiver can reconstruct the words sent out by the source. If someone is talking on a ham radio and says, "John lied out of fright," and the noise and static are such that the receiver of the message decodes it as, "John died last night," the message was unintelligible. Of course even an intelligible message must be interpreted or understood, but intelligibility is a minimum requirement for understanding. The reason the mumbler is not understood is often that the receiver simply cannot hear the consonants well enough to decipher what words the source is saying.

For example, if you are talking over the telephone and find that, because of a bad connection, the person on the other end of the line cannot make out the words you are saying, the best procedure is not to yell the vowels more loudly but to articulate the consonants with great care and clarity. The vowels are probably being heard but the consonants are what counts. Talking more loudly to slightly deaf people often makes them angry; articulating your consonants more slowly and more clearly helps people with hearing impairments understand what you are saying.

To communicate effectively, a person must both articulate clearly and pronounce the words correctly. Of the two skills, clear articulation is the more basic. If a person articulates clearly, others will probably be able to decipher the words even though they may wince at the way a dialect's conventions for saying those words are being broken by mispronunciations; but if a person does not articulate well, the receiver may not be able to decode the word the source intended.

The major articulation errors consist of (1) the omission of a phoneme, (2) the substitution of one phoneme for another, and (3) the distortion of the phoneme. As a child learns a language, he tends to begin speaking by omitting certain sounds and may first say something like "I wa I tee tone" for "I want an ice-cream cone." As the child becomes more proficient, he tends to add the sounds, but because some consonants are more difficult to form than others, he may substitute easier sounds for the more difficult ones. Notice that the child who is saying "I wa I tee tone" is substituting the easier /t/ sound for the more difficult /k/ sound. Finally, at the latter stages, a child may realize the substitution is an error and try to say the right sound but fail in the effort and, as a result, distort the sound.

Sometimes because of bad habits we continue to omit, substitute, or distort sounds on into our adolescent or adult years. No one bothers to point out our error, and we do not listen to ourselves critically as a rule. A common word illustrating two articulation problems is *just*, which ought to have a final /t/ sound, but is often articulated as "jis." When one says "jis" for "just," not only is he omitting the sound at the end, he is substituting the easier sound /i/ for the /u/ sound. Learn to listen for this in your own speech and that of others. You will hear "jis" frequently. Other common substitutions include "git" for "get," "goin" for "going," "runnin" for "running," and "beaudy" for "beauty." An occasional misarticulation is of little importance, of course, but many people have evolved bad habits of articulation and their speech is filled with such mistakes.

When a person consistently omits and substitutes sounds in running speech, the result is a mumble that is difficult to understand. Read the following sentence aloud to see how difficult misarticulation is to understand: "Hey, Joe, jeet yet? Lesgo grabbasanwish." Now read the following sentence carefully forming each phoneme: "Hey, Joe, did you eat yet? Let's go grab a sandwich."

Poor articulation is found in every dialect. You should not confuse a dialect's rules for pronunciation with errors in articulation. Recall that every dialect has a group of speakers who use the dialect well and who set the standards and a large group of speakers who use the dialect in substandard ways. A person who speaks a black inner-city dialect may articulate the sounds of the dialect clearly or may mumble in a fashion that makes it difficult for others *who also speak the same dialect* to understand him. No matter what dialect or dialects you speak, you ought to check your articulation, and where it is inaccurate, you should work to improve it simply for the sake of being understood—to make your speech intelligible.

PITCH

Pitch is the perception of changes in a sound wave as tones on a musical scale. The pitch of a speaking voice should be neither too high nor too low for general, comfortable use, and every speaker should learn to use variations in pitch to best advantage.

The way a speaker varies the pitch of his voice is an important nonverbal technique to emphasize the meaning in a message or to indicate that the meaning one would normally associate with certain words is to be discounted or interpreted as irony or sarcasm.

One can communicate a great deal by the skillful use of changes in pitch on such vowels as "oh" or "eee." You can experiment with the usefulness of pitch variations as a nonverbal technique of communication by saying "oh" so that it expresses different emotions and meanings: "how delightful," "I don't believe you," "that's nothing new," or "how disgusting."

Pitch inflections can be thought of as consisting of three main types: (1) a downward inflection, (2) an upward inflection, and (3) a circumflex, or upward *and* downward, inflection.

Downward inflections require that the voice start a sound on a relatively high note for the speaker and then slide down the scale while the sound is prolonged. Downward inflections add the nuance of assertion, certainty, and solidarity to meanings. Try the sentence, "I am quite certain about that," and use a strong downward inflection on the words toward the end of the sentence. Notice that the pitch variation supplements the verbal message, making the total message, both verbal and nonverbal, more emphatic.

Upward variations of pitch are useful to add nonverbally a questioning, tentative, light, or sprightly tone to the verbal message. Experiment with saying the sentence, "I am quite certain about that," with an upward inflection. Because the sentence is a statement rather than a question, you may find it difficult to read with a rising inflection or pitch, but with some practice you will be able to do so. Notice that sometimes the rising pitch alone makes the sentence sound like a question, and sometimes the rising pitch makes the remark sound tentative and unsure even though the words themselves assert certainty. Questions are emphasized by an upward inflection of pitch.

The circumflex, or upward and downward, movement of pitch is more complicated in its nonverbal connotations. Usually the verbal context and the situation influence the interpretation of the circumflex. The primary function of the circumflex is to make a portion of the message in which it appears stand out from the context. (Interestingly enough, in English we seldom use a pitch inflection that starts high, glides downward and then slides up the scale. You might experiment with a U-shaped tonal glide and see if you can interpret its nonverbal meaning.)

Pitch changes are among the most important voice techniques for nonverbal communication. Generally pitch changes are a result of stepping up or down in pitch either from syllable to syllable or from word to word, or of gliding from one tone to another while prolonging a vowel sound. (Recall that the vowels carry the musical quality of connected speech and that pitch changes within syllables are usually associated with vowels.) The pitch variations in oriental languages often convey different meanings: The same sound pitched at four different tonal levels may be decoded by an oriental listener as four distinct words.

You should select some sentences, experiment with shifting pitch in a step-like way from word to word, and then read the same sentences and shift pitch on the vowels in order to get the feel of the two major techniques to suggest mood and meaning with pitch variations.

LOUDNESS

The ear perceives changes in air pressure in the sound wave as changes in loudness. Loudness levels of voice have one basic and vital function in speech communication. The message must contain enough sound energy to travel through the channel to the intended receiver so it can be picked up and decoded.

Above the minimum required for intelligibility, loudness changes provide another technique of nonverbal communication. Loudness variations add emphasis by making certain ideas within a message stand out. In addition, a generally loud tone communicates excitement, high emotion, boisterous feelings, anger. A soft tone connotes calm, reverence, peace, boredom. We must always be careful not to view the nonverbal codes as though their meanings were as clearly defined and understood as the meanings of words. In a given culture, we tend to interpret nonverbal communication such as loudness or softness of speech in terms of how people talk in given contexts under the stress of certain emotions. Excited spectators at a basketball game may speak loudly, shout, and yell. Mourners at a funeral tend to speak softly.

A speaker can make important elements in a message stand out by saying them either more loudly or more softly than the surrounding verbal padding. We sometimes forget that speaking for a time at one level of loudness and then suddenly dropping the voice and saying the important words softly, can emphasize them as much as suddenly raising the voice to a shout.

Try reading the following line in the two ways suggested by the stage directions in parentheses, to get the feel of loudness variations as a nonverbal communication tool:

(normal level of loudness) When you say that, Mister, (drop loudness some) you better (pause, then very softly) smile.

(normal level of loudness) When you say that, Mister, (louder) you better (very loud) *smile.*

RATE

The speed at which one utters syllables and words is the *rate* of speech. Rate is the third major dimension of voice related to non-verbal communication. A rapid rate is usually associated with excitement, danger, the need for sudden action. A slow rate often communicates calm, tiredness, sickness, resignation. Speaking rates tend to vary depending on what section of the country you were brought up in, and much of what we call speech accents is actually a variance in rate.

In many respects, variations of rate function, like variations in pitch and loudness, to add emphasis.

PAUSES

Pauses can be thought of as part of the rate of utterance, but they play such an important role in the nonverbal encoding of messages that they deserve separate treatment.

Perhaps the most important feature of the pause is its function as oral punctuation. Comedian-pianist Victor Borge had a comedy routine in which he substituted strange and bizarre sounds, such as whistles, squawks, and clicks, for the various punctuation marks. The result was a hilarious example of the fact that the spoken as well as the written message needs to be properly punctuated to carry meaning successfully.

Generally short pauses are useful as dividing points to separate short thought units or modifying ideas, much as commas are used in writing. Long pauses serve to separate complete thought units much as periods, question marks, and exclamation points do in writing. Notice how pausing punctuates the following sentences so their meanings are changed:

The captain (pause) said the mate (pause) was drunk again last night.

The captain said (pause) the mate was drunk again last night.

Woman (pause) without her (pause) man is a beast.

Woman without her man (pause) is a beast.

Pauses of longer duration may communicate nonverbally in the context of an interview or small group meeting or before an audience. The famous "speaker's pause"—when a public speaker takes the podium and before starting to speak, looks out over the audience and waits for several moments—communicates confidence, a collecting together of important thoughts; it often catches the attention of the listeners, who expect something to happen at once, when it does not, grow curious about why the speech has not begun.

Within the context of an interview, also, a pause may be interpreted as meaningful. An interviewee who pauses for an appreciable length of time before answering a question may be communicating something such as, "That is a difficult question and I am not sure I know how to answer it," or, "I know how to answer that question but I am not sure I want to do so right at this point." When a respondent stops talking and the interviewer does not say something in turn, the pause may be interpreted as, "Please go on; I would like to hear you continue talking about this matter."

PROBLEMS OF NONVERBAL COMMUNICATION

Voice and articulation problems can be generally divided into two categories: those which are the result of some illness or malformation of the parts of the body that produce speech, and those, far more numerous, which are the result of habits of speech that do not utilize the vocal mechanism as well as possible. A tone-deaf person will probably never be a fine singer, but even a person endowed with a fine musical ear needs training to reach his maximum potential. If you have a severe voice or articulation problem, you should consult a trained speech clinician or correctionist. The advice we give here is directed at the vast majority of students who have perfectly normal voices but wish to retrain faulty speech habits to make their voices more expressive and to increase their effectiveness at nonverbal communication.

The same general procedure can be used to retrain bad speech habits regardless of whether they are associated with poor use of pitch, time, or loudness, with poor articulation or poor voice quality. The first step in any program of improvement is to train the ear to hear the errors. Most of us are so used to speaking that we ignore the way we sound. Few students are aware of the common voice problems. Because speaking is, by nature, imitative, we speak as our friends speak and copy one another's bad habits of articulation and lack of variety.

An excellent way to hear yourself is to record your voice and play the tape back while you listen critically. You ought to take advantage of every opportunity to tape relatively long passages and listen to them. Eventually, however, you must come to the point where you can monitor your own speech—*while* you are speaking. The feedback principle discussed in Chapter 2 is relevant here. You must become the actor in a feedback loop with the objective of improving your own voice. Your ear becomes the perceptor, and the sounds you utter are continually monitored to allow you to bring your practice on target.

The steps in the process go something like this:

1 / Train your ear to hear the problem.

2 / Gain control of the problem by learning to produce a sample of poor speech whenever you want to.

3 / Learn to produce the better sound.

4 / Practice the good sound and the poor sound, thus increasing the power of your ear to discriminate and at the same time teaching your vocal mechanisms how it feels to produce better speech.

5 / Once you can control your vocalization so that you can produce poor speech and good speech whenever you wish, begin to introduce the new speech habits into conversation with others— during lunch, for example.

6 / Gradually you will find the new speech more comfortable, and as it becomes more habitual, you can introduce it more often into your daily routine.

Eventually, you will use your new speaking voice without having to think about it consciously, and you can concentrate on the ideas you are framing in your message, assured now that you are using the best vocal technique you can build to communicate your ideas and feelings nonverbally.

This general pattern can be used to correct slovenly articulation of certain sounds, particularly the tendency to substitute easy sounds for more difficult ones such as /i/ for /e/ and /d/ for /t/. The general pattern can be used to correct monotony of pitch, time, and loudness. It also works with voice quality problems. Difficulties of rate are the easiest to remedy.

If a person speaks too rapidly, for example, careful attention to speaking more slowly, drawing out the vowel sounds in a smooth way during drill sessions, will soon enable him to train his ear. One can speak more rapidly or more slowly without difficulty. A good feedback loop can bring the rate on target quickly. Often a person who speaks rapidly also speaks in a jerky, staccato fashion so that the articulatory mechanism—the tongue, teeth, and lips, in particular—are asked to form the consonants so rapidly that they are poorly articulated. Slowing the rate and forming the consonants more carefully many times solves an articulation problem as well as a rate problem. Generally a good rate for reading to audiences is between 140 and 185 words per minute. Daily speaking should not exceed this maximum, and speaking slower than 140 words per minute should be restricted to occasions when one is addressing a large crowd and must overcome problems of general noise, echo, and the like.

A good drill for breaking the monotony of time, pitch, and loudness is to read a passage first in a monotone and then with great expressiveness, much as a Shakespearean actor might read an emotional speech from a play. Overdoing the flexibility of your voice in drill sessions does two good things for your nonverbal communication: (1) it forces your vocal equipment to stretch its range just as daily exercise stretches muscles and makes them more flexible, and (2) it teaches your ear to discriminate changes in emphasis at the same time it teaches your vocal equipment how these new sounds feel.

A whole cluster of voice problems may be improved by finding a suitable pitch level for your voice. Poor pitch flexibility and low levels of loudness may result from speaking at the wrong pitch level for your vocal equipment. Using the wrong pitch habitually may also strain the vocal folds, and one response to such strain is failure of the valve in the larynx to close completely, producing a breathy voice quality. Another typical response to vocal strain is tightening of the throat and forcing the voice to be loud enough to be heard, producing a harsh or hoarse voice.

We must first note that a person may speak at or around one pitch level habitually, even though that level is not the best one for his vocal equipment. For example, if a girl has a natural alto singing voice but is placed in the soprano section of a choir, she may be forcing her voice to reach the high notes and thus be straining her voice. People learn to speak largely by imitation, and a child may model her speaking voice after her mother's or an older sister's and thus learn to speak at a level that is unnatural for her. Sometimes people adopt a good pitch level as children but fail to adopt the lower pitch level that should come with growth. Sometimes people consciously strive to adopt a low pitch level because they feel it is more attractive. The pleasant voice is not necessarily the low-pitched voice. A man may have a good tenor voice if the vowels are resonant and if he varies the pitch, time, and loudness skillfully.

The *habitual pitch level*, therefore, is the pitch around which a person talks. Somebody with a good musical ear can help you discover your habitual pitch by finding on the piano the tone you tend to use as you speak or read. Contrasted with your habitual pitch is your *natural pitch level—that pitch best suited to your voice.* Just as a certain hair style may make a girl look more attractive because it emphasizes her best features, so will the best (natural) pitch level for you make your voice more attractive.

We have no sure method for discovering a person's natural pitch level. One way to approximate it is to sing the lowest note you can, and the highest, including falsetto, and then find the tone one-fourth of the way up that range for men and one-fifth of the way up the range for women. Somewhere in the region of the lower fourth or fifth of the range is the place where most people's natural pitch level falls. Another way to approximate your natural pitch is to say a vowel such as "ah" with as low a pitch as you can and then move easily up your pitch range. At some point you will discover you can make a louder sound more easily than you could at the lower pitches; proceed up your range until you again find yourself straining to reach the pitch. Your natural pitch is in the region of the scale where you produce a good, loud tone easily.

A good drill to improve pitch level is to take ordinary prose material and read it in a low tone, then a middle tone, then a high tone. (Sometimes doing this will also reveal whether your present habitual pitch is too high or too low.) If you discover you need to raise or lower your habitual pitch, you should proceed just as you do with other voice problems by first training the ear to hear the difference, and then in your drill sessions, reading at the old pitch and then the new pitch.

To have a good resonant and flexible voice, a speaker must provide adequate breath support for the vocal cords. Since pauses are part of our language code and function as punctuation, a person who runs out of breath at the wrong place in a sentence and must pause for another breath will punctuate his thoughts in a confusing way. The technical name for punctuating your ideas improperly is *faulty phrasing*. To phrase properly, people who do not have good breathing habits for speech often tighten the vocal folds and try to conserve breath in that way. The result of tightening the vocal cords and throat muscles, as we have seen, is harshness, or hoarseness. A tight throat also reduces resonances and creates a relatively flat or weak and thin voice. If your voice lacks resonance, the fault may well be bad breathing habits.

Many features of contemporary life contribute to the generally bad breathing habits of Americans. A young lady often consciously sucks in her waistline to improve her posture and figure. A girl who is pulling in on her tummy has no chance to use her diaphragm to draw in a breath or to pull across her stomach to support a tone. She is forced, therefore, to lift her shoulders when she breathes and use only a little bit of the upper lungs to support her speech. She may have a gorgeous figure, but when she opens her mouth she either screeches like a shrew or sounds like a preschool child actress. Athletes who compete in sports that require sudden bursts of energy, such as basketball or track, often develop a habit of breathing in quick, shallow upper-chest pants. The result is often a husky athlete who speaks in a weak, thin, harsh, or husky voice. The common tensions of life also cause people's stomachs to knot up and reduce their use of the diaphragm and stomach muscles in breathing. Indeed, when a person wishes to relax, a good way to start is to take several slow deep breaths.

Good speech requires an adequate supply of air in the lungs and sufficient skill to control the air pressure during phonation. Singers, who face the same problem as speakers, spend much time learning to support a tone properly. The same general approach will work for anyone wishing to improve breathing for speech. You should use the entire breathing mechanism, including the diaphragm, while speaking. To get the feel of diaphragmatic breathing, stretch out on the floor and place a book on your stomach. Now try to get the book to rise when you inhale and sink when you exhale. With a little practice you will discover you can begin to breathe naturally. (You breathe with your total respiratory system when asleep). Notice that as you breathe slowly from the diaphragm, the tensing muscle inside your body forces the expansion of your waist. The muscle you feel tensing under your lungs is the diaphragm.

Having discovered the feel of diaphragmatic breathing, your next step is to begin to practice support and control of your speech while actually speaking. While breathing exercises by themselves are not harmful and may even be good for your health, alone they do not improve your voice. What is required is a training of the habits of breathing during speech. (Interestingly enough, a singer who has excellent breathing habits while singing may have bad breathing habits when speaking.)

A good exercise is to take the old nursery rhyme "This is the house that Jack built," and, taking a good breath before each phrase, try to read the phrases in one breath as they get longer and longer. Thus:

(breathe) This is the house that Jack built.

(breathe) This is the malt that lay in the house that Jack built.

(breathe) This is the rat that ate the malt that lay in the house that Jack built. (And so on.)

Another good exercise is to count in a whisper in a slow, deliberate manner. See how far you can count on one breath. Practice taking another breath and try to count farther. Several minutes of drill each day will soon increase your ability to support speech with your breath. After you have counted in a whisper, repeat the exercise while phonating. Be careful to count only as long as you can do so with a relaxed throat. The minute you begin to tighten your throat and strain your voice, stop counting.

Quite often, improving the breath support for the voice encourages the speaker to keep the throat open and the vocal cords relaxed. A good athlete is relaxed even when playing a vigorous game of basketball. A good speaker is relaxed even when projecting his voice a long distance. With a relaxed throat and good breath support, a person can speak loudly for long periods without strain. If you find yourself hoarse after shouting at a ball game, you are probably not using your throat properly. When a speaker uses a relaxed and open throat and an adequate breath supply, the vocal quality of his voice tends to be improved. Often simply opening the throat and using more of it as a resonator causes less of the sound to go through the nose, and a nasal voice quality is corrected by the change. Another way to improve the vocal resonance is to be sure to open the mouth when articulating the vowel sounds. Again, singers are trained to open their mouths wide to improve the quality of their singing voices. The same principle holds for speakers. Too often we develop lazy habits of articulation and speak through clenched teeth with a rigid jaw. A good drill is to read prose material opening the mouth in an exaggerated fashion and overarticulating both the vowels and the consonants.

Articulation problems require first a careful analysis. The best procedure is to record your voice reading a passage of prose that contains all the sounds of English arranged so they fall at the beginning, the middle, and the ends of words. Listen over and over again to the recording. You should be able to pick out the omissions, substitutions, and distortions. If you are fortunate enough to have a voice expert listen to the tape with you and give you a vocal diagnosis, fine. If you typically, for example, substitute /d/ for /t/, you should then practice making the two sounds in isolation. Then drill, saying them one after another. The drill in which you say the correct sound first, then the wrong sound, trains your ear to hear the difference and trains you to associate the correct sound with a certain position of the articulatory mechanism.

If you wish to change your voice into a pleasant and ex- pressive instrument for nonverbal communication and acquire the technique needed to add subtle nuances to the meanings in words you utter, you must drill upon the fundamentals of voice and articulation improvement. You should look at your weekly schedule and select short periods several times a week when you can go off alone somewhere and chant, read, shout, and make weird sounds. Even if you can spare only 20 minutes on Mondays, Wednesdays, Fridays, and Saturdays, and then only in the early evening or just before going to bed, you ought to do so. No one can improve your voice for you. You have to do it yourself. And now you have a good idea of what you need to work on and how to go about im- proving those things that need improving. So set up a schedule and decide which of your problems require immediate attention. Next develop a list of drills to work on these problems. This is not something you have to do the rest of your life. You can improve your speech noticeably in a matter of months, and you can enjoy the rewards that better speech can bring you the rest of your life without having to fret about it any more.

You will find that after several months of drilling for short periods your ear will become much better able to discriminate the sounds you are making; your voice will become a major tool of

the key ideas

Most dialects have some unique vocal patterns.

Generally we emphasize ideas by making them stand out from the context.

A person might as well communicate in writing as speak in a monotone.

The key to the successful use of vocal flexibility is: *Get your meaning across.*

An expressive voice is the result of natural talent, good vocal equipment, and training.

Most of us are lazy about speaking and can greatly improve our voices with study and drill.

Proper articulation is a matter of being intelligible, of being understood.

The vowels carry the quality of the voice.

The main function of the consonants is to distinguish among various words in a language.

If you want to be understood, you must articulate the consonants clearly.

If you want to have a pleasant and expressive voice, you must articulate the vowels clearly and vary their pitch, loudness, and duration.

---

nonverbal communication. You will become a much more effective communicator in all the communication situations in your life— interviews, group meetings, social conversations, over the telephone, and if the occasion should arise, in public speeches and meetings and over the mass media.

SUGGESTED PROJECTS

1 / Each student records his or her voice both talking informally and reading. The reading should be from simple prose exposition, *not* dramatic reading. With the help of the instructor and the other students, each class member analyzes his nonverbal communication in terms of vocal monotony, flexibility, quality, pitch, rate, loudness, and clarity of articulation. Each student writes a

in chapter 4

When a person consistently omits and substitutes sounds while speaking, the result is a difficult-to-understand mumble.

Poor articulation is found in every dialect and ought always to be improved in the interest of intelligibility.

Pitch changes are among the most important voice techniques for nonverbal communication.

A speaker can make important elements in a message stand out by saying them either more loudly or more softly than the surrounding verbal padding.

The most important feature of the pause is its function as oral punctuation.

The same general procedure can be used to retrain most bad speech habits.

A person may learn to speak habitually at a pitch level that is unnatural.

When a person habitually speaks at a level that is natural for him, his voice quality and flexibility are generally quite good.

Good speech requires an adequate supply of air in the lungs and enough skill to control the air pressure during speaking.

---

brief paper describing his own vocal strengths and inadequacies and in consultation with his instructor if necessary plans a program of exercises that can be used to improve his nonverbal vocal communication.

2 / The class makes a list of popular television newsmen, local or national. After discussion, the list is narrowed to the five the class decides are best. Members of the class then make tape recordings (audio only) of these five and play them back for the whole class, which ranks the five and analyzes their strengths and weaknesses in voice and articulation. To insure that the verbal elements and the meaning of the message do not sway the class, the tapes may be played backwards so that only the nonverbal elements can be judged. How much of the appeal these newsmen had when first chosen seems to come from voice quality and articulation alone?

3 / Divide the class into coeducational pairs if possible. Each pair

has 2 minutes to communicate an emotional relationship between two people using only a variation in the intonations of the words "John" and "Mary." No other words may be used. The male member of the pair will say "Mary," and then the female will say "John," and they alternate these words for 2 minutes. Gestures and facial expressions should be kept at a minimum. The situation portrayed could be as impersonal as two strangers meeting on a bus and striking up a conversation, as personal as an intimate family incident, a lover's quarrel, or merely two friends gossiping. The class tries to figure out the relationship between the two people from the verbal intonations alone.

SUGGESTED READINGS

Addington, D. W. "The Relationship of Selected Vocal Characteristics to Personality Perception," *Speech Monographs*, 35 (1968), 492–503.

Birdwhistell, Ray L. *Kinesics and Context*, Philadelphia: University of Pennsylvania Press, 1970. "Stress in American English," pp. 128–143.

Bronstein, Arthur, and Beatrice Jacoby. *Your Speech and Voice*. New York: Random House, 1967.

Eisenson, Jon. *The Improvement of Voice and Diction*, 2nd ed. New York: Macmillan, 1965.

Fairbanks, Grant. *Voice and Articulation Drillbook*, 2nd ed. New York: Harper & Row, 1960.

Mehrabian, Albert. "Communication Without Words," *Psychology Today*, 2 (September 1968), 53–55.

5 how to improve nonverbal communication through body language

In addition to the paralanguage of voice and articulation, nonverbal communication includes body motion—the silent language of gesture, posture, facial expression, and the way people position themselves in relation to one another as they talk.

Three factors are involved in the body language of each of us:

1 / We learn a general body language from our particular culture. We learn this general body language as children, just as we learn to speak in the verbal code of our family. The cultural body language refers to such things as how closely people stand when they talk to one another, whether people touch one another when talking, whether people look one another in the eye when they are angry or embarrassed, whether a vigorous nodding of the head accompanies agreement or disagreement.

2 / Every individual, within his culture, develops a nonverbal language to help him communicate. He may use nonverbal gestures while talking to emphasize his verbal messages, or he may use nonverbal gestures alone to convey his meaning. To some extent, nonverbal communication is cultural, but to some extent, it is individual and varies from person to person. Some people are skilled and can use nonverbal communication to emphasize, even to contradict, what they are saying.

3 / Every person develops characteristic ways of talking and moving, of standing or sitting while listening, of using the hands while excited. This is highly individual, and often nonverbal communication of this sort is more an interference than a help in conveying meanings to another person. If an individual's gestures call attention to themselves, not to the message intent,

these gestures should be modified to allow the more meaningful gestures (discussed under 2, above) to enhance communication.

Birdwhistell, a leading scholar in the field of communication through body motion, tells of a study to investigate possible differences in the nonverbal communication of a mentally disturbed family compared with a mentally healthy one. Careful observations revealed that the mentally upset mother was sending out contradictory messages. The investigators filmed the way the mother handled a baby girl. They discovered that in changing the baby's diaper, for example, the mother placed her arm around the baby so that her hand was between the baby's arm and body as she was pinning the diaper. As the mother pinned the diaper, she both pushed upward on the baby's arm, sending a message to the infant to raise the arm, and put pressure on the baby's body in such a way that the baby would think the arm should come down. The child was in the unsettling position of being unable to obey either message without disobeying the other.

If this example of Birdwhistell's seems far-fetched, stop and think how a child often learns from his family to do things that are directly counter to the parents' pious pronouncements. "Don't," a father says, "make the mistake I did and drop out of high school. Get a good education. You can't get anywhere these days without it." At the same time the father says this, however, much of what he does suggests to the son that he thinks reading books is a waste of time, that he views colleges with suspicion, and that he sees college professors as strange, impractical people. The father communicates in a thousand nonverbal ways that he does not believe his own advice, and then this same father is unable to understand why his son quits school just as he himself did. There is much truth in the old saying that "teachers teach as they were taught, not as they were taught to teach." You must be sophisticated indeed in all aspects of communication to be totally aware of what you are communicating, nonverbally as well as verbally, when you send out messages.

Examples of the cultural basis of much body-motion communication are numerous and striking. Middle-class white teachers in urban-ghetto schools had difficulty communicating with the black children because they did not understand some of the black nonverbal cultural traditions. The teachers were from a culture in which eye contact while conversing indicated interest, sincerity, careful listening, and genuine concern. The teachers thought of a person who looked down or even away as being shifty-eyed, insincere, perhaps even untruthful. The children were from a culture in which eye contact indicated anger. No wonder the children were disturbed by teachers who always seemed to be angry with them!

The Japanese tend to smile in a certain way when apologetic, embarrassed, and disturbed. When a manager in a Japanese factory calls a mistake to an employee's attention, the latter smiles. Before American managers working in firms in Japan learned of this cultural way of communicating, they often were upset by the smile. One manager broke off, reprimanding the employee with a curse, and forbade the employee to smile like that when discussing an important problem.

When you talk with someone from a different culture, whether that culture is within the United States or outside it, you need to be aware that the culture-based silent language of body position, relationships, and motion can hinder successful communication. We have many different cultures within the United States that affect the nonverbal part of communication. Some authorities maintain that poverty produces its own culture. We are becoming increasingly aware of, and are emphasizing, cultural differences in the minority groups in our national culture. Regional differences affect communication. The dialects of the Deep South are not just matters of forming sounds; they also relate to the vocal inflections and the body motions that accompany them. The same is true of the Yankee dialects of the New Englander or the speech of the Far Western Mountain Region.

PROXEMICS

Edward T. Hall, who studies nonverbal communication, uses the word *proxemics* to stand for the way people communicate by their use of space in relation to other people. Hall points out that we are comfortable in some communication situations only if there is a certain amount of space between the other person and ourselves. He describes four distances which are common in four different communication situations. The first is *intimate* distance, which varies from touching to a space of 1–1.5 feet. Intimate distance is appropriate only for the most intimate conversations, usually between a man and a woman who are well acquainted and friendly, or between parents and children, particularly young children. When we are placed in such close contact by being forced into a crowded bus or elevator, we usually protect ourselves by not conversing. For important and personal communication situations, however, the intimate distance is often the most rewarding.

The second distance Hall refers to as *personal* and suggests that the space is roughly 1–2.5 feet. When two people meet in an office building or on the street and strike up a casual conversation, they usually remain approximately this far apart. Watch the people around you for the next day or so and see if your own observation bears out this theory, and if you behave this way too.

The third distance, *social* distance, varies from about 4 to 7 feet. The social distance is good for impersonal business. The job interview, for example, is often conducted at this distance.

The final distance is the *public* distance, which starts at about 12 feet and extends as far as is feasible in a large room or auditorium. (You may wonder what happens in the areas between the zones covered, such as the distance from 7 to 12 feet. Other things must be taken into account, and the student of nonverbal communication might be able to determine whether the design of a given room for a speech, a presentation, or a discussion will place the participants in a public or personal zone even though they are going to be talking to one another at a distance somewhere between 7 and 12 feet. These distances are simply rough rules of thumb to indicate that distance is an important feature of communication.)

As important as distance is the geographic location of the participants—where people are in relation to one another. If an employer calls an employee into his office to discuss something in a two-person situation, the arrangement of the furniture and the seating of the two people influences the communicative setting. If the boss sits behind his desk and the worker sits in front of the desk, the fact that one is the boss and the other the employee is always part of the situation. With the nonverbal dimension, the proxemics, so strongly a part of the interview, a discussion of personal matters would be difficult. Clearly, the boss who sets up a conference on this basis wishes to keep some distance from the employer as a person and to stress the status difference between them. If the boss comes from behind his desk, pulls up another chair, and sits beside the employee so they can talk at a distance of 1 or 2 feet or even touch (a tap on the shoulder to indicate personal concern or emphasis), the situation has been drastically altered by the changed geography of the communicative setting.

The geography of the small group meeting is a fascinating study. In some settings, a place at one end of a rectangular table is viewed as a position of power. Watching the way people sit at a meeting tells a wise observer a good deal about who likes whom and who is competing with whom for position or influence. During the course of the discussion such gross bodily movement as leaning back in the chair, leaning forward and placing the elbows on the table, turning slightly and pulling away from the speaker, or turning toward the speaker each indicates interest, boredom, acceptance, or rejection.

In a large group, the position of the listeners in relation to one another and to the speaker is a matter of considerable importance. If the speaker is located on a stage, standing behind a podium some distance from the audience, the proxemics of the situation says something about it. Should the speaker jump down from the stage and walk up and down the aisles as he speaks, such bodily movement would communicate a desire to break the public distance and move in the direction of more personal space to convey his message.

The distances among the members of the listening audience also affect the suggestibility of the audience. If a few individuals are scattered throughout a relatively large room, with many chairs empty, the effect is much different than if the audience is packed tightly together and some people are sitting on the floor around the edges of the room or standing along the walls. When the audience reacts sharply to a speaker by a sudden tightening of bodily tension on the part of a majority of the listeners, a sudden intake of breath, a sigh, a laugh, or a groan, the speaker and the listeners get the message and respond with emotion as well as with interest.

When the nonverbal body-motion codes are sent by television waves rather than directly face to face, the changes are important, but our knowledge of the differences is as yet relatively intuitive and undeveloped. The two major media for communicating body language are television and film. The actress in a television commercial selling shaving cream is stretched out on a beach blanket; she wears a bikini. Her slightly mussed-up hair falls over one side of her face. With an inviting smile and half-closed eyelids, she says in a husky voice, "Take it off, take it *all* off." Certainly she is communicating a great deal nonverbally that has little to do with shaving. The director can have the camera take a full shot of the actress, or he can have her lift herself up on her elbows as he brings the camera in for a shot which includes her face and the top of her bikini, or he can have the camera take a tight close-up of her face. If the message is to be, "Use this shaving cream and you will be successful with beautiful, sexy girls such as this one," the director's decision about which part of the total nonverbal communication of the girl he is going to show his audience is important. Not only that, but the nonverbal gestures he asks the actress to make if he chooses to use a shot of her entire body viewed from some distance will differ from the gestures he requests if he chooses to use a close-up.

Despite increased interest in, and study of, kinesics, proxemics, and body-motion communication in recent years, little information useful to the student trying to improve his interpersonal speaking skills has resulted. We now know that body motion is important in communication, particularly as it pertains to the vital areas of overcoming protective-filter devices and communicating trust and support. We will discuss these matters in considerably more detail in the next chapter. For now we have to state that the implications of nonverbal body movements for the success of human interaction are much more complicated than we at first thought and that they hold many clues to the problems involved in intercultural communication.

The day may soon come when we will have enough knowledge about body language to teach people how to communicate more effectively in two-person conferences, small group meetings, and other intimate and informal settings. We have two traditions, however, that have long recognized the vital importance of body movement in communication. In our culture the traditions stem from Ancient Greece and relate to the theater on the one hand and to public speaking on the other. Actors and directors of theatrical productions learn the art of communication through gesture, facial expression, eye movement, and positioning of actors on a stage. Students of public speaking also learn to use body motion in delivering a speech effectively.

For the remainder of this chapter we will describe ways in which you can learn to use body movement to communicate effectively while giving a public speech. We will give directions that have been worked out over years of study and practice of the art of rhetoric. Since the public speech is a special cultural event, it has certain expected norms of behavior and certain conventions of gesture and movement to guide the speaker. Future study of more informal interpersonal communication settings may yield similar knowledge about how to communicate nonverbally under such conditions. Meanwhile, if you study the information and drills used by students of public speaking, you can take their approach as a guide to your own study of the body language of interpersonal communication.

STAGE FRIGHT

Most beginning public speakers find that the thought of talking to a large group of people makes them nervous. Perhaps nothing about a speech-communication course is more on the beginner's mind than this worry about stage fright. It is not an insurmountable problem. There are many things you can do to keep stage fright from showing to the audience, to make it work for you rather than against you.

If the beginning speaker is anxious, the audience finds out about it largely through nonverbal cues. The speaker's hands may shake, his voice may quiver, he may have difficulty looking at the audience, and he may remain poker-faced, wooden-looking. An audience is quick to pick up cues about the way a speaker feels about himself. If the speaker regards his own nonverbal cues as showing that he worried about his performance, the audience will get the correct impression that the speaker has stage fright. They will begin to worry about him and his feelings and be distracted from the ideas in his speech. Then the speaker not only has trouble getting his ideas across to the audience, but also must combat their view of him as someone with not much to offer them; someone they need to help through the difficult task of giving a speech. Interestingly enough, the same body motions, if perceived by the speaker as symptoms of his intense involvement with, and high regard for, his subject and the occasion, can make a strong positive impression on an audience. We cannot stress too much the importance of how the speaker perceives himself. This perception of yourself is the first thing you communicate to any audience.

If the speaker can control his tension so that his gestures, posture, and facial expression are appropriate to what he is saying, the audience will seldom know he is anxious. Every good speaker gets keyed up before he goes on; even able, professional public speakers get stage fright before they start. Every teacher confesses to some nervousness before meeting a new class for the first time. But like the athlete who is nervous and keyed up in the dressing room but feels fine 2 minutes after the game starts, the good speaker uses these feelings of nervousness and tension to key him up to do a better job.

The point is that you do not want to stop feeling nervous about giving a speech or standing before a crowd. You want to learn to use this nervous tension to make your mind sharper and less likely to forget and to give your whole body more focus and concentration on communicating with your audience.

A good way to get the tension under proper control is to feel satisfied about the preparation of your speech. Each of us has a way that works best for him, but if you can feel you have something worthwhile or fun to say to your listeners, something they will enjoy and use, and if you feel you know exactly what you want to say, you will find it easier to get past the few difficult moments as you begin. Throughout the book, particularly in Chapters 7, 9, 10, 14, and 15, there is more specific information to help you prepare speaking material.

Another good way to get the tension under control is to pick a spot in the front of the audience, and when you are introduced, get up from your chair, pause, pull yourself erect, and firmly and calmly force yourself to walk to the spot. When you reach the spot you picked, pause again, stand erect, and with the weight balanced comfortably on both feet, look out at the audience and, for just a moment, let your eyes run over the listeners. Be sure and look at the people in the audience *until you can see them.* Some beginners, when they feel particularly nervous at the start of the speech, are unwilling actually to look at the audience. Since they do not know what the people look like or what they are doing, they find themselves growing more and more nervous as they proceed. We are all afraid of the unknown, and if the speaker is not watching the audience, he has no way of knowing what it is doing. In all speaking situations, it is far better for you, the speaker, to look at your audience, to see the friendly faces, the smiles, the frowns, the questioning looks—to realize that an audience is made up of human beings much like yourself, that they usually wish you well (particularly in a speech-communication class), and that they want you to be a good speaker.

And so, having looked directly during this pause at the people to whom you will be talking, take a good deep breath as quietly as you can and begin your speech in a strong voice. By standing erect, by acting confident, by pausing, and by beginning in a good strong voice, you complete the illusion of confidence for your audience.

Furthermore, you will discover that if you can give the audience the impression that you are a poised and confident speaker, their impression will affect you and you will soon feel more confidence and find that you can keep your tension under control.

Several final hints may help you in controlling nervous tension and using it to make your nonverbal communication more effective. Pick topics that excite you. If you talk on subjects you feel strongly about, you will soon discover that your interest in what you are saying is genuine and is taking your mind off yourself.

Develop an audience-centered approach to speaking. Keep your mind on the listener and his response. Watch individuals. Did the audience like some example you used? Did an analogy work well in getting one of your points across? (Was there nodding of heads in agreement, for example?) Can you think of other such examples or analogies that you might insert to increase audience interest and involvement? Is the audience geting bored? Do any members of the audience look confused? As in the trite but true advice to young people who want to learn how to get over self-consciousness in social situations, get your mind off yourself! By concentrating on the audience, the speaker takes his mind off himself and his performance. Self-centered attitudes are primary causes of stage fright. We devote Chapter 14 to the important matter of audience analysis. Obviously, you must learn how to analyze your audience before you can become audience-centered.

Finally, the fright mechanism is an old one that we have inherited from our prehistoric ancestors who often had to fight or take flight from personal danger. The person who is frightened generally has an increased heartbeat and increased adrenaline in the system and is charged up either to run fast or to fight hard. When we speak in front of an audience, however, neither flight nor fight is advisable. But if you are by nature a person who gestures in conversations, or if you tend to move about when taking part in a discussion, use this habit of moving when you speak to dissipate some of the nervous energy in strong, purposeful gestures.

POSTURE

The way a speaker stands and holds his shoulders and his head as he speaks communicates a good deal nonverbally to the audience. If the speaker is standing in the region of public distance (12 or more feet from the first row of the audience) and is delivering a speech in a relatively formal setting, the audience expects him to stand erect, with his weight evenly balanced on both feet. The feet should be relatively close together with one foot slightly in front of the other.

The speaker should not lean on the speaker's stand, slouch on first one foot and then the other, rock back and forth or from side to side, or stand with feet widespread.

If the speaker is in the position of social distance and in a relatively informal setting, and if he wishes to communicate nonverbally that he does not want to give a carefully prepared speech, but plans to ramble on a bit and throw out a few ideas and then ask for questions and comments, he may sit on the edge of a table, sit in a chair, lean on the speaker's stand, take off his coat, and so on.

FACIAL EXPRESSION

One of the most important tools any speaker has for nonverbal communication with an audience is his range of facial expressions. Smiles, grins, smirks, frowns, grimaces, and raised eyebrows can all add emphasis or, conversely, suggest that the descriptive words in the message are to be discounted. Unfortunately, one of the beginner's most common reactions to nervousness is failure to use facial expressions. As a result, the anxious speaker often talks in a monotone, sighs a great deal, and has a blank expression on his face.

The person who is vivacious in conversation, smiling, frowning, whose face is alive every second in animated talk with one or two others often tones down his facial expressions when giving a public speech. He should do just the opposite. An expressive smile or grin in the region of intimate space (1–2 feet) or even personal distance (1.5–2.5 feet) is often lost on an audience 12 feet or more away. Thus you ought to overdo the smile, the grin, the frown when you are giving a public speech in a good-sized room or auditorium. You have to overdo your platform personality to achieve the effect you ordinarily produce in the more informal and intimate situations.

EYE CONTACT

One of the most expressive regions of the face is the area around the eyes. Again and again the eyewitnesses who reported their impressions of such great American speakers as Daniel Webster, Henry Clay, Stephen Douglas, and William Jennings Bryan noted the arresting and powerful effect of the speakers' eyes.

Generally the speaker ought to give the illusion that he is looking directly at the members of the audience. To be sure, direct eye contact may be a culture-bound nonverbal convention and you may wish to modify the advice for special situations. However, you are well advised to look a middle-class white North American audience in the eye.

In almost all situations, random eye movements are distracting. Looking over the listeners' heads for no clear purpose, looking out the window, looking at the corner of the room, looking at the floor, or looking always at your speech notes can prove distracting. We have already noted that when the speaker looks away from the audience for the greater part of his speech, he has no way of judging its response, of utilizing the feedback from nonverbal cues.

GESTURE

The beginning speaker often makes an unsettling discovery when he gets in front of an audience. He finds that attached to his shoulders are two arms to which he normally pays little attention, but which now suddenly cannot be ignored. At the ends of his arms are two conspicuous hands. His first thought is to hide his hands, so he puts them both behind his back. When he does this, he feels tied up, and every move he makes with his shoulders seems awkward. He then tries to hide his hands in his pockets, but he still feels restricted and his hands seem as obvious and as useless as ever. He may fold his arms over his chest or try to hold them rigidly by his sides in the hope that nobody will notice them, but there is no hiding either the arms or the hands. The only solution is for the speaker to learn to use his arms and hands to make gestures in support of the material in his speech.

Once the beginner realizes he must move his hands and arms, he may make a second mistake by keeping his elbows close to his sides, using only the forearms for short, jerky gestures. His nonverbal communication at this point is that he wants to use some gestures but feels inhibited in front of his listeners.

You can get the feel of good ways to gesture by practicing at home in front of a mirror. When you practice gestures suitable for a speech, you should make them broader than you first feel necessary. Experiment with gesturing with both arms. Remember to use the space above your shoulders, particularly if you are speaking from a stage and are some distance from your audience. Move your hands to express ideas. Make sure the movement flows through the entire arm to the tips of your fingers. Do not let your hands and fingers flop about loosely; do not use gestures that distract from, rather than add to, the meaning of what you are saying.

The entire body can gesture to suggest nonverbal meanings. The speaker may hunch his shoulders and crouch to suggest a certain mood or feeling. He may step toward the audience, pull back, turn to one side or another, or stand on tiptoe. A good speaker may use the techniques of pantomime, the art of getting across emotions, actions, and feelings by mute gestures. He may turn slightly, crouch, and make an imaginary pistol out of his extended index finger to suggest to the audience the character of a holdup man in a story. He might next turn, stand rigidly erect, and hold both hands high, this time suggesting his own response to the feeling of having the gun in his back.

THE USE OF NOTES

The question of whether to have notes for a public speech may seem a minor matter. Yet in the hands of a speaker who does not know how best to use them, notes can inhibit eye contact, facial expression, posture, and gesturing, and thereby affect the speaker's total skill at nonverbal communication. Many speech instructors prefer that students not use notes in class simply because notes hinder development of good habits of nonverbal communication through body language. Some instructors also feel that beginning speakers should learn to keep the outline of their ideas in mind, without notes, as they speak. We do not use notes in most interpersonal communication situations. We may use notes for formal speaking situations, however, and the Teleprompter and other devices provide ready notes, even whole speeches, for television performers. It seems to us that the situations calling for speeches, formal or informal, without any notes, are rare. However, listeners are impressed when a speaker uses no notes, and you should keep this in mind for your most polished and important speeches. If you can develop a way to prepare speeches that allows you to keep the main points of your outline in mind, you can usually easily remember the examples and other supporting material that fit under the main point. If you can speak extemporaneously without notes, you can keep your eyes on the audience and gesture more freely.

Many students find it difficult to speak without notes and plan to use notes in the speaking they will do after they finish the class, so they prefer learning to speak well using them. The most important point about using notes in a speech is not to pretend that you have no notes. Few things a speaker can do distract an audience as much as the pretense that he has no notes. Sometimes a speaker writes his notes on small cards and stacks them on the speaker's stand or holds them hidden in the palm of his hand. He cannot fool anyone. The first time he sneaks a look at his notes the audience picks up the cue and watches for him to steal another look; he may create more suspense with this nonverbal behavior than with what he is trying to say! So if you need notes, bring them out into the open, then use them naturally, trying not to cut down on the eye contact and facial expressiveness any more than necessary. Perhaps in the instance of quoting a statistic or a special sentence from some authority, the speaker can even hold up the notes and point to the place where he has his information; this communicates nonverbally that what he is saying is absolutely correct and he has it written down to make sure he says it correctly.

Avoid the common pitfalls of using notes. Do not look at them whenever you feel embarrassed; look at the audience, keep your poise, and pause to collect yourself. To the audience, your poised look at them as you pause communicates that you are about to say something important and are thinking about exactly the right way to say it best. Do not play with your notes; a nervous speaker with something in his hand is often tempted to fold it, roll it, tap it, or bend it. The audience may, again, become more interested in what you may do next with your note cards than in what you are saying.

Do not clutch your notes tightly in front of you with both hands; you cannot gesture with your hands if they are in this rigid position. Hold the notes in one hand and use the other arm and hand for gesturing, although you may certainly gesture with both arms if it seems appropriate, and the notes, held up in the one hand, will not distract from the gesture; if anything, a vigorous arm gesture that includes the display of notes may communicate that you are prepared, you have in your hand what you are going to say, and you are very much in charge of the situation.

The more imagination you can develop to enable you to see yourself as the audience does, the better your nonverbal communication will become.

Nonverbal communication is sometimes called the silent language. We are all vaguely aware of the implications of gesture, facial expression, and body attitudes when we talk with people from day to day. When we are involved in public communication

the key ideas

We all learn a general body language from our culture.

The body motion which accompanies verbal messages may emphasize, deemphasize, or even contradict what the words say.

Children often do as their parents do rather than as their parents say to do; nonverbal messages are powerful.

People from different cultures often have difficulty understanding one another because of differences in their nonverbal communication.

A comfortable distance for talking in a given culture depends upon how well the participants know each other and how intimate their conversation is.

The way people sit in relation to one another in a small group meeting often mirrors the dynamics of the group and the relationships among the members.

The distances between the members of an audience for a public speech affect the suggestibility of the audience.

---

events, we need to become more sophisticated about the implications of nonverbal body-motion codes so that if we are speaking, we know what to do to make our nonverbal communication support our intention. If we are viewing and hearing someone else speak, we need to be aware of the many signals given by the speaker's body, eyes, and vocal intonations. All these are elements of nonverbal communication, and they are important components of messages; there is much truth in the saying, "What you *do* speaks so loud, I can't hear what you *say*."

SUGGESTED PROJECTS

1 / The class divides into groups of two or three, and each group selects a brief emotional scene one of the members has witnessed. (An example would be the reactions of downtown shoppers who witness a serious automobile accident, or of ardent basketball fans watching a local hero take a final shot at the basket with the score

in chapter 5

The rhetorical tradition of study and practice of public speaking contains much knowledge about the art of using body motion to communicate non-verbally.

Audience members often think the speaker is nervous because of non-verbal indications.

A speaker should watch his audience and see how they are responding to his remarks.

One of the most important ways a speaker can communicate nonverbally with a listener is by means of facial expressions.

Whether or not we look at the other person affects how he interprets what we say.

Random body motion unrelated to either cultural norms or meaning tends to distract the listener.

tied and 2 seconds remaining. Or the scene might be much more intimate, involving a tense and critical interview between a doctor and a patient, a parent and child, or a lawyer and a witness.) For 1 minute the group tries to communicate the emotions involved to the rest of the class, using only hand and body gestures. No facial expression should be used at this stage of the exercise. For a second minute, the group continues to use hand and body move-ment to convey the emotions but also adds facial expression. The third minute, they add movement in relation to one another (proxemics.) The class then discusses the importance of various elements of body language in communicating emotion.

2 / Five members of the class are given a current, preferably con-troversial topic to discuss. They go to the front of the classroom and conduct a brief unrehearsed discussion. Half of the remaining members watch and make notes about the proxemics of the dis-cussion group, their nonverbal gestures, postures, and facial ex-pressions. The other half of the class watches the nonverbal proxemics and gestures of the entire classroom, including the instructor. After the discussion, a general class meeting analyzes

the nonverbal dimension of the discussion group and the entire classroom setting.

3 / Prepare a stage fright analysis of yourself. Show this initial analysis to your instructor, then keep it throughout the course. It is to be a personal record, so be frank and honest. Begin with a brief discussion of the types of communication experiences in which you feel most anxious. Write a brief description of physical symptoms that you notice at such times such as shaky knees, a dry mouth, sweaty palms, or trembling hands. Keep a record of your communication experiences throughout the quarter or semester and describe in some detail your feelings during each class exercise. Prepare one of your final communication assignments with the express purpose of achieving maximum control of your tensions. Select a topic about which you have strong feelings, prepare your message carefully, use strong, convincing language. Concentrate on the audience response. Write a final progress report of your tension during this final assignment. Compare your response to communication tension toward the end of the class to your initial analysis and particularly note your progress in controlling and using stage fright.

SUGGESTED READINGS

Birdwhistell, Ray L. *Kinesics and Context.* Philadelphia: University of Pennsylvania Press, 1970.

Bosmajian, Haig A. *The Rhetoric of Nonverbal Communication: Readings.* Glenview, Ill.: Scott, Foresman, 1971.

Clark, Margaret L., Ella A. Erway, and Lee Beltzer. *The Learning Encounter: The Classroom as a Communications Workshop.* New York: Random House, 1971. "Nonverbal Behavior," pp. 52–65.

Fast, Julius. *Body Language.* Philadelphia: Lippincott, 1970.

Hall, Edward T. *The Silent Language.* Garden City, N.Y.: Doubleday, 1959.

Jensen, J. Vernon. *Perspectives on Oral Communication.* Boston: Holbrook Press. "Perspectives on Nonverbal Intercultural Communication," pp. 133–160.

Mehrabian, Albert. "Communication Without Words," *Psychology Today,* 2 (September 1968), 53–55.

6 how to talk to another person

In Chapter 2 we presented a general theory of communication which included a model of the communication process. The general model is applicable to most any communication, from television commercials, to public speeches, to small group meetings, to casual conversations. Here we adapt the communication theory from Chapter 2 to the most common and probably the most important communication situation of our daily lives—the two-person setting.

When we talk with another person, the source of the message is clearly one person, and the receiver is clearly another, each having all the individual characteristics of human beings. When we examine a television commercial, for instance, we are never sure how many people worked on the message and thus we have difficulty analyzing the source in personal terms. The two-person situation, on the other hand, provides the chance for maximum analysis of both source and receiver.

In our discussion we will restrict ourselves to those times when one person wishes to talk with another. On occasion, messages are encoded in a way that closely approximates our model of communication, but these messages fail to illustrate all the key parts and all the process. Communication events are not like those occasions when a person *expresses* himself. When a person says something in the presence of another, it is usually because of some want or impulse within the message source. If one person wants to tell another something about the world, the speaker, or the listener, we have the possibility of communication. If the person has an impulse to express his feelings or emotions, with no desire to tell anything to the other person, we have an instance of personal expression.

When a source encodes a message to communicate, he aims to achieve some level of common meanings, denotative or connotative, between himself and his listener. When a person expresses himself, he gives vent to feelings and ideas, for example, with a grunt or a shout, by crying, or even by forming words into sentences. The person expressing himself has no interest in arousing common meanings. The attention of others, either positive or negative, often satisfies the impulse. A child in a temper tantrum is not communicating; he is expressing himself. When the parent asks, "What's the matter? What's wrong?" the child continues to kick, scream, and roll on the floor, yelling, "No, no, no." The parent may read some meaning into the tantrum and try to explain it; the child, however, makes no attempt to tell the parent what is troubling him. The act of giving vent to his personal feelings is his goal. Consider the nonrepresentational painter; he does not care what the viewer thinks of his picture as long as it means something to him. He is expressing himself. The student protester who makes nonnegotiable demands and does not care to talk about them is expressing himself rather than communicating. Self-expression is neither good nor bad; often it is valuable, fun, and necessary. We must, however, be clear about the differences between self-expression and communication and understand that while self-expression may be artless, communication always requires artistry. We must work at effective human communication and learn the craft if we hope to succeed consistently. Some problems in getting along with one another could be avoided if people could preface all self-expressive messages with, "I just need to hear myself talk. Don't pay any attention to me. I'm riled up and boiling over. Just plug up your ears." The trouble is, of course, that when we are emotionally upset, we are often least able to preface an outburst with such a reasonable explanation.

THE BASIC PROCESS OF TWO-PERSON COMMUNICATION

In two-person conversation, the source encodes a message in words and nonverbal codes. As he talks, he can watch for the response of the other person. The receiver provides the speaker with continuous feedback as the message unfolds. Since the channels in a face-to-face conversation include both sight and hearing, the speaker can get a reading throughout and *at the same time* he is speaking, from the nonverbal feedback cues of the listener. We cannot stress too strongly that the two-person communication provides ideal conditions for close-range, continuous feedback. In many communication situations, as when you are writing a letter, memorandum, or report, or are watching television or listening to the radio, such efficient feedback is missing. The opportunity for high-fidelity and deeply significant communication is thus greatest in the two-person situation.

As the receiver listens to the message unfold, he does not simply absorb the other's meanings. He interprets the message by calling up meanings from his experience and fitting them into the forms suggested by the structure of the message. We come, therefore, to the important question: What are *meanings*? Philosophers, psychologists, and linguists have puzzled about the meaning of meanings and discovered that the definition is much more difficult than might at first be supposed. For the student of interpersonal communication who wishes to improve his daily conversations with other people, however, the basic question has been answered.

When two people talk to each other, the meanings aroused by their interaction are within them. When you talk with another person, what you derive from the talk is something within your consciousness, and what the other person derives from the talk is something individual and personal for him. We are islands of consciousness and cannot break out of the boundaries of self to experience directly another person's interior life. For example, when you see a color and call it "red," you have learned from experience that when other people talk with you in the presence of flowers of that hue, they call them red. You thus come to call flowers of a similar color red, and when you give your date flowers and say these red roses mean something special, she accepts your characterization of the roses as red, whereas had you labeled roses you have learned to name *yellow* with the word *red,* she would have corrected you. You and your date both know what the word *red* means in the sense that you agree in the presence of a particular flower that it has the property, "red." Such agreement is the basis for much common meaning when we communicate with one another.

However, even after you both agree that the rose is red, you have no way of knowing if the red you see is anything at all like the red the other person sees. Logically we have no evidence that when Mr. A. talks with Mr. B, they may not have radically different worlds of color, sound, taste, and feeling. Mr. A's world may be full of bright and garish colors, while Mr. B's is full of muted tones. Mr. A's world may be a noisy, raucous one, full of violent and clashing sounds, while Mr. B's world is muffled and quiet. Mr. A and Mr. B may agree that the rose is red or that the musician is playing a Beethoven sonata, but in an important sense, neither one can know what the color red means to the other or what the music sounds like or means to the other. The point is made by the old unanswerable question, "How do you tell a color-blind person what 'red' means?"

Within his island of meanings, the source discovers a desire to tell another person about something. He encodes a verbal message and supports the *meaning* with nonverbal intonations and body language. Quite often the speaker finds that, for what he wants to say, his tools are clumsy. He struggles to find the right names and right properties and relations. He casts about to form the words into the right kinds of sentences. Still he cannot put everything he wishes into his message. His island of meanings is too complicated; the ideas are so complex. He tries to pattern a message that reflects the complexity and the subtle richness of his ideas. The task is difficult. The world within the message source is changing, shifting, dynamic; the language he encodes is frozen once it leaves his lips. The sentences are set, static. He resembles the painter who tries to put a great idea and deep feeling into a series of static forms on a flat canvas. How can he catch the motion, the shifting relationships? The answer is, of course, that he cannot do so completely. The source approximates his ideas and meanings into the form of the verbal and nonverbal message codes.

Some sources encode messages better than others. The encoding of messages is an art that can be learned. Language is limited, but most natural languages are flexible and have great communicative power when handled by a well-trained and talented speaker. English is a particularly rich and powerful tool of communication. The source's language facility, the size of his vocabulary, the rules of his dialect, his creative ability to combine words into novel patterns and to associate ideas and make new meanings by coining figures of speech all affect the kind of verbal message he encodes. Also, some people use nonverbal communication better than others. The source who has a flexible voice and an expressive face, and who uses appropriate gestures naturally, enhances the effectiveness of his communication.

All of us when talking with another encode our messages from within our islands of meanings. We have biases, interests, prejudices, needs, and wants, all of which affect the way we encode messages. If we are trained as policemen or medical doctors or legal secretaries or automobile mechanics, our training and the kind of work we do begin to enlarge certain areas of our vocabulary, and that part of our internal world likewise grows in size and complexity, while the areas we seldom think about or discuss gradually dwindle in our perception. Our ability to talk technically and with understanding and complexity about the things we do most often increases as our ability to talk about those things we seldom do or think about decreases.

Each of us has to accept his ignorance as he communicates with someone else. I know little or nothing of you until you tell me. You are ignorant about me, also. Ignorance is simply what we do not yet know. You are bound to know a great deal about something I know nothing about. If I pretend I am not ignorant about something, I mislead you. We can expect communication problems. We have to learn to broadcast our ignorance on occasion and not try to conceal it. Only when we admit ignorance can someone else begin to tell us about what we do not know. Admitting ignorance is a vital key to providing feedback to improve communication.

The source's problems of finding the right message to communicate his meanings are mirrored to some extent in the receiver. The receiver of any message also has a personal island of meanings. The receiver has a certain language facility, a certain dialect, certain biases, interests, and prejudices. The listener tends to read into the messages those meanings associated with his personal biases and interests.

The receiver finds some parts of the message easy to associate with a denotative meaning. Generally if the name is specific, "My dog, Rover, sitting over there by the chair," the listener associates a part of his perceptual world quickly and easily, and both the speaker and the listener know what is being discussed. The receiver feels confident that he understands the message and he may nod his head to indicate understanding. Problems arise because some words are abstract and difficult to associate with a denotative meaning. Messages that are not firmly anchored to clear denotative meanings may trigger the listener to call up a large pool of meanings and their emotional associations. The source may say, "I've just come from a long talk with my personal God. Are you a born-again Christian?" and the receiver may respond with a recollection of his evangelist father and call up his meanings for "born-again Christian," which may be personal and quite different from those the speaker was trying to communicate. Another source may say, "The communists really hate democracy and all it stands for." The listener associates his own meanings for communists and for democracy, and the potential for misunderstanding is great.

Just as the speaker finds his verbal and nonverbal codes clumsy for the task of encoding messages, so the receiver finds the interpretation of messages difficult, but it is through this interpretation that human understanding can come about. Perhaps the listener interprets a nonverbal hint as a clue to some deep and important idea within the consciousness of the speaker. The excitement of discovery regarding a fellow human being begins. The listener strains to find a verbal key to the idea. He asks for more messages. He strives to interpret these and seeks additional comments. He thinks he sees the shape of the idea; he gets a glimmer of the feeling within the source. Somehow he manages some contact through the self-protective walls of biases, dialect, background, interests, and motives. The interchange has proceeded until the two people feel they have achieved genuine understanding. Both are excited, moved, touched by the experience. They have transcended the human condition, disclosed themselves to one another. They have glimpsed the interior island of another person's meanings.

Such high moments of communication come too seldom for most of us, and little wonder, considering the difficulty of the task and the fact that we often take the skills required for granted. We turn now to the factors that cause our efforts to talk to another to go astray.

AN ISLAND INVADED

How many times have you heard someone mutter when he is called to by another person, "What does he want *now?*" The tone of the intended receiver indicates that previous messages from that particular source have been unpleasant and the person is not willing to enter into a communicating relationship because of too many bad experiences. Homeostasis is the tendency to preserve things as they are if we are comfortable, plus the struggle to get things back into a comfortable state when we are uncomfortable. If you irritate a person, he usually tries to get away from the irritation. All interpersonal communication is potentially irritating and sometimes punishing. Communication often upsets the *status quo,* asks us to rethink our pet ideas and prejudices, challenges our self-image, and questions our habits.

To some extent all of us adopt a self-protective wary attitude as we begin to talk with other people. We develop a protective filter through which we hear everything said to us and which strains out meanings that would be too painful for us to admit to our inner selves. The thickness and complexity of the protective filter vary from person to person. Someone who has a good, comfortable feeling about his worth as a person has a relatively large-screen filter. A person whose self-image has been damaged by the problems of life has a fine-screen filter. Rarely is a person so mature and clear-eyed in his self-awareness that he is able to tell you what all his filters are. Most of us have some degree of self-knowledge, but most of us need to work at becoming more aware of the way we distort our interpretations of messages because of such protective devices. As instructors in colleges and universities who try to tell students about their various inadequacies in communication skills so that they can begin to improve themselves, we have had abundant opportunities to watch the fascinating operation of protective filters and the defensive communication that results. An instructor criticizes a student's speech, first pointing out that certain aspects were good. The student accepts this praise without flinching. Next the instructor criticizes the content and organization of the speech and the articulation of the student. The student immediately says he was nervous, that he was well prepared and had much good information, but forgot it because he was nervous.

If the student was well prepared he should not have forgotten, the instructor persists. The student then says he is working 20 hours a week, had to stay up until 3 o'clock in the morning to get the speech ready, and was therefore tired and could not do a good job. No matter how the instructor tries to convey the idea that the student has certain inadequacies in his ability to communicate that can be overcome by coaching and practice, the student meets each attempt with an excuse or an explanation that blames the problem on something other than his own inabilities. More than likely as he leaves the conference, the student thinks to himself, "That instructor just does not like me. Why do I always end up with instructors who pick on me because they do not like me?"

Everyone has a sense of self. Our image of ourselves is important to our mental and emotional health. Our self-image is modified as we go through life, certainly, but it can change somewhat even from hour to hour, depending on our experiences. As you will learn in the two chapters about small group interaction later in the book, a person's behavior is always affected to some extent by those with whom he happens to be. This is just as true in two-person interpersonal communication.

Some students become upset because, when they learn to be more analytical about their communicating behavior, they discover that they communicate differently with different people; they wonder, "When am I acting, and when am I the real me?" The answer is that two-person interaction is dynamic. Just as we examined in Chapter 2, the circular flow of signals in a communication event, so we repeat: Communication involves a source and a listener, and you are a different source, to some degree, when you interact with a different listener. This is not hyprocrisy, as some students fear, it is simply normal human adjustment to a complex part of human behavior. It is still valid to call that general feeling we have about ourselves, taking into consideration the many variations we all experience, our self-image.

If our self-image includes the notion that we are not good at performing, we may respond by withdrawing from activities that call on us to perform or, in an opposite way, by overdoing our efforts to impress people. We all search messages to determine what they mean in terms of our self-image. Because of this natural protective response, when interpreting a message, the listener often reads into the words meanings that have to do with himself as a person. Is the other person saying or implying something about me? Is he saying that he likes me? That he dislikes me? That he respects me? Values my work? Thinks my work is mediocre? Thinks that I'm attractive? That he wants to know me better? A lot of questions about *me as a person* intrude into my interpretation of the other person's words.

The message source is often as preoccupied with himself as the listener is with himself, and therefore the speaker is putting his own excuses, explanations, interests, biases, and prejudices into the message. The speaker may be wondering about the impression his communication is making. Does the listener find me attractive, interesting, and competent? Does he sees the depth of my feeling? The great humor in my personality? Little wonder that the moments of glimpsing the other person's inner self in the course of our conversations come as seldom as they do. Learning to be message-centered is a first step beyond the natural self-centeredness we all bring to communication interaction. Learning further to be listener- or audience-centered is an art requiring constant awareness and practice on the part of any message source.

In a given communication event involving two people, the way they perceive one another is as important in their conversation as the way they see themselves. Let us take a situation in which John is talking with Mary. John has an image of himself which influences his manner and approach to the communication; John also has an image of Mary; John, further, has a dream image of the way he wishes Mary would see him; and finally, John has an estimate of the way Mary really does view him. Mary, likewise, has a set of images which mirror those of John. She has a self-image, an image of John, a desired image of herself which she wishes John to have, and an estimate of the way John does view her. Each person, thus, has four images of important selves involved in the conversation. If the four images of John and the four of Mary are more or less alike, they can talk in a relaxed and trustful way. You might call this an ideal basis for good two-person communication.

Much communication takes place, however, with one or more of the images in conflict. We will illustrate several possibilities leading to conflict—there are many more, of course—and suggest that you try to see what other images might be out of phase and what other communication difficulties are likely to follow. When John's self-image is much less attractive than the impression he wants Mary to have of him, he may overdo everything because he feels inadequate. He may talk too much, drive his car too fast, and generally come across as overbearing. If John thinks Mary has an attractive image of him as a handsome, brilliant, witty fellow, whereas she really thinks he is plain, dumb, and boring, John will have trouble talking with Mary. Mary's internal response may be, "Brother, does he think *he's* God's gift to women. Yuck!"

IMPROVING TWO-PERSON COMMUNICATION

Most freshmen and sophomores in college are, according to a thoughtful, war-veteran student recently in class, at about the worst time of life in regard to knowing who you are, what kind of a person you hope to be, what your self-image really is. "When I was 16 I had all the answers," he went on to say. "When I was 18 I had a different bunch of answers. Now I've been around the world and back, I'm 21 years old, and I know less now than I used to, about me, other people, life, you name it." To ask you, particularly if you are in the usual age group of college freshmen and sophomores, to try to figure out what your self-image is and to keep it in mind when communicating with others, is a big order. Learning to know yourself is a lifetime job, but there is no better place than college to start a more sophisticated, systematic examination of yourself and the way you respond. Many college courses have the examination of one's self as the not-so-hidden item on their agenda. Certainly any course in interpersonal communication must include this probing of one's own basic reactions to life, to situations, and most of all, to people.

One way to improve the agreement among the various images involved in a conversation is to open up oneself to the other person. We call the revealing of self the process of *self-disclosure*. We know certain things about ourselves and sometimes we disclose some of these things to another, and sometimes we decide to hide most of them. Often we hide the unpleasant truths about ourselves to protect the image we want the other person to have of us. We fear the truth will keep us from gaining the liking and respect of the listener. Oddly enough, there are some things about ourselves that we do not know. We may not know, for example, about our little nonverbal mannerisms that disturb other people when we speak. We often do not know what someone else may have told the listener about us.

When two people talk with each other, therefore, they both know some things about each other. When they share much the same information about one another, their communication is easier and their talk tends to be free and less protective. Communication becomes protective and less open when one person knows something about the other that is unknown to him, or when the person knows something about himself that is unknown to the other. Take the first instance: Bill knows that Harry has damaged his knee cartilage to the extent that he will never be able to play football again, but Harry does not know his injury is permanent and will partially disable him for life. What Bill knows and Harry does not know makes it difficult for the two of them to have a free and open talk about Harry's future as a professional athlete. Take the second instance: Mary knows something about herself that Ann does not know. Mary knows she is an alcoholic who has controlled her drinking problem through membership in Alcoholics Anonymous. As Mary and Ann discuss plans for a party, the hidden fact of Mary's alcoholism means her communication is always, to some extent, protective.

When a high level of communication is desirable between two people, the goal of both should be the widening of the area of what they both know about one another. The technique for such widening or sharing of inner experiences is called self-disclosure.

How does one go about creating a communication climate in which self-disclosure is possible, even encouraged? Psychologist Carl Rogers, working as a clinical therapist with patients who had mental and emotional problems, developed a technique of counseling which he called nondirective. He did not lead or direct the patients in their conversations with him; rather, he encouraged them to pour out things in a free, uncritical, nonjudgmental atmosphere. He learned how to build trust between the patient and himself so that the patient came to know he could say anything he wished and not be punished for saying it. What Rogers began as a therapy technique, he and others have now modified into a general technique for working with normal people to improve communication. The heart of the humanistic approach in psychology is to release the human potential within individuals by eliminating the threatening, critical, evaluative communication which brings out a listener's protective filters and produces defensive or counter-threatening messages, and using, instead, supportive comments to encourage honest discussion.

Because of the manner in which many Americans have come to communicate with one another, we can say that most of us need to develop skills in being consciously supportive of others in those moments of deep and serious talk that are so important to us. We tend to leave things unsaid, to drift through our conversations leaving many loose ends. Through sheer bad habit we often knock the props out from under one another without meaning to do so and sometimes without even knowing that we have done so. One of our friends who has lived in the Middle East for a decade commented, upon returning to live in the United States, that she was more than ever impressed with the coldness and reserve with which we interact socially. "We touch so seldom," she said, "we seem to fear getting personal when people don't want us to, so we stop talking just when people in the Middle East would begin to open up and really help one another. When something really bothers Americans, we tend to clam up." Her comments apply more to the Scandinavian, North European heritage of many people in the Upper Midwest where we now live, than to the many other groups of people in our complex, pluralistic society; nevertheless, what she said is true of many subcultures in our country.

The feeling of holding back, which our neighbor found inhibiting upon her return to the United States, is sometimes called *alienation*. Today many people feel alienated. All of us are handling more sensory stimuli, in the form of messages, sounds, and emotional assaults, every single day, than our ancestors had to handle in a week or more. Much of our interaction grows impersonal because we simply cannot devote our full attention to every new person we meet, every conversation we take part in, and every message we hear on radio or see on television.

Our feeling of alienation is increased by the impersonality of urban life. When several generations of a large family live together or nearby, as they may in a small town and as they did a generation ago in the inner-city ethnic communities, there is a feeling of belonging, of having many people who care how you are, how you behave, what you do, and what happens to you. Today, our mobility from place to place, class to class, group to group has resulted in a loss of the feeling of community. The burden of providing the feeling of closeness and belonging has been placed on the nuclear family. One father and one mother are supposed to give each other and their children all the warmth, support, love, and care each needs. The rising divorce rate is one result. When, for any number of reasons, the family is not able to fill our need for close and important human relationships, we go out into the world somewhat crippled in our ability to interact and communicate with others. We fail to be warm and supportive; others, in turn, fail to be warm and supportive to us. People close emotional doors, begin to turn away, and do not care about one another.

Mutually supportive communication between two people is extremely difficult; certainly the degree of maturity each has attained influences its success. The strain caused by the demand that all the supportive human interaction each of us craves must come from just one other person has led to the development of life styles other than the traditional nuclear family. These experimental communes, trial marriages, and multimarriages attest to the difficulties involved when two people interact; many of these experimental life styles are attempts to broaden the bases for supportive communication, or in the case of the trial marriage, to acknowledge the possible inability to develop a continuing relationship and give both parties an option to stop it without the need for traditional proceedings of divorce. Despite the development of these new life styles, the majority of Americans plan to marry, and the requirements for sustaining a supportive dyadic (two-person) relationship are important for most of us. And to a lesser degree than is necessary in marriage, all of us are involved in two-person relationships with family members, good friends, and coworkers.

If we can learn to communicate accurately and meaningfully with those around us, we will find that our skill in human relations is greatly improved. Much of what people feel about us is related to the way we communicate with them. People who make us feel good, we tend to like. People who make us angry or depressed, we tend to avoid. The more genuinely supportive communication we learn to give to others, the more we are liked. If we remember that the other fellow wants to be talked to as a worthwhile person, we are more likely to be a successful communicator. Even if the other person misunderstands us at the start, if we have made clear, verbally and nonverbally, that he is a person we value, he is more likely to mention his confusion, to voice his doubts, and generally to disclose his real response to us, often leading to better understanding. Once trust has been established, even unpleasant communication can take place, not without discomfort, of course, but with a feeling of mutual respect.

We believe that good communication must be based on trust—which is not to be confused with liking, necessarily. Initially we all learn basic communication habits from our own families. If the early examples we use as communication models are good, our chances of being effective communicators are increased. If our parents relate well verbally with each other, they also probably communicated pretty well with us. When the person you should be able to trust most of all, your parent, or if you are married, your wife or husband, lets you down, the experience is a terrible instance of taking an important risk and being punished because of it. If for no other reason than to learn what is supportive and what is damaging in the interpersonal communication within your immediate family and circle of friends, you should begin to build a good understanding of healthy communication and learn how to create good interpersonal relationships with free and open discussions. In his play *Hamlet,* Shakespeare urged his actors to suit their actions to the words. The advice is good for real-life interpersonal communication as well as for successful acting. If you say one thing and do another, you set up contradictory responses that cause misunderstandings. If you say "yes" and then do as you say you will, you build trust. If you say "love" and act "hate," you set up discord.

Some communication problems come about simply because people avoid talking about what really bothers them. In these instances, people often pretend that when they talk with one another, they are primarily interested in discussing facts, events, and "business." Suppose a teacher and a student have arranged a conference to talk over the student's courses for the coming term. The stated object of the talk is to find out about hours, requirements, and scheduling. To be sure, the topics are important and of concern to both teacher and student. Of equal importance to both, however, are some questions about *self*, and these questions have not been stated. The student may feel isolated and alone in the new environment of the college. He may have liked the teacher's course he took the previous term and he may have found the teacher an interesting, reassuring person. A personal problem is troubling him greatly: His father has always wanted him to become a lawyer and he has now decided he does not want to study law. He would like to talk to the teacher about this.

The instructor also has some personal interests he would like to talk about with the student. He had taught the course the student has just completed in a different way and he would like to have the student's opinion of the course. He has some new projects in mind and would like to ask the student's opinion about them.

Because the stated object of the meeting is to talk about the student's next-term courses, both the student and the instructor feel a certain pressure to stick to the stated business. The conference could very well end with neither of them discussing their more important concerns. We speak of the stated business of a conference (interview, meeting, committee session) as the *agenda*. The agenda of the student and teacher we have been discussing concerned what courses the student should take next term. When people talk, they often have hidden items on their agendas. In this example, the student's hidden item was his career problem, and the instructor's hidden item was the student's reaction to the course just finished. Often, bringing what speech people usually call the *hidden agenda* into the open through the process of self-disclosure is a good way to improve communication. The responsibility of centering communication interaction on the subject you really want to talk about is *yours*. If you wonder why the other person is acting and talking in unexpected ways, and you sense some hidden agenda item, our advice is simple: *Ask.*

Much talking that passes for communication is merely people talking *at* other people, because the speaker and the listener demand neither feedback nor clarification. One of the surprising discoveries of people who study two-person communication is that so many people are so poor at providing and interpreting feedback to aid understanding.

Several important factors operate in two-person communication to keep people from providing the essential feedback. One is the mistaken notion that talking with another person is a simple matter. After all, we reason, we have probably spent more of our total communication time in such two-person talks than in any other form of communication. We ought to be good at it by now, we tell ourselves. Besides taking such interaction for granted, the situation itself is often informal, relaxed, and seems much less difficult than giving a good formal speech to an auditorium full of people. When we do misunderstand something in an informal conversation, we often blame our failure to find out more on some inherent trait of the other person or some factor beyond our control: "I guess George didn't hear me," or "We were interrupted about then and I guess it wasn't clear," or, "I don't know what it is about Lorraine but she just never can get anything straight."

Another factor that operates to prevent feedback is our assumption that our first attempt to tell another person something has succeeded. We often interpret silence as understanding and acceptance. We even interpret mumbling or other unclear answers as acceptance. Actually, our first attempt to communicate is *likely to fail*. The more completely we have failed, the more likely it is that the listener will greet the communication with silence. Silence itself often should be interpreted as feedback indicating not that the other person understands or agrees with you, but rather that he is confused. If you give a directive to someone else, particularly if you are in a position of authority, you should be as suspicious of a simple "yes" answer as you are of silence. When a policeman has been called to an apartment because of a domestic argument and he "lays down the law" to the couple and then demands of them, "Now, is that clear?" what can their answer be but, "Yes." As one young policeman said in class, "And then I had to go back five nights later and spell it out again." He was disgusted, until he realized that he had left little opening for the couple to express their real failure to understand his advice and their refusal to appreciate the need for working out their problems in some way that would not disturb their neighbors at 4 o'clock in the morning.

An additional factor in poor feedback is concern for protecting the self. We have discussed protective and defensive communication at length. One of the important effects of the need to defend self is the unwillingness to reveal lack of information, knowhow, understanding, or skill by providing feedback. We have to learn to be comfortable admitting what we do not know in any situation.

A final factor in poor feedback is lack of skill. Watch a television play or go to the theater and watch the actors who are *not* speaking at any given moment. The good performers are acting every minute, reacting to what the speaker is saying, responding nonverbally, *communicating* to the audience what they understand and how they feel about what another character is saying or doing. A good communicator does much the same thing when listening to another person; he responds in such a way that the speaker can see and hear and understand his response. We will talk more about this sort of creative listening in Chapter 13.

One of the more important verbal methods of providing good feedback is the use of questions. Asking questions is an art all of us can use, and most of us could study and improve our skills in the techniques employed. In our classes we sometimes make the point about asking questions to provide feedback by having the students prepare short speeches which are to be interrupted by members of the class when they fail to understand or when they disagree with the speaker. The class members are allowed to ask only one of three basic questions when they interrupt: (1) what do you mean? (2) how do you know? and (3) so what? Many a student has been astonished to hear, "What do you mean?" so soon after he begins his speech. Many have found the question, "How do you know?" difficult to answer, and almost all students discover that their 5 minutes of prepared remarks take 20 minutes to get across when the listeners ask honest questions and thus provide feedback to achieve a high level of understanding. Without direct and explicit feedback in the form of questions, many of the students would have delivered their 5-minute speeches, sat down, and assumed the audience had understood them.

We have stressed throughout this chapter the need for self-disclosure to build trust because, too often, the importance of the *relationship* between two people trying to talk with one another is overlooked. The need for openness and trust is, without question, great. We do not want to leave the impression, however, that maximum self-disclosure, honesty, and openness are desirable at all times and under all circumstances in every communication situation. The thrust toward instant trust is, we feel, being misunderstood and misused by many people. There *are* limits to what we need to tell others about ourselves. Psychiatrists trying to help mentally ill people rebuild a good enough self-image to get by in the world, day by day, find themselves not only allowing people to keep certain inhibitions, certain established ways of responding to life, but encouraging them to rebuild many of the defenses they found fairly useful before becoming ill. While not all the defenses these people had constructed could be considered good, even desirable, the point is that the defenses enabled the people to get along, and to some extent, all of us have built into our personality structure defenses which enable us to face life. These defenses are there for a reason, and anyone working to break them down had best be prepared to provide replacements or face trouble.

Many people do not care to go about belaboring the world with their innermost thoughts and feelings, and these people should have the right to keep whatever they want to themselves. Few of us who have passed through adolescence do not remember at least one painful truth session with "a good friend," who, after telling us all our faults, assured us that "it was for our own good," and left us hanging emotionally, wondering if that was what all our friends thought of us!

Good communication then, we feel, requires restraints and respect as well as, on occasion, self-disclosure. Part of the trust needed in supportive communication comes from knowing that when we are interacting with this person, he will *stop short of hitting below the belt.* He knows the limits of privacy set by me, and he respects them. The wife who tells her husband's secret worry to outsiders is headed for real trouble; so is the husband who repeatedly reminds his wife about her worst habit. This sort of communication hurts and is extremely destructive to the relationship between two people. There are limits of self-disclosure in good interpersonal communication and they are drawn just at that point where we take a swipe at the underpinnings of the personality of the other person. You have to know someone else pretty well to know just where to direct such a verbal hit.

Differences must be talked out, and verbal battles are useful when they serve the purpose of clearing the air. Verbal battles fought within agreed-upon limits can be useful, even fun, when they help dissipate the natural hostilities generated in any close relationship. Nonetheless, when two people want to maintain good communication, they both have to know where to draw the line. Naturally, as a relationship deepens, each can cross the line a little more from time to time, but no matter how close any two people become, each has privacy limits across which no other human should ever intrude.

SUGGESTED PROJECTS

1 / This is a job-interview project. The instructor may have interviewers come from companies in the community and conduct

the key ideas

When a person expresses himself he gives vent to feelings or ideas and has no interest in arousing common meanings in listeners.

While self-expression may be artless, communication always requires some artistry.

Two-person communication provides ideal conditions for close-range, continuous feedback.

The opportunity for high-fidelity and deeply significant communication is greatest in the two-person situation.

We are islands of consciousness and cannot really break out of the boundaries of self to experience directly another person's meanings.

Our interior world is changing, shifting, dynamic; the language we use to encode our meanings, however, is static.

The encoding of messages is an art that can be learned.

The English language is a particularly rich and powerful tool for communication.

Admitting ignorance is a vital key to providing feedback for improved communication.

Listeners often read into messages the meanings that fit their personal biases and interests.

Interpersonal communication is potentially irritating and sometimes punishing.

We all search messages with an eye to what they mean to us personally and, particularly, what they mean in terms of our self-image.

---

simulated job interviews with some or all of the students individually in front of the class. (Many businesses consider a request for an interviewer excellent public relations. If local businessmen are not available, a fairly realistic situation can be created if the college's personnel officer will interview for student employment, or if the school newspaper editor will interview prospective reporters, ad solicitors, or business managers.) If no outside interviewers are available, the class can be divided into pairs with one

in chapter 6

The way two people see one another is as important to their conversation as is the way they see themselves.

Self-disclosure widens the area of what two people know about one another and thus increases the possibility of high-level communication.

Threatening, critical, evaluative communication brings out a person's protective filters and produces defensive communication.

Deep and serious talk requires consciously supportive communication.

Through bad communication habits we often knock the props out from under one another without meaning to.

Once trust has been established between two people, even unpleasant things can be discussed openly, not without discomfort, but with a feeling of mutual respect.

Some communication problems come about simply because people avoid talking about what really bothers them.

Often bringing the hidden agenda of a conference into the open through self-disclosure is a good way to improve communication.

Many people are unskilled at providing or interpreting feedback.

Our first attempt to communicate with another person is likely to fail.

Silence should usually be interpreted as feedback telling the speaker the other person is confused.

Maximum self-disclosure, honesty, and openness are not desirable at all times and under all circumstances.

Each of us has limits of privacy which no other human being should ever cross.

student playing the role of interviewer while the other presents himself or herself as the job applicant. Roles can then be reversed. Our students often make the simulated job one they are actually hoping to qualify for in the future, so that the role they play is meaningful and a rehearsal of things to come. If possible, the interviews should be video or audio taped, so that each student can evaluate his own communication skill as a job applicant. If the instructor and the viewing class members write critiques of the interview while it is taking place, the student can compare his own appraisal, which he makes from the tape recording, with the comments of his peers and instructor, and write a short paper evaluating his performance.

2 / The class is divided into pairs. One person in each pair selects an important idea or process to explain to the other. The idea should be something that the first person knows from a course he has taken or from a personal experience he has had but the second person has not. The first person acts as a message source and tries to explain the idea or process to the other. The second person concentrates on providing feedback, both verbal and nonverbal, to the first. The second person can only ask these three questions: What do you mean? How do you know?, and So what? at the appropriate times.

3 / Write a brief paper describing an instance when you became thoroughly angry with someone and could not communicate your anger to him. What happened? Why couldn't you communicate it? (Was the person someone you feared or someone who had some power over you that you feared?) Do you think that if you could have communicated your anger and brought it out into the open it would have helped? How?

SUGGESTED READINGS

Giffin, Kim, and Bobby R. Patton. *Basic Readings in Interpersonal Communication*. New York: Harper & Row, 1971.

Goffman, Erving. *The Presentation of Self in Everyday Life*. Garden City. N.Y.: Doubleday Anchor, 1959.

Jourard, Sidney M. *The Transparent Self*. Princeton, N.J.: Van Nostrand, 1967.

Keltner, John W. *Interpersonal Speech-Communication: Elements and Structures*. Belmont, Calif.: Wadsworth, 1970.

Matson, Floyd W., and Ashley Montague (eds.). *The Human Dialogue: Perspectives on Communication*. New York: Free Press, 1967.

Rogers, Carl. *On Becoming a Person*. Boston: Houghton Mifflin, 1961.

7 how to inform

Often when we are the source of messages we have as our basic purpose telling the receiver something about the world. We are emphasizing the first face of language usage—the denotative. For example, when we tell someone how to get from one place to another, we are informing him about the geographic location of various places. The basic content of a message discussing facts is *information*. A common dictionary definition of information is a message about facts.

What are facts? *Facts* are those things which two or more people can see and agree on. We encode factual messages about such things as chairs, tables, cars, people, buildings, and their relationships to one another. Someone may come to a meeting, look about the room and ask, "Where is John?" If you have the information, you may encode a message in reply as follows: "John just called. His car is stuck in the ice in his driveway and he will be late." The information in the message relates to things such as the human being called John, his automobile, his driveway, and the relationships among these things, for example, the relationship contained in the words "he is stuck in his driveway." Further, the message provides information about John's relationship to the building in which the meeting is being held: that he is in his driveway, that the driveway is some distance from the place of the meeting, and that he is there now and will be here somewhat later than expected.

A message to inform consists of information about facts. We need to understand and have skills in the denotative use of language in order to make ideas about facts clear. We begin our study of how to inform by examining techniques for describing and explaining facts.

DEFINITIONS

One of the most important tools a speaker has to help make ideas clear is the ability to define a word. Before a person can tell someone about facts, he must decide whether his listener understands the words he hopes to use. If the listener does not know what is named by a word in the speaker's message, he is likely to misunderstand or be confused by the message.

When a speaker defines a word he tries to make clear to his listener the thing, property, or relationship he means to indicate when he uses the word in their conversation. A basic way to define a name is to say the word and at the same time point to the object named. Thus, if we are defining names for someone who does not know English, we might point to an object and say, "telephone, telephone." When our listener understands that when we use the name *telephone* we are referring to that object or one like it, we have defined the word, and now we can both use the term in our future conversations. Defining properties in a basic way is sometimes more difficult. We might define the property of "red," for example, by pointing to a red chair and asserting, "red, red." The trouble is that the listener might not know that we mean the color rather than the texture of the material or the shape of the object. We may have to also point to a patch of color in a picture on the wall above the chair and again assert, "red, red," until the listener makes the connection and discovers that what the things all have in common is a certain color.

Once the source and receiver have the same meaning for the content words in messages—that is, they both use the same words for naming things and the same words to stand for properties and relationships—they can talk about the facts of their common experience. They can then talk about the things in a room. For example, one person might say, "Please sit in that red chair." Or, "Be careful of sitting on that red chair because it is weak and may break." People can also speak about chairs that are not present at the time of their conversation. In this instance, the source may write a message to a receiver, in which he describes the color, size, and shape of a chair. Should the receiver decide to buy the chair, he will expect it to have certain properties because of the information he decoded from the message. If the chair is not what he expected, either the source misled him by claiming that the chair had certain properties it did not possess (his information was false) or they did not have the same definitions for the words in the message (the receiver misunderstood).

When you are trying to make an idea clear you must look carefully at the words you use in your messages. You must ask yourself, "Will all the people taking part in the communication decode a name as standing for the same thing?" If not, can you use another word for the same thing that everybody will understand? If not, you must select the best word, in your opinion, for the thing to be discussed and carefully define it for your listeners.

One way to define a term is to find other words that say the same or nearly the same thing, and by using these other words, clarify how you plan to use the term in the communications to follow. Many of the terms that we have used earlier in the book have been defined in other words. The dictionary definition of a term usually supplies other words that mean the same thing. For example, one of the meanings of *communicate* supplied by a good dictionary is to give thoughts, feelings, or information by writing, speaking, and so forth.

If one can describe the thing or events named by the term clearly in other words, the result is a definition. An interesting by-product of the process of definition used to talk about things in the world is that we can describe an imaginary thing, person, or event, and give it a name. For example, we can describe a person who is "the present king of the United States" and refer to such a person in our messages. Of course, the United States has no king, so no real person is named by the definition. Yet we can go on talking about "Samuel Rex, the present king of the United States," as though such a person existed. We can also pick a name such as *unicorn* and supply such a precise description of the beast that an artist can draw a picture of one, even though the animal does not exist.

Take the case of the *rockslide cornberet,* a strange, gray bird the size of a crow with a crown of feathers resembling a beret. The rockslide cornberet gets its name from its love of corn, its beret-like headdress, and the female's peculiar practice of laying a single egg in some stones at the top of a mountain and then kicking egg and stones over the edge, thus starting a rockslide. When the rockslide comes to rest in the valley, the pile of stones serves to protect and incubate the egg so the female does not have to sit on it. Since neither source nor receiver can observe the nonexistent rockslide cornberet, they may argue about it because they are talking about individual impressions and not about anything in the world which they can observe to correct their impressions.

We do not get into serious trouble talking about mythical animals or the present king of the United States, but we do get into difficulties when we talk about *the Establishment, a racist society, the New Left, duty,* or *Black Power* and cannot find any observations to correct our impressions. Much misunderstanding and many arguments come from discussions of terms that, like the rockslide cornberet, stand for nothing but the meanings we put into them. Equally important is the problem posed by defining terms such as *democracy, capitalism,* or *communism* without reference to actual events. The process of definition allows us to name a nonexistent economic system called *pure capitalism* or a governmental arrangement called *pure communism.* Having named these fictitious things, we can go on to discuss them as though they were real events with real implications. If we define something called *world communism* in terms of a powerful force of millions of people dedicated to the violent overthrow of capitalism and the destruction of the United States, we may act as though the thing we defined actually exists in the world. If the thing defined is as unreal as the rockslide cornberet, we might act foolishly because we are responding to definitions and not to things. (What of the man who spends years in the Rockies with his camera trying to get a photograph of the rockslide cornberet?) The same thing can happen with definitions such as the *conspiracy* to kill Black Panthers or the *conspiracy* to overthrow the government by violent means.

If you wish to inform people, therefore, you should be sure that both you and your listeners understand whether the terms defined refer to the things of the world that can be observed to check on the definitions, or are names for fictitious people or events.

One final problem relating to clarifying ideas and conveying information concerns confusion resulting not from lack of skill in definition, but from the intent to mislead. On occasion a source uses words that all his hearers understand and says something about the things under discussion which is not true. In short, the source asserts something about the world which he knows is not true and he does so with intent. The information contained in his message is *false,* and the result of the intent to mislead is a lie. A communicator who exploits the situation where the receiver expects clarification and information by purposely telling a falsehood has been unethical, not lacking in communication skill.

EXPLANATIONS

One of the most important ways in which a person can make something clear to another is to explain it. Perhaps the most basic and important way to explain something is to describe it. When we describe something, we find a suitable name for it—one that all involved in the communication understand—and then proceed to use descriptive words that denote properties or relations to explain the thing. When either the source or the receivers of the message (or both) have fewer words for the properties or relations (that they wish to assign to the thing under consideration) than they need, they use comparisons (figures of speech) to indicate that the thing is like something else in certain respects; they may also point out how the thing differs from other commonly understood things and thus, by pointing out what it is not, begin to explain what it is.

When we describe a situation, a thing, a happening, or an event, we can use language to appeal to the listener's imagination. One of the most important ways in which people acquire information about their world is through their senses. By skillful descriptions of how a thing appears, sounds, smells, tastes, or feels, a message source can make a receiver understand the thing almost as though the listener were experiencing it himself. When trying to explain a complex experience or situation, we ought to use descriptions that appeal to as many of the senses as possible.

We can also explain something by *listing its parts*. We explained communication by using the S M C R key to the parts of the process. We might explain the government of the United States by listing the three main branches: the legislative, the executive, and the judicial. We could then go on to list the parts of the legislative branch such as the House of Representatives and the Senate.

Another good way to explain certain things is to *describe the way they work*. We could explain an internal-combustion engine by showing how the gasoline is changed into a mist as it moves through the carburetor and is drawn into the cylinder by the vacuum created by the stroke of the piston moving out of the cylinder. We could go on to describe how the stroke of the piston pushing back into the cylinder compresses the mixture of air and gasoline until the spark from the spark plug ignites it and the resulting explosion drives the piston forward.

We can explain some things by pointing out the *causes or scientific laws* that account for them. Why do some people who shoot heroin get hepatitis, or inflammation of the liver? We could explain that hepatitis is caused by small organisms that can be transmitted from one person to another through the bloodstream and that such small organisms can live for a time on a dirty injection needle.

We can explain some human behavior on the basis of the *goals and desires* of the people involved. Why does a student become nervous before giving a speech in front of the class? We might explain stage fright in terms of the student's desire to get a good grade and to make a good impression on the others in the class. Since the student knows that the opportunity to get up alone in front of everybody and have the spotlight on him for a short period of time offers a great chance to impress the others (and the instructor), he realizes that much is at stake. What if he forgets his speech and makes a fool of himself in front of everybody? Since he is risking a great deal, he approaches the speech with mingled hopes and fears. He might win a great deal but he might lose as much. He feels something like a gambler who is risking a lot of money in a crap game or at poker. He is tense, excited, and fearful.

We can explain some things by telling a *plausible story* that includes all the facts to be explained and makes them hang together so they sound possible. Children who like to do things they are not supposed to do sometimes get caught. A child might become adept at telling stories to keep from being punished. Bill comes to school late after playing hooky, and he has not done his homework. He tells a story about how he overslept because he had to stay up late taking care of his sick mother and how, because of all the extra work taking care of things at home, he cóuld not do the homework. The Ancient Greeks explained many important events in their lives through stories about the gods on Mount Olympus. Lawyers often explain the events surrounding a crime by placing them into a plausible story. Thus the prosecuting attorney might account for the events by saying that the accused had the stolen property in his apartment because he was the boss of a ring of burglars and that when he met with them at his place he laid the plans for future crimes. The defense attorney might say that the accused knew some of the burglars but was an innocent victim because one of his friends had asked him to keep the stolen stuff. The accused did not know where the goods came from and had no idea they were stolen. The meetings in the apartment were to play cards, and while the accused may have been unwise in his choice of card-playing friends, he is not guilty of any crime.

We may also explain something by *fitting it into a class.* If we take a number of things and divide them into several classes on the basis of some common feature, we can explain some characteristics of an individual thing by fitting it into the proper class. For example, if we take a number of children and divide them into classes on the basis of their ages, as is often done in an elementary school, we could further divide the fourth graders on the basis of reading ability, so that we would have bluebirds (fast readers) and redbirds (slow readers). We could explain some things about Johnnie by saying he is a fourth-grade bluebird. We use classification systems to help explain things in a number of different areas. In botany we divide plants into classes and subclasses. In biology we divide animals into genus and species. In sociology we divide people into socioeconomic classes.

Definition and explanation are basic ways of clarifying a point and informing others. We have discussed some important ways to define and explain. Several additional tools are available to the person who is trying to make ideas clear. These additional tools can be used to define terms and explain things, but they are so important for other purposes as well that we will deal with them separately and in some detail. The most important tools for clarifying ideas are the example, the analogy, and the narrative.

EXAMPLES

One of the most important skills you should develop to improve your communication is the ability to recognize and use examples. What we call *examples* are sometimes also called illustrations.

An example is one (of a number of things) taken to show (the nature or character of) all. The example illustrates some important points about all the things like it. An example may also be an instance that illustrates the operation of a law or a general principle. As you become more professional in communication, you will find yourself noting the technique others use to support an idea or make a point clear.

Earlier in the chapter we used several examples to clarify an abstract idea. In discussing the notion that the process of definition allows a person to describe a fictitious event or person and supply a name for it, we used the examples of the "present king of the United States" and the "rockslide cornberet."

When a person submits an example to make a point clear, he may select an instance that actually happened or he may invent an example much as an author makes up a story. When a speaker uses nonfictional accounts of actual events or people, he is using a *real* example. When he dreams up a fictitious incident that might have happened, but in fact did not, he is using a *hypothetical* example.

Real examples are useful in making a point clear, but they may also be evidence to prove a point in an argument. If a person wants to prove that the smoking of marijuana does not necessarily lead to the use of heroin, he might submit as proof the real examples of a number of people who have smoked marijuana but have not used heroin. Hypothetical examples, on the other hand, are not proof, because if you were in an argument and made up a number of examples to support your side, another person could make up an equal number of examples to support his side. Suppose one person argues that juvenile delinquency is caused by poverty and miserable living conditions in the inner city. "Take the case of Johnnie," he says, "growing up in the ghetto. Johnnie is much more likely to become delinquent than a child in the suburbs." "Not at all," answers the other person.. "Take the case of rich Billy whose parents have no time for him and who give him every material thing he wants instead of giving him enough love, time, guidance, and discipline." Both parties in such an argument can dream up make-believe characters such as Johnnie and Billy as long as they like and match hypothetical example with hypothetical example. When using real examples, however, the debaters could submit only actual happenings as evidence.

Real examples carry more weight because they are factual and because the person in a conference, interview, group discussion, or public speech who explains ideas by using real examples gives his listeners the feeling that he is speaking from a firm basis of facts and that he is an expert.

We may have trouble using real examples, however, when we take part in informal talks and do not have notes with us. If a point comes up in a conversation or an interview and we need an example to make the idea clear, we may not remember the details of a real example and may not have time to look them up. Even if we have time to prepare for a discussion or business meeting or public speech, we may search the library in vain for exactly the right example to make a point.

We can tailor the hypothetical example to the needs of the audience, the point to be clarified, and the time available. Thus, although hypothetical examples are not evidence, they are a good way to make a point clear.

Why are examples so important to basic communication skills no matter what the setting or the occasion? Examples are concrete and make broad principles and laws easy to hear, smell, see, taste, and feel. When we stop talking about the law of gravity and start using the example of the falling basketball, the listener can visualize the event and see how the law works in actual practice. Examples add interest to the message. A good example makes a difficult idea easier to understand. We enjoy the understanding that comes from seeing how or why something works. We like to be able to understand things, and so an example which brings understanding also brings interest.

People appreciate the skillful use of example. Most of us enjoy watching an expert perform. Even though we may not be good musicians, we probably enjoy watching and hearing a skillful pianist. Although we may not care much for baseball we may enjoy watching a talented shortstop field ground balls. When a talented and skillful speaker uses a good example—one well suited to the listener, the occasion, and the point under discussion—we get a similar sense of interest and appreciation.

The use of examples is an art that can be acquired through practice. Some aspects of communication discussed in this book are difficult if not impossible to change; the most you can hope to do is understand them, take them into account, and develop the right attitude about them. We cannot change time limitations; we cannot change the way dialects reflect social and geographic differences; we cannot control the complicating effects of status on communication situations; and we cannot change the basic rules of the dynamics of small groups. We just have to allow for these things in our conduct within the particular situations. But some aspects of communication can be controlled, and a good communicator has learned to encode messages more skillfully than a poor one for a given receiver (or receivers), and for a given purpose, and in a given situation. One of the arts of communication is the invention and use of examples to make a point clear. Any speaker can pick one from a large number of possible examples to clarify the same idea. A good speaker is able to pick an example that interests the listener and is within the listener's experience and level of understanding. By skillful use of examples he can connect even abstract, difficult ideas to the experience of the other person.

When you pick examples to clarify a point you ought to be receiver-oriented. A good speaker has a number of different examples available for illustrating the same point. He invents examples from different situations. The speaker who picks an example that interests the listener helps ensure the success of his attempts to inform. By selecting examples of different lengths, the speaker can make his comments shorter or longer. The speaker who has a good supply of examples can be guided by feedback and then supply the listener with additional examples until he is sure he has been understood.

Suppose we wish to clarify the point we made in Chapter 3 that each person should carefully decide whether to learn the standard general American dialect if he does not already speak it. Suppose, too, that we know quite a bit about the people who will hear our message. We know how old they are, whether they are male or female, what jobs they have, their hobbies, their social and economic class, whether they are from the South or the North, from the city, the suburb, or a rural area. We have available the following examples to clarify the point about the decision to learn a new dialect:

An actual person who is a network television announcer and grew up in tidewater Virginia

A hypothetical person who is an education major from Brooklyn and plans to teach in Brooklyn

An actual person who is a business major at Louisiana State University and speaks with a Cajun accent

An actual person who is a community-college student with no major as yet and comes from a suburb in Los Angeles

An actual person who is a black star in the National Basketball Association, attended a Big Ten university, and was originally from a ghetto of New York City

A hypothetical person who is a chicano from New Mexico and attends a junior college there

An actual person who is from an aristocratic old family in North Carolina and proud of her background, and is studying art

An actual person who is a militant black from an inner-city ghetto in Detroit, studying to be a social worker

Each of the above examples contains a great deal of additional information. Some are quite detailed and take longer to explain than others. Some are humorous, some serious, and some full of conflict. When we prepare to talk to a given group of people, we have to pick the example which seems best for this audience, in this setting, at this time. Decide which of the above examples would be best for each of the following occasions:

A meeting of the Parent-Teachers Association in a wealthy suburb of Detroit

A meeting of the Parent-Teachers Association in an inner-city school in New York City

A speech-communication class in a Los Angeles College

A group of students at a high-school careers-day convocation in Atlanta, Georgia

A meeting of the Black Student Union at a Big Ten university

Since examples can add interest and emotional tone to a message, the source must consider the occasion as well as the audience when selecting which examples to use. If a person plans to discuss a topic in an informal two-person conversation over coffee in a cafeteria, he might use a light, humorous example. If he plans to clarify the point in an important presentation before a large group in a formal setting, he should pick an example which has a different tone and treatment. One should not use humorous or sexy examples on solemn occasions, nor should he use serious, weighty, or complicated examples in an after-dinner speech.

ANALOGIES

The analogy is another important way to clarify ideas. If you become good at using examples and analogies, you will be able to meet 80–90 percent of your needs in making a point clear. An *analogy* is an extended comparison. When a speaker takes two things or two events and points out that they are the same in important respects, he is making a comparison. If he continues to point out several similarities, he makes an analogy. The short comparison is a figure of speech. "She has a neck like a swan's" is a figure of speech. If we take the figure of speech about the girl's neck and extend the comparison, we might invent an analogy as follows: "She has a neck like a swan's. She swims with the grace of a swan but when she walks she waddles like a swan. Her voice is a swan-like screech and her nose looks like a swan's beak."

Analogies are like examples in many respects. Like examples, analogies come in two major types—the literal and the figurative. A literal analogy resembles a real example. The *literal* analogy is a comparison between two things, people, or incidents drawn from the same class or genus. The speaker who compares Metropolitan Community College to North Oaks Community College in regard to size of student body, quality of instruction, courses offered, and extracurricular activities available is using a literal analogy. He can find and verify this information. A *figurative* analogy, on the other hand, resembles a hypothetical example. It is a comparison between two things that, at first glance, do not seem comparable. A girl's neck is not really like a swan's neck. A girl does not have feathers on her neck, nor is a girl's neck as thin and long as a swan's. And yet we say something the listener understands when we say that the girl's neck is like a swan's. Life is not really like a football game, although many a coach has used that figurative analogy in his annual speech for the team.

The literal analogy, like the real example, is an important tool to prove a point as well as to inform or clarify. If you know a great deal about one event you can often reason about what will happen in a similar situation. Let us say that a student did well in science courses at a small liberal-arts college in the East. In his sophomore year he transfers to a small liberal-arts school nearer his home in the Midwest. We might argue that since he did well in science courses at the first school he will do well in science courses at the second; this argument is based on a literal analogy.

We often think in terms of analogies and try to reason from past experience to the present and future on the basis of literal comparisons. The literal analogy is an important way to make ideas clear to a listener. The ability to identify literal analogies is basic to better thinking. If we practice inventing analogies and saying them, we can improve both our thinking and our communication.

The literal analogy can build on the past experience of a listener. A good way to make a new idea or a new situation clear to another person is to compare the new idea to the old. Moving the listener from the familiar to the unfamiliar creates interest and understanding. The listener often finds familiar material dull. If the content of a message is unfamiliar, on the other hand, the listener is often so confused that he rejects the material and makes no attempt to understand it. In a good message the content is familiar enough so the listener can keep his bearings, yet is novel enough to create interest.

If a recent graduate returns to his high school after his first semester at college, a young friend still in high school might ask, "What is college like?" The college freshman might answer with a literal analogy comparing the high school they both know to the college only the speaker knows.

Literal analogies, like real examples, usually depend upon factual material for their development. You cannot always find a good literal analogy to use in an informal conversation or discussion. When you do find an apt literal analogy, however, you have a powerful tool for making ideas clear.

Figurative analogies resemble hypothetical examples in that they are largely fictitious. Often the message source can express an emotion or an attitude toward some person or event more by comparing two things that might not, on the surface, seem comparable. For example, the president of a large steel company might argue:

My company is criticized because we have a large share of the market for steel. I can't understand the criticism. The steel industry is like the National Football League. If a team wins a large share of its games in the league everybody thinks it is a great team because that is what football is all about—winning games. But when we win a large share of the steel market we are criticized for being a monopoly. Yet that is what the steel industry is all about—winning a share of the market.

The comparison of the steel industry to the football league expresses a strong positive attitude toward the industry on the part of the speaker. Try to invent an analogy that would express a different attitude toward the steel industry on the basis of this following hint: "Big steel is like an octopus that has its tentacles into every aspect of our lives including the government!"

Figurative analogies add interest to a comment designed to clarify an idea. They reveal the speaker's basic communicative skill, and we enjoy the artistry of a good comparison whether it is a short figure of speech or an extended figurative analogy.

Figurative analogies can help make complex notions and principles easier to understand. One common figurative analogy is to compare the functioning of the human nervous system to a telephone exchange. Another is to compare the structure of an atom to the structure of the solar system.

NARRATIVES

The final important device for making a point clear is the narrative. *Narratives* are stories, either true or fictitious, long or short, that contain characters, situations, and action. Stories are about one central character who draws the audience's interest. Usually the main character has a clear object in view and attempts to achieve his goal; in the process he runs into trouble, and the story tells about his good and bad times as he works for his objective. The old formula for a love story, for example, is boy meets girls, boy falls in love with girl, boy loses girl, boy gets girl. The fun of the story is in the many different ways in which the boy may lose the girl and the unusual ways in which he may win her back. In a good story the forces that keep the boy from getting the girl ought to be evenly balanced with the chance the hero has to get the girl. Conflict and suspense result from the hurdles the character must overcome to win his objectives and the even odds on his success or failure.

Narratives may be factual; among the real-life stories, some of the most effective are the speaker's personal experiences. Perhaps he was trying to get to school for a big examination, but stayed up late studying and slept through his alarm. When he did wake up he had only a short time to get to school. Racing to make it in time, he was stopped by a policeman, and so forth. The personal-experience story is one of the most common and effective ways to make a point clear. A well-told personal-experience story can amuse, illustrate, clarify, and present the speaker in an attractive light as a person of insight and humor.

The *anecdote* is a short narrative concerning one particular happening of an interesting or amusing nature. When the anecdote is amusing, it also may be called a *joke*. Both serious anecdotes and jokes tend to have a sudden twist at the end which is called the *punch line*.

Narratives may be used as explanations by fitting the facts into a plausible story, as we noted earlier. Narrative material is often worked into analogies and examples to add human interest, conflict, and suspense. Narratives also play an extremely important role in the process of persuasion, as we shall see in Chapter 9, where we discuss the way dramatic stories present heroes and villains acting out dreams which people often strive to achieve.

A BASIC MESSAGE UNIT

In discussing communicating to inform we must consider any technique, such as an example or an analogy, in terms of the point the speaker wishes to make. The basic building block for messages consists of two parts: the point to be made and the material to support it. Sources may encode messages composed of single blocks placed in some order or structure. The basic building block is used in talking with another person informally, in casual conversation, in a conference or an interview, in a small group discussion or a business meeting, and in a presentation or a public speech. No matter what the reason or setting for your message, you need to know how to construct the basic message units.

When a communication source says only his main points without supporting or amplifying them, his messages sound and read like a telegram or an outline of the major headings for a theme in an English class. Brief comments on points to be made are hard to understand. Telegraphic talking has the advantage of brevity but usually produces so much confusion that the time saved is used up in trying to clarify meaning.

A point to be made clear should be expressed in a complete, simple, declarative sentence. We use the terms *complete, simple,* and *declarative* in their technical meaning for English grammar. A complete sentence is one in which all the parts, such as a subject and predicate, are included. A point for a message unit should not be phrased as are the following: "black English," "the numbers racket," "walking on the moon." Complete sentences include both subject and predicate, as follows: "You must know black English to teach black students," "The operators of the numbers games pick the winning numbers from common experiences," "The moon's gravity affects the way a person can walk on the moon's surface."

Remember that a simple sentence has but one subject and one predicate. Put another way, the point to be made in a message unit ought to contain only one idea. The following sentence would make a poor point for a message unit: "The operators of the numbers games pick the winning numbers from common experiences and generally pay off the police to keep in business."

A declarative sentence states something, as contrasted with a question, which asks for information, or a command, which tells somebody to do something. "How do they pick the winning numbers for the numbers game?" is not a good point for a basic message unit. Neither is the command, "Stop playing the numbers."

Never underestimate the importance of finding a good clear way to state the point you wish to make. If you can express what you want to say in a good, clear, simple sentence, you have gone a long way toward getting your point across.

After you have found a good statement of the point to clarify, provide supporting material to make the idea clear. Give an example (real or hypothetical) an analogy (literal or figurative), or a narrative that applies directly to the point. (Of course, if the idea is difficult for the receiver to understand, you may give several examples or analogies or stories to clarify one point.) An important mistake of beginning speakers is to use an example that does not have much to do with the point they are trying to make. Here is a hypothetical example of the does-not-apply mistake:

The operators of the numbers game in my neighborhood pick the winning numbers from most anything. For example, I

the key ideas

One of the most important skills in making ideas clear is the ability to define words so that your listener fully understands you.

A description of a thing or event named by a term results in a definition of the term.

Definition can also be the process that creates imaginary things and assigns them names, as in the case of unicorns and other mythical beasts.

Abstract names such as *democracy, capitalism, communism, youth,* and *the Establishment* cause communication problems when used without reference to actual events and things.

People get false information because of inept communication or because the speaker intentionally lies to them.

The most important tools for making ideas clear are the example, the analogy, and the narrative.

The example illustrates some important points about all things like it or provides an instance of the operation of a law or general principle.

When a person uses an example he may select one that actually happened or one he made up.

Real examples not only clarify points but can be used as evidence in an argument.

We can tailor hypothetical examples to the needs of the listener, the point we are making, and the time available, but since they are fictitious, we cannot use them as proof, only as clarification.

A good example makes a difficult idea easier to understand and arouses the interest of the listener.

know this one bookie who pays protection money all the time and he's been working this one place for a long time and nobody has bothered him or given him any trouble.

In the above instance, the so-called "example" has nothing to do with the point made before it.

in chapter 7

The use of examples is an art that can be learned.

A speaker can often pick one or two examples from a large number that may all be used for the same purpose.

A short comparison is a figure of speech; an extended comparison is an analogy.

Literal analogies are comparisons between things from the same class or genus.

The literal analogy can build on the listener's past experience by comparing the thing to be explained to something the listener already knows.

If we know a good deal about one event, we often use a literal analogy to reason about what will happen in a similar situation.

Figurative analogies are based upon comparisons that are unusual; they add interest to a message because of their novelty.

In a narrative, conflict and suspense result from the hurdles the main character must overcome to win his goal.

Stories may be factual or fictitious.

Among the most effective factual narratives for a message source are those dealing with the speaker's personal experiences.

The basic building blocks for messages consist of a point to be proved and the material that supports, explains, or illustrates it.

A message that consists only of main points sounds like a telegram or an outline for an English theme.

A message can be too brief, because points that are not explained or illustrated are hard to understand.

The basic message units can be formed in several ways. The following four patterns are often used:

type 1
Point to be made clear
Supporting material (examples, analogies, stories)

type 2
Supporting material (examples, analogies, stories)
Point to be made clear

type 3
Supporting material (examples, analogies, stories)
Point to be made clear
Further supporting material

type 4
Supporting material (several examples, analogies, stories)
The point is never said in so many words, but the audience is supposed to be able to figure it out from the mass of supporting material; the point is made *by innuendo*

As a general rule, the patterns that state the point to be made clear first or last are the best; certainly you seldom will go wrong using message-building blocks of these first two types. Burying the point in the middle of a message block often hinders the receiver's efforts to dig it out and follow your comment. Leaving out the point entirely is quite risky. However, if you are reasonably sure of your listener's ability to identify the point on the basis of your clear examples and analogies, the 4th pattern can be effective, partly because it provides variety and partly because it creates the illusion that the point is the listener's own notion and facilitates his willingness to accept it. We recommend, therefore, that you use the basic message unit without a clear statement of the point primarily for persuasive situations and that you stick to Types 1 and 2 for most efforts to inform.

SUGGESTED PROJECTS

1 / Write ten statements illustrating good points to be made clear. Make sure that each statement is phrased as a simple, declarative sentence.

2 / This is an oral exercise in making ideas clear. Select a complex concept from one of your other courses, such as the concept of comparative cost advantage in economics, or the concept of valence in chemistry, or the concept of mitosis in biology. State the point to be made clear, and using only one extended real example or one extended hypothetical example, make the point clear to the class. Your example should be 2 minutes in length and you should announce to the class *before you begin* which form of example you will use.

3 / This is another oral exercise in making ideas clear. Select a concept similar to the one used in project 2 above. State the point to be made clear, and using only one extended figurative analogy or one extended literal analogy, make the point clear to the class. Again your analogy should be 2 minutes in length and you should announce which analogy you will use before you begin.

SUGGESTED READINGS

Braden, Waldo, and Mary Louise Gehring. *Speech Practices.* New York: Harper & Row, 1958.

Jeffrey, Robert C., and Owen Peterson. *Speech: A Text with Adapted Readings.* New York: Harper & Row, 1971. "The Use of Supporting Material: Exposition," pp. 266–285.

Olbricht, Thomas. *Informative Speaking.* Glenview, Ill.: Scott, Foresman, 1968.

8 how to persuade: the persuasive power of personality

No aspect of communication is more important to our daily lives than persuasion. We are urged to vote for political candidates, to support reforms, to buy products, and to establish relationships with other people. The message with persuasive intent comes at us in two-person conversations and interviews; in face-to-face small group conferences; in public speeches and business presentations; in newspapers, magazines, letters; in films, radio shows, and television programs. Billboards proclaim suggestions about how we should act or believe; neon signs entice us to drink, eat, or buy. The lyrics of popular songs sell a point of view or a life style. We go to a job interview and try to persuade the interviewer to hire us. We take a job as a salesman and try to get a customer to make a purchase. We see an attractive person and try to persuade her or him to go to a movie.

PERSUASION DEFINED

Persuasion is sometimes called changing behavior. It can also be defined as changing attitudes or belief, as winning friends, influencing people, gaining cooperation, or selling a product or an idea. When we talk somebody into doing something, we have persuaded him. When we suggest ideas or beliefs or argue for a position with evidence and logic in such a way that the listeners change their behavior, attitudes, or beliefs, we have persuaded them.

We will define *persuasion* as communication to influence choice. When we speak to inform (make a point clear), we often provide the listener with information that opens up new horizons and increases choices, but when we speak to persuade we try to influence the listener's choices and narrow them to the one we prefer.

Notice that persuasion is communication intended to get a response from the receiver, to change the receiver's attitude or beliefs. The source of the message, the person giving a persuasive comment or making a persuasive point, has a specific purpose in mind and drafts the persuasive message to achieve that goal.

Persuasion is not the same as force. We can control human beings to some extent with the use of force or the threat of force. Coercion restricts choice. If you are forced to do something, your options are closed. Coercion eliminates choice, while persuasion influences it. Coercion does not require artistry. "Do this or I will bash in your head" may get results, but requires little skill—only the brute strength and the desire to deliver the blow. A good salesman, on the other hand, is skillful and has developed the art of persuasion to a high level. If selling were as easy as bashing in heads, more people would be making $30,000 a year in commissions.

Persuasion is not the same as inducing somebody to do something by offering a powerful reward. A father might get his son to cut his hair by promising him a new car. Offering a large reward is similar to offering a threat of force. The boss who says, "Come to work on Saturday or I will fire you," is operating on the same level as the one who says, "Come to work on Saturday and I will give you a bonus." Neither offering a large reward nor threatening punishment involves much communication skill or selling ability.

PERSUASION AND PERSONAL RELATIONSHIPS

One of the most important factors for persuasion in a communication situation is the quality of the personal relationships that are established. If the people who are discussing a topic like and trust one another, attempts of either one to influence the other are more likely to succeed.

Persuasion often consists of advice. When we receive advice, we usually face some risky choices. Many of the big decisions in life pose some risks. Should I enlist in the army? Should I take a job with Pulver Motors? Should I get married? Should I go to college? Should I take a shot of heroin? When the choices are risky and I need advice, I turn to someone I trust. Trust assumes that the other person will give me advice that seems to him best for me. When I trust a person, I can count on his strength, integrity, sincerity, and expertness, and on his concern for me.

PERSUASION AND LIKABILITY

Often liking and trusting go together, but they are not necessarily always connected. We might find some people likable but not trustworthy in important matters because we know they are forgetful, unreliable, or easily swayed by emotions. On the other hand, some people whose advice we take and whom we trust are not likable. We might trust a certain medical doctor because we know he is well trained, sober, and a talented physician, even though we do not like him much as a person.

Nonetheless, if we like a person, we are tempted to believe and accept his ideas and his advice. We often *feel* better about taking the advice of someone we like than about accepting the recommendation of someone we dislike. An important part of the study of persuasion, therefore, concerns how people who talk with one another come to *like* one another.

Picture in your mind a person you like. Recall your conversations with that person. What do you talk about? How do you talk? What is your attitude toward the person before you start a given conversation? Does the likable person have certain characteristics, such as physical appearance and habits of dress, that carry over from conversation to conversation? What does the likable person do and say that is attractive?

Physical beauty is a factor in being likable. Peoples' ideas about what is beautiful are as individual as people. Just the same, Americans spend billions of dollars each year in the search for beauty because, for many, physical attractiveness is the key to popularity and friendship. Physical beauty is not enough by itself to assure likability, but other things being equal, the beautiful people have an advantage. Slogans such as "slim is beautiful" and "black is beautiful" clearly tie physical beauty to persuasive messages. Advertisers often use the persuasive power of handsome men and beautiful women shown using the product or simply being present in the same picture with an advertising slogan. The persuasive message is clear enough: "Beautiful people use this product; buy this product and you too will be beautiful."

Speaking ability is a factor in being likable. A pleasant, flexible, resonant voice quality communicates a dynamic personality, an alive and vibrant person. The person who can find the right word at the right time and who can express an idea clearly and with interesting examples or analogies draws attention and interest. The person with a lively and vivid imagination, who can make small talk, spin out dreams or fantasies, dramatize characters, tell interesting stories, and ask unsual questions, is interesting and can be likable.

Listening ability is a factor in being likable. Listening is a real talent and is often underestimated. The person who is willing to listen to others and find out who they are, what they are interested in, and what they are worried about is often liked. Genuinely good listeners are always welcome.

People who come to like and trust one another often do so by means of serious, deep conversations that take place over a long time. To be sure, some try to achieve such liking and trust in a week or two, or even a few days, by means of the intensive sensitivity or encounter groups we discussed in Chapter 6. Such forced feeding of significant communication is usually less successful than the growth of a relationship over more time. Instant trust is much like instant coffee; it just does not have the same flavor as a well-brewed cup. One of the charms of alcohol, drugs, and other consciousness-lowering mind changers is a "let's pretend" state of instant trust, but the feeling is the result of the altered mental state; it is not real. Trust cannot come without testing over time.

THE IMPORTANCE OF OUR ATTITUDE TOWARD OTHERS

All the basic personality characteristics mentioned above, such as physical appearance and speaking and listening ability, enter into our significant communications, but equally important is the attitude people bring to their interpersonal communications. When we engage in significant communication, we let others know what we think, where we stand, and how we feel. We disclose our hopes, our dreams, and our fears. People are more likely to disclose themselves to those whom they think have a real interest in them. The salesman who seems interested in us only as long as he thinks we will buy something so he can make a commission irritates us. People who use the others in a working group for their own ends or who treat others like things rather than like authentic persons seldom create trust and liking.

An attitude of willingness and ability to help creates a feeling of trust and liking in others. A genuine offer of help is a powerful force of persuasion. A good salesman often has a sincere and dedicated desire to help the customer. Well-managed stores instruct the salespeople to ask, "May I help you?" The may-I-help attitude in reverse works to build trust also. "I *need* your help" is another persuasive message. A person who asks for help accepts it without bitterness and then thanks us, makes us feel good. When people have helped one another, they feel freer to ask for help when they need it. When we create a climate of trust, we often accept the people we are talking with for themselves *as they are*. Acceptance does not mean approval of everything said or done by the participants in a communication; it means that the worth and importance of each person are unquestioned.

People who wish to persuade others in order to exploit them often try to cover up their real intentions. In face-to-face situations like the interview or small group meeting such persuasive tricks usually fail. No matter how hard the manipulator tries to make the others believe he is sincere, unselfish, and dedicated to the welfare of all, his facial expression, vocal intonations, and bodily posture and gestures give him away. Others come to think of the manipulator as slick, oily, phony, insincere. If a person is only pretending to be interested in another, the nonverbal messages communicate his real feelings. A common example of pretended interest is the child who courts another child only to ride his new bicycle. The result is that the receiver dislikes the person more than if the speaker had been honest in the first place.

Sometimes, a speaker's nonverbal cues create a wrong impression so that he fails to establish friendship and trust without knowing why. Often if several people are having trouble talking with one another because of unintended nonverbal mannerisms, they can discuss the things that bother them and come to an understanding.

PERSUASION AND SOURCE COMPETENCE

In addition to being likable and working to engender trust, the speaker should suggest competence, expertness, and credibility, if his advice is to be persuasive. We expect a competent person's talk to contain a wealth of good and relevant information about the topic under discussion. The speaker who is clear, whose comments are easy to follow because they are well organized, whose language is precise, and who has a fluent and expressive way of speaking, further suggests to us that he is competent. This is as true of the person talking to us face to face as of the person speaking in a more formal setting to a group of people in an audience.

PERSUASION AND SOURCE CONVICTION

Finally, a powerful force for persuasion is the speaker's deep personal conviction that he is right. The first person a good salesman persuades is himself. The father who discusses the dangers of the use of tobacco and advises his son not to start smoking as he himself drags on a cigarette is not persuasive. The persuasive power of dedicated reformers is in large part a result of their willingness to make great personal sacrifices for the cause. William Lloyd Garrison, a leading figure in the fight to free the slaves in the nineteenth century, once wrote of his own part in the battle to abolish slavery:

It is my shame that I have done so little for the people of color; yea, before God, I feel humbled that my feelings are so cold, and my language so weak. A few white victims must be sacrificed to open the eyes of this nation, and to show the tyranny of our laws. I expect and am willing to be persecuted, imprisoned, and bound for advocating African rights; and I should deserve to be a slave myself if I shrunk from that duty or danger.

Since Garrison was writing from a jail cell in Baltimore, his sincerity was obvious and his credibility was increased. One of Martin Luther King's most persuasive messages was his "Letter from Birmingham City Jail."

PERSUASION AND THE SPEAKER'S REPUTATION

Up to now we have been talking about persuasion as it applies to the man in the street, to you and me. When an important public figure takes his platform to the people, persuasion moves from interpersonal communication, where people talk directly to one another in what we called in Chapter 4 intimate and personal space, to communication from the region of public space.

Two factors influence the public speaker's ability to persuade his listeners: his reputation and the particular speech he is making. When we study the persuasiveness of well-known public figures, therefore, we must examine both the effect of the speaker's reputation and the impact of the message itself. If we hear from others of a basketball player's skill and high scoring ability, his reputation affects the way we watch the start of the game but our final opinion is also influenced by how well he lives up to his reputation in the game we are watching. The reputation of a speaker influences our acceptance of his ideas, but our final decision usually depends upon what he says to us.

Scholars have used a number of different terms to stand for the concept of the source's reputation. A popular term is *image*. Most politicians have professional help in building an image (reputation) that will gain votes. Business firms, motion-picture stars, rock musicians, government agencies, and other institutions often try to create a favorable image of themselves.

Another term for the speaker's reputation often used in communication research is *source credibility*. A large number of studies have examined the influence of a source's reputation on audience attitudes. The researchers first gave the experimental subjects a test to find out their attitude on a topic. Next the investigators told different groups of subjects that different people (sources) had produced the message they were about to hear. (The message was tape-recorded so it was the same for each group.) They then played the message to the subjects and tested them again to determine whether listening to the recording had changed the listeners' attitudes. Since the content of the message was the same (controlled), the investigators argued that measurable changes in the attitudes from group to group resulted from the fact that each group believed a different person had been speaking.

Advertisers talk of image, communication researchers refer to source credibility, while students of rhetoric use the term *ethos* for much the same concept. Because the Greeks studied the arts of rhetoric thoroughly, we often still use their terms: *ethos,* according to Aristotle, refers to a person's *character*—his disposition to act in certain ways.

A communicator's ethos or image is not static. Rather, when people talk with one another, they develop images related to that talk. For example, in the two-person conversation between John and Mary, developed in Chapter 6, their images of one another grow out of what they say to each other and how they say it. The images involved in conversations are thus more like motion pictures than like still snapshots in which a given message source has one image now and forever and in which that image has a certain persuasive impact regardless of the receiver of the messages.

The personality of the listener influences the effect of a persuasive message, as well. Research reveals that the listener's scores on dogmatism tests (which show how bullheaded or inflexible a person is) or personality inventories correlate with how much the listener changes his attitudes after hearing a message.

A listener's prior opinion of a speaker comes from many sources: previous in-person communications between them; what others have said to the listener about the speaker, what the listener has read about the speaker, and biographic information the listener may know about the speaker. Sources of information need not be individuals, of course. We receive communication from organizations, as well, and they too have prior reputations. The Defense Department has a reputation that affects all messages sent out by that particular unit of government, just as the John Birch Society, the Black Panthers, the United States Steel Corporation, the Communist Party, the Republican Party, and the Students for a Democratic Society all have images or reputations that affect the persuasive impact of messages they send.

Consider the images of two mythical candidates as they have been created on television and in the national publications. One is a senatorial candidate named Wayland, who is said to be young, slim, handsome, educated at Harvard College, dynamic, polished, a man who inherited wealth but who has been giving his life to public service. Photographs of Mr. and Mrs. Wayland attending cultural and social events often appear in the slick magazines. They have several attractive young children. Wayland has appeared more and more frequently in recent months on television news shows in brief scenes that show him stepping off airplanes, talking informally to reporters at airports, or speaking before audiences. His voice is pleasant, his manner serious but with some lightness and humor. He has a good smile and looks like someone you would enjoy knowing. Wayland's enemies say he is a lightweight and has gotten as far as he has largely through the power of his inherited wealth and social connections. There are ugly rumors about an impending divorce and about his extramarital sex life. Wayland is a liberal and he is strongly committed to international disarmament.

Wayland's opponent, also mythical, is the incumbent Senator Homer Beardsley. Beardsley is approaching 60 but is said by his friends to be amazingly vigorous and young at heart. He is frequently shown jogging, playing tennis, and chopping wood for the fireplace of his cabin in the western mountains. Beardsley is a self-made man, the son of a poor tenant farmer; he worked his way through college and law school, won a scholarship, and went abroad to study. Beardsley is said to be a brilliant man, but he has some difficulty expressing himself in speeches. He is a man of few words and he has something of a poker face. He is by no means a charmer. He has the reputation of being a powerful member of senate committees, although he does not get many headlines. Mrs. Beardsley is a plain but pleasant woman who likes to recall her farm background. They both enjoy country music and camping trips in wilderness areas. Their children are grown; they have grandchildren. Beardsley has been a strong defender of what he calls "preparedness" and is suspicious of all plans to disarm the country.

Some students in a speech class (with our myth in mind) are presenting a debate on disarmament, and the student speaking *for* disarmament quotes candidate Wayland. The student speaking *against* disarmament quotes Senator Beardsley. The reputation of each man influences your, the listener's response to the statements. However, should Wayland appear on campus to give a speech, his reputation would be a factor as you *begin* to listen to him, but his platform personality and his demonstration of the personality traits others have attributed to him would be important factors in your final image of the man.

THE BUILDING OF IMAGES

Building a good image of candidates and institutions is the object of much organized persuasive campaigning. As an individual, you are projecting a public image every day. You can learn much about how your own image appears to others and how you can improve your projection of it by studying the professional image-makers' techniques. What are they primarily interested in doing? Professional persuaders often go to great lengths to discover attractive images for clients. Obviously, you are also trying to project your own image in the most favorable way.

Interestingly enough, images for persuasive impact vary from audience to audience and from culture to culture. You will certainly try to project your most responsible image to your father when you ask for the family car for the evening, but 10 minutes later, on the telephone, you may try to project your most exciting, devil-may-care image to the date you expect to pick up in an hour. Consider our mythical political candidates once more. Did you find Wayland's image more attractive than Beardsley's? If so, you might well be from the suburbs of a metropolitan area. If you found Beardsley more attractive, you are probably from a small town, rural, or midwestern area. Psychologists tell us that we identify with people with whom we feel we have much in common. In this instance, the word *identification* refers to the feeling that you and another person could walk a while in one another's shoes. Consider a candidate who is black, was raised in an urban ghetto, went to college on a basketball scholarship, became a star in the National Basketball Association, and subsequently worked with ghetto youths and became a militant advocate of Black Power. Would you find his image attractive? Anyone wise in the arts of persuasion takes a close look at the image he wishes to project and then works hard to find out what images will be attractive to the audience he hopes to persuade.

You are all familiar with the national public-opinion polls —Gallup, Harris, and others. These polls are national trend-takers. Many campaign experts hire private survey firms to make depth studies of public reaction to images. In these studies, the experts collect responses from a group of people and, using those responses as a guide, estimate the responses of the large group that will be involved in the actual voting. The use of computers has, according to the pollsters, increased their accuracy and effectiveness in predicting actual voter performance. The methods they use to discover why people choose this man over that man are often unique. One poll-taker showed his respondents a list of some of the more popular television characters and asked them which of these personalities they would most like to represent them in Congress. On the basis of their findings (by whatever method) about what the candidate's public considers attractive, the image-builders select the elements in the candidate that they feel will be most attractive to the voters and stress these elements in news releases, in television commercials, and in the candidate's speeches.

From all this, however, you must not conclude that image-makers are creating false impressions of candidates or institutions. Persuasion must work within the limits of reality. The basic personality of the candidate or the nature of the institution being "sold" forms a framework within which the persuaders must operate. The best public-relations firm in the world cannot make Homer Beardsley appear to be a member of the jet-set or socialite Wayland appear as a soul brother. If a public realizes it has been fooled, the reaction is always swift and disastrous for the unwise candidate. All the persuaders can do, but this is of considerable value to candidates and to you as an individual, is to learn what is attractive in a personality being "sold" and to help a person stress the attractive portions of his image and minimize the less attractive elements.

Our society has been undergoing a refreshing scourging of phonies. If you consider it hypocritical to sell yourself when you wish to persuade, you should remember that there are times when a man believes in a cause so strongly that, if he finds his personality is alienating people, he will work hard to change his image in order to build more favorable response for the cause he is promoting. Thousands of college students hoping to stop the Vietnam War "went clean for Gene," cutting their hair, dressing conservatively, talking at length, quietly and without profanity, to potential voters as they campaigned for Senator Eugene McCarthy for President in 1968. By emphasizing the positive features of their cause and themselves, the students improved their ethos in an ethical way. They were able to level with the voters and still be honest with themselves. Accenting the positive is no sin; accenting what does not exist, on the other hand, is unethical. If a potential candidate sells himself to the voters as a church-going, sober man, when in fact he never goes to church and drinks heavily in secret, he will be found out and his ethos will be damaged.

We all form first impressions of people we meet. On getting to know these people better, we often change our opinions of them as the friendship grows or does not grow. In the case of national political figures, we are given much information from news media and magazines, and we are given information by the political figures themselves. We form opinions about all sorts of well-known people because we see and hear them or read about them; but about many people we have little information prior to our initial communication.

What happens when we know little or nothing about the source of the communication? We often decide how much to accept from such a source on the basis of the stereotypes we have all built in our minds since childhood.

We accept or reject messages because they come from people whose roles in society we accept or reject. We know that many professional people have spent years acquiring the knowledge needed to label themselves landscape architects, medical doctors, lawyers, certified public accountants, or college instructors, and when they speak to us as professionals we tend to accept what they say as being useful (truthful or persuasive) whether or not we find them personally attractive. We are accepting the image of the expert rather than the image as a personality, and we accept messages from such experts more readily when they are speaking about their particular area of competence. When a professor of economics argues that the Federal Reserve Board is following the wrong policy to get the country out of a recession, we listen to him and tend to think he knows what he is talking about. We expect his judgment to be professional and based on careful research. When this same professor argues that the salaries of economics professors ought to be increased, we may not accept his message as being as persuasive, since in this second instance, he is speaking as a man with vested self-interest, and not as a scholar making an objective study of a subject. The authors watched with interest one evening as a well-known surgeon nearly tore up his hat in anger and frustration after the elementary-school building committee wisely declined his carefully worked out plans for the new school. Used to having his judgments accepted immediately in his day-to-day hospital world, his expertise dropped dramatically when he spoke as another parent in the school meeting. The parents preferred the opinions of the teachers, administrators, architects, and city planners present, and wisely so. An expert, to be persuasive, has to stay within his area of competence.

DIRECT KNOWLEDGE OF THE SOURCE

In the final analysis, of course, a great deal of any speaker's ethos is generated by how he talks and what he says. Any speaker can do much to make his image more attractive right at the moment he is communicating. He can use nonverbal suggestion to make himself more influential with his listeners, more persuasive. The speaker should work hard to appear to be in charge of the situation and his material, though in a relaxed and friendly way, not in a dictatorial or wise-guy manner. Remember that we are more likely to be persuaded by someone we accept as a person—a person we feel we could like. If the speaker's manner conveys the impression that he is calm, confident, sincere, and honest, we are more likely to trust and to believe him. In a question-and-answer period after a formal speech, or in any face-to-face communication event, if the speaker's manner of fielding questions, dealing with disagreements, and handling challenges is fair and confident, his credibility with the listeners is increased. If, under such stress, he loses his temper, his credibility often correspondingly plunges. If, further, the speaker can communicate to the listener that he genuinely appreciates questions and respects the questioner, and if he responds fairly and candidly to the best of his ability, admitting honestly when he is stumped, he tends to build good will. If the speaker's manner suggests that he has something to hide, that he is irked when his expertise is challenged, or that he is angry when his opinion is contradicted, or if he hedges in such a way that he appears insecure and afraid of making a mistake, then his ethos is damaged. All these instances refer mostly to the manner in which the speaker conducts himself, to his nonverbal signals.

What the speaker says, his verbal message, certainly has a considerable effect on whether we like and trust him, whether we accept what he is saying and are persuaded by him. If the speaker is to be trusted he must say things that reveal him to be unselfish, interested in us, guided by a suitable code of ethics. (A suitable code of ethics would vary somewhat from situation to situation, depending on the speaker and the audience.)

If a person communicates verbally and nonverbally that he is trying to control us, that he is trying to outwit us and make us do something *he* wants but that we do not know about, that he is interested not really in us but in what he can get out of us, that he thinks he is a lot better and smarter than we are, or that he is so set in his ways he will not be changed, no matter how wrong others may feel him to be, then we are likely to reject him as a person and to reject his message as well. He will not persuade us because we do not think much of him or his ideas.

On the other hand, if the speaker communicates verbally and nonverbally that he is absolutely fair, candid, and honest, that he is not defensive about his status or his expertness, that he is deeply involved and dedicated to the common objective we share (why he is speaking to us and why we are there to listen); that he is willing to make personal sacrifices for our common good; that he is competent; that his advice is good and is given in our best interest, then his ethos is likely to be persuasive for us. He just may persuade us as he speaks because he inspires confidence that he knows what he is talking about and wants to share his know-how with us for our own good.

The speaker may well create an advantage by reminding the audience of factors in his background, experience, and training that make him particularly competent to discuss the topic. This should not be done in a boastful way, of course. Often the speaker's expertise is known beforehand, either from advance publicity or from an introduction before he speaks.

The speaker may also imply his status. For example, he can add as he talks about what kind of tires we should use on our cars, "I've been racing stock cars for some years, and I've found that. . . ." A speaker can dramatize his or her expertise as in the following example. A woman, a special counselor in the welfare department, was being introduced as a speaker to a group of young mothers, all newly receiving aid to dependent children benefits. These mothers were more than a little wary of listening to another expert tell them how to manage their lives, particularly their finances, now that they were on relief. The program chairman introduced the speaker as a woman who had earned a degree in social work from the university and whose experience in the field was extensive. The listeners were only mildly impressed. The speaker won their attention and hearts at once when she began. "Fifteen years ago I was sitting in your seat. I'll tell you how I got up here, and I'll tell you how you can get yourself back on your own two feet, and I know that's where you want to be. I *know* each of you wants to do the absolute best you can for your children, and for yourself, and that's why you are here." Wiping away the feelings of guilt that had washed over the young mothers as they had filled out the myriad papers necessary to obtain public assistance, the speaker had immediately told them: "You are great girls with problems; I had the same problem a while back, and I learned a lot of answers which I am going to pass on to you."

If a speaker can rise above the self-absorption that comes when one is the focus of attention and can work to raise the status of his listeners with genuine compliments about the organization they represent, warm comments about individuals in the audience, or requests for help and advice (giving every indication that he plans to take such suggestions seriously), then he will certainly build good will.

One final element always useful in constructing the persuasive ethos of a speaker comes from the fact that we all like to laugh. If a speaker can amuse us, if he can share his sense of humor with us, we are going to find him more likable. If he can communicate to us that he takes the subject, but not himself, seriously, we will be drawn toward him. If his humor is gentle rather than cutting or sarcastic, if he turns his humor back on himself rather than using it against others, we will trust him more. A person who can amuse his audience seems secure and in command of the situation. You must be careful not to overdo the use of humor, of course, particularly if you have a serious point to make. People love comics and clowns and try to place in that role any person who has some talent for comedy. The rewards for amusing speakers are great—laughter, congeniality, and the knowledge that they are well liked. But just as the expert must stay in his area of expertness, so the comic is expected to stay the comic. If the clown tries to make a serious point, to give advice

the key ideas

Persuasion is communication designed to influence choice. Coercion, like persuasion, restricts choice but, unlike persuasion, requires little artistry.

Little persuasive skill is involved in offering a reward or threatening punishment.

Much persuasion is dependent upon the quality of the personal relationships established among the people involved in the communication.

When the choices are risky and a person needs advice, he turns to someone he can trust.

People who come to like and trust one another often do so by means of a series of deep conversations.

Trust seldom comes without a period of testing.

People are more likely to disclose themselves to those they feel are really interested in them.

A genuine offer to help is a powerful force for persuasion.

We tend to believe people whom we think are competent, expert, and interested in our welfare.

A powerful force for persuasion is a person's deep personal conviction that he is right: Sincerity is persuasive.

about important matters, we feel uncomfortable and tend to ignore his advice. Funny guys are not listened to on serious matters. Use humor in your persuasive speeches, then, but keep in mind your over-all purpose.

There is much persuasive power in the personality of the source of the message. In the next two chapters we will consider the other components of persuasion in communication: the power of suggestion and the use of evidence.

SUGGESTED PROJECTS

1 / Select some important personal decision such as which college to attend, whether to get married, whether to buy a car, or which

in chapter 8

The image of a public figure is closely related to his credibility as a source of messages.

Organizations and business corporations also have images that affect their believability when they issue corporate messages.

The persuasive impact of a public figure's image varies from audience to audience.

If a public realizes it has been fooled by misleading image-building, the reaction is usually swift and disastrous for those involved.

We accept or reject persuasive messages from some sources because they have professional credentials which we respect.

Much of a person's ethos is created by how he talks and acts in our presence.

A message source creates a credible image to a large extent by his non-verbal communication suggesting he is interested in the listener, expert in the subject, and admirable as a person.

Funny guys are not listened to on serious matters, but a judicious use of humor in a speech increases a speaker's credibility as a human being.

---

career to pursue. Think of the one person whose advice you would be most likely to accept in regard to the decision. Make a list of reasons why this person is a credible authority for you in regard to this particular decision.

2 / This is actually a project within a project. Using the personal experience oral narrative, tell the class in 2 minutes about some exciting or emotional thing that has happened to you. Your aim will be to portray yourself through your participation in, or response to, the incident in such a way that demonstrates that you are wise, sympathetic, strong emotionally, understanding, dependable, friendly—whatever characteristic you feel will enhance your ethos with your intended audience. You should use the most effective verbal and nonverbal communication you can. Your purpose is not to entertain, however; you should select the experience and develop it in such a way that will make the audience accept you as

a credible message source on some undisclosed topic. After you have finished giving your narrative, tell the class what persuasive point about what topic you have in mind, and explain how you believe the personal experience narrative you have just related to the class would serve to enhance your persuasive position if you were to develop the whole topic on another occasion. Here is a brief example of what this exercise could be like (this is the personal narrative I tell): "I had always been a loner, and I am very interested in science and technology. I was put in charge of our high school Ecology Day and had to learn how to organize student committees and work with others. I discovered I enjoyed it. We had poster exhibits and class discussions and films; we also had a big all-school program in the auditorium. I introduced our visiting speaker. Unfortunately, I had worked so late every night all week making sure everything was ready, I was exhausted, and I fell asleep while the speaker was talking." I would tell this incident in a speech to students asking them to vote for me for student senate. I would hope to show them, with this story, that I am a person who becomes very committed to a job and works very hard at it, but that I am also human, have a sense of humor, and can tell a story about myself when I became the butt of the joke.

3 / Attend a speech given by some prominent individual. Write a paragraph about the speaker *before* attending the speech analyzing what you think of the speaker and deciding how credible a message source the speaker is for you. Keep notes on important comments relating to the speaker's ethos that occur *during* the speech. *After* you have heard the speaker, write another paragraph describing any changes in credibility that resulted from the speech itself. Write a third paragraph explaining these changes in terms of things the speaker said or did during the speech—how his personality influenced your judgment of his credibility.

SUGGESTED READINGS

Andersen, Kenneth, and Theodore Clevenger, Jr. "A Summary of Experimental Research in Ethos," *Speech Monographs*, 30 (1963), 59–78.

McCroskey, James C., Carl E. Larson, and Mark L. Knapp. *An Introduction to Interpersonal Communication.* Englewood Cliffs, N.J.: Prentice-Hall, 1971. "The Source-Sender," pp. 78–92.

9 how to persuade: the persuasive power of suggestion

PERSUASION AND PROPAGANDA

Much of the power of a personality to influence others in communication situations can be thought of as nonrational or unthinking. People often accept the advice or direction of someone they like and trust without examining the content of the message for consistency of reasoning or soundness of evidence. Some people use *propaganda* and *persuasion* as synonyms and contrast *bad* and *good* propaganda to show that it is not always undesirable. In the years before and during World War II, Germany, Italy, and Russia used communication in a ruthless psychological war against their enemies within as well as outside their borders. The Nazis established a ministry devoted to propaganda warfare under the direction of Joseph Paul Goebbels, who along with the Führer, Adolf Hitler, left documented evidence of the cynical and unscrupulous manipulation of the masses by the restriction of freedom of speech and the studied application of persuasion. Since the time of Goebbels and Hitler, the term *propaganda* has had a generally undesirable connotation, and when the United States government established an agency for war propaganda it was named the Office of War Information.

We will use the term *propaganda* to refer only to the irresponsible and unethical use of persuasive communication techniques. The unethical features of propaganda include the intentional assertion of falsehoods and half-truths, the misrepresentation of facts, the exploitation of the human tendency to act without thinking, and the use of every additional sort of technique that promises to achieve the propagandists' ends and to thwart their enemies.

Persuasion refers to a wider range of communication than does propaganda, and in our study of persuasion we will include those situations in which the people who communicate through the mass media are truthful, represent facts fairly, assume that human beings are capable of reflective and creative thinking, and use the techniques of communication to work cooperatively for a common good. As a student of communication, you should become alert to the differences between persuasion and propaganda, and we will explore them in this chapter. Persuasion will influence you for the rest of your life. One always has to make choices about such little things as which toothpaste to buy and about such big things as which candidate to vote for. We sometimes have trouble recognizing the distinctions, but you must be able to recognize propaganda devices for what they are and refuse to be persuaded by less than the best evidence and reasoning. If you are not consciously aware of propaganda devices, you will react to propaganda without thinking. That is just what the propagandist wants. He has many good reasons for believing he can make you do what he wants you to.

APING BEHAVIOR

People often do or believe something because other people around them are doing or believing it. Follow-the-leader behavior is so primitive we will call it *aping* behavior because the stereotype of an ape is that it will mimic behavior. If a person walking down a street stops and peers up toward the sky, some people may walk on past the sky-watcher, but several other people will stop to see what has caught his attention, and soon a knot of people will be standing, peering upward.

How often have you been a part of this next scene? A siren sounds in a quiet neighborhood. People go to their windows or doors or out on their porches to see what is happening. One person runs from a house and dashes up the street. Soon several more follow, and if enough of the watchers are pulled into the parade, the pressure for you to go along with them grows strong. You probably go, too.

When people communicate with one another in a small group for the first time, they develop ways of proceeding on the same follow-the-leader basis. Someone says, "Let's introduce ourselves." Someone else says, "Okay. You go first." The first person tells her name and then a good deal about her background and manages to convey to the others a good idea of the type of person she is: chatty, informal, and friendly. The group has a chance to laugh with her and relax a bit. Finally she says, "That's about it for me. How about you?" She looks with interest at the person next to her; she seems genuinely interested in what the others have to say. She has broken the ice. The next person then describes as interesting a version of "me" as he can, and as the introductions continue around the group, no one resents the time being taken because each feels his turn will come; everyone begins to feel comfortable about the group and each acquires a good notion of what the other members are like. But consider another group that does not get off to such a good start. One person says to another, "Why don't you tell us about yourself?" and the second person simply mumbles her name in an embarrassed way and seems to have nothing to add. She looks at the next person immediately, as though her name is all she need give, and so the next person gives his name, and so on, and the group members' first attempts to get acquainted are not notably successful. In both groups the results stem from aping behavior; what one person starts, the others follow.

Beliefs and ideas can develop in the same fashion. So can norms or ways of behaving.

Laboratory studies have shown the extent to which the behavior of others persuades us to do things we otherwise would not do.

A candid film made in the 1960s included a scene in which, when actors planted in an employment office waiting room began taking off their clothes in a matter-of-fact way, as though this were the usual procedure in that situation, a number of unsuspecting clients, after initial reactions of surprise and bewilderment, also began to remove their clothes.

You are probably not enjoying this evidence of how often we simply ape others in how we behave, what we do, even what we think. Aping behavior smacks of *1984* and Big Brother and totalitarianism. But human beings *do* behave this way. Aping behavior is often harmless and normal. However, you should resist being manipulated by propaganda that is designed to induce you to ape behavior which, if you stopped to consider, you would *not* choose to copy. You should particularly watch for the propagandist's use of the so-called "band-wagon" technique, which asserts that "everybody is doing it, so come on along."

FOLLOWING DIRECTIONS

Another common human behavior pattern is to do and believe as we are told. Again, this is an immediate and natural response. If one person gives another directions about what to do or what to believe, the second person tends to do or believe as directed. Directed behavior occurs without thinking. If the sign says "STOP," you stop. Often people are hardly aware of what has taken place when they unthinkingly accept directions. As parents, you will tell your children what to do. As children, you were told by your parents what to do. Much of our educational process is a matter of following directions. Carried to extreme lengths, controlling people by telling them what to do and think is like pushing buttons to direct the movements of a mechanical toy. Under deep hypnosis, people blindly follow the directions of the hypnotist, reacting much as a machine would to programed instructions.

Even so-called "rational" man is surrounded by persuasive messages capitalizing upon this tendency to follow directions. Particularly on radio and television we are ordered to:

Buy Buick!

Buy bonds!

Elect John Doe!

Vote Republicrat!

Shop downtown!

Throw the rascals out!

Save today!

ACCEPTING SUGGESTIONS

Directions, as shown above, are clear, blunt, and unequivocal. You are given no option. Directions are phrased and delivered as commands. Suggestions, on the other hand, recommend a belief or an action, but are phrased in such a way that the receiver has an option, some choice about doing or not doing what is suggested. The direction, "Quit your job!" becomes the suggestion, "May I suggest that you consider resigning." Suggestion slips the idea into the mind more gently than the jarring direction, and although suggestions encourage the growth of the idea or action, they do so less directly.

Thinking up and developing good suggestion requires considerable artistry. Suggestion skillfully done is efficient. Suggestion puts positions or points into the mind so they are hard to attack logically. We have observed many student discussion groups trying to find a good topic to present as a group for a class discussion. One member suggests a topic and immediately, another makes a face showing his disgust with the idea and says, "Let's not do that. Let's do something new and interesting for a change." The first participant then has to present good reasons and make a big effort to overcome the effect of the second member's suggestion that the topic is trite and uninteresting.

The process of suggestion, however, like that of direction, involves getting the listener to accept without thinking an idea, belief, or action. Suggestion is one of the most commonly used persuasive techniques in advertising and propaganda. See if you can think up a strong suggestion in behalf of some service or product in 25 words or less. Can you better these paraphrases of Madison Avenue masterpieces? "Glamour toilet tissue is like facial tissue. It doesn't *feel* like toilet paper." "If she kisses you once, will she kiss you twice?" "Clean odor, the Cologne of Mouthwashes." One we have always liked is the brief persuasive spiel of the hawker selling cheap inflatable pillows to people attending the big show in the state fair ground grandstand. "Four hours on a board," he drones. "Four hours on a board. May we suggest a pillow?"

Many of the people who bought pillows after hearing about the 4 hours on a board probably never consciously reasoned through their decision. This board-and-pillow example is of further interest because the hawker's spiel contains the two major kinds of suggestion used in persuasion, direct and indirect. The sentence, "May we suggest a pillow?" is *direct suggestion* telling the potential customer what the seller wants him to do. The phrase, "Four hours on a board," is *indirect suggestion* that the potential customer will be uncomfortable shortly if he does not buy the pillow and, moreover, will be quite comfortable throughout the show if he does buy and use the pillow.

Directions and suggestions may be positive or negative. Positive persuasion results when a belief or a course of action is urged. "Save today at the Daisy sale!" Negative direction and suggestion urges the listener not to believe, or not to do something, such as in the slogan, "If you smoke, stop! If you don't smoke, don't start!" Positive suggestion and strong direct urgings have persuasive impact. Negative suggestions or directions are often less effective than positive ones. Negative urgings call attention to the belief or action you do *not* want to encourage and, in so doing, may arouse a curiosity about the subject which had not been in the listener's mind before. There is a line from a Carl Sandburg poem we often quoted to one another when our children were toddlers. The line well describes the unwanted effects of negative suggestion. Paraphrased a little, it reads, "Why does the child put molasses on the cat when the one thing I told the child *not* to do was put molasses on the cat." The sign, "Do Not Open This Door" often prompts more than one person to open the door simply out of curiosity. You would be wise to consider *all* possible results when you use negative suggestions in persuasive communication.

When a speaker hints at a point without actually saying it, the suggestion he is using is indirect. The listener is led to discover the point rather than told directly about it. If a propaganda campaign maintains a steady barrage of indirect suggestion over a long time, the listeners may gradually come to believe something or begin to form a new attitude, almost without knowing what has been happening to them. When television was still advertising cigarettes, one brand was sold for some time as the cigarette for sophisticates. Its advertisements showed a woman dressed in the current high fashion, surrounded by luxurious furnishings, holding this particular brand in a long cigarette holder. Then, the company decided to change the cigarette's image, and a whole new advertising campaign was launched. Sophistication was out, and the ads now showed virile he-men working in oil fields, punching cattle, fighting forest fires, logging, or building huge bridges in high mountains. Gradually many viewers came to associate this brand of cigarettes with strong young outdoorsmen. Little was said in either campaign about the cigarette's flavor or its nicotine content. Both advertising pitches were expensive campaigns of indirect suggestion designed to persuade people to smoke the brand if they, too, wanted to be, at first, sophisticated, and later, ruggedly masculine.

TECHNIQUES OF INDIRECT SUGGESTION

Indirect suggestion is an important technique of both propaganda and persuasion. Direct suggestion tends to be explicit, simple, and repetitive. The propagandist who uses direct suggestion searches for suitable slogans and then repeats them endlessly. Hitler and Goebbels masterminded the propaganda of Nazi Germany, and for the mass audience they often used slogans, repeated over and over again. Indirect suggestion, on the other hand, requires considerable more artistry and skill. One important persuasive tool for the person using indirect suggestion is the ability to select exactly the right word to name a thing or event or to describe its properties and relationships. Mark Twain is supposed to have said that the difference between the right word and the almost-right word is the difference between lightning and a lightning bug; certainly that is the case with indirect suggestion: It must be subtle enough to be indirect, yet obvious enough to make your point.

In Chapter 7 we examined the way language can be used to discuss our world. We divided words into form words and content words and pointed out how content words can name something and then discuss its properties or relationships. When you study indirect suggestion as a valuable tool of persuasion, you will use this knowledge about words in a practical way. Suppose people are talking about the same thing, but are using different names for it. Even with these different names, they may all understand what is being discussed. Say that several people are talking about a college. They might name it *the college, the old alma mater, the institution, the nut house, the playpen with ash trays, the ivory tower* or any one of the names by which this college is known to its many students and alumni. No matter which name the person in the group chooses for labeling the college, all the others present know it is *the college* he is talking about. What, then, do we learn from the different labels? By the selection of a particular label for a thing, the source of a message indicates a great deal about how he feels about the event in question.

If several men are discussing female acquaintances, a given woman might be referred to as *darling, honey, my old lady, the little woman, that broad, my chick, slut, real dog, a sow* or whatever happen to be the current slang words for attractive and unattractive females. And, of course, women would have a comparable vocabulary to describe the males they know. The point is the same: The name selected for the girl, or for the man, is powerful indirect suggestion to all others present. The words we use are important parts of our indirect suggestion persuasive messages.

Propagandists often use names that reflect attitudes. Two hostile bordering countries report an armed clash of their troops. Country number one calls the event "shameless naked aggression," while country number two calls the same event "a defensive retaliation." One country names the government of another "a totalitarian regime"; the latter government refers to itself as "a democratic peoples' republic."

Some revolutionaries set off a bomb in a public building. Sympathizers with the revolution call the bombing "a courageous act by heroic freedom fighters." Those who oppose the revolutionaries and dislike the destruction of public buildings call the same bombing "a cowardly, criminal act by mindless anarchists."

Selecting names heavily loaded with suggestion is but one way in which the choice of words is important. The words a speaker uses to describe the properties of the things, events, or people designated by the names are equally important. One person says, "This cheese has a rich bouquet." Another remarks, "This cheese stinks to high heaven."

Compare the following properties as ascribed to a given individual by the words used and see how words work to carry suggestion to the listener:

John is prudent.
     versus
John is a tightwad.

John is courageous.
     versus
John is reckless.

John is sensitive.
     versus
John is emotionally unstable.

We can also suggest attitudes by the words and phrases we use to describe relationships among things, people, and events. Consider these examples:

John was a love child.
     versus
John is a bastard.

John and Mary have a deep and satisfying personal relationship.
     versus
John and Mary are living together like a couple of alley cats.

In the last example we used a figure of speech to describe the relationship. Figures of speech are important techniques to suggest or state a comparison between two things. By associating a thing, person, or event with something pleasant, admirable, or good, we suggest that the thing itself is also desirable. By associating the thing with something unpleasant or bad, we make the opposite impression. Compare "this cigarette has a spring-like freshness" with "this cigarette reeks like a dumpyard incinerator."

One important propaganda technique is to describe a person in terms of an adjective or noun that connotes a positive or negative attitude toward that individual. Much of what people do when they persuade is to attack or defend other people and their actions. We often say that a friend has good qualities and an enemy has bad character traits. When a propagandist uses words with negative connotations to describe an enemy, we call the technique *name calling*. A politician using the name-calling technique might refer to an opponent as a "political hack," a "crook," a "left-winger," or an "arch conservative."

In addition to calling good or bad names, a speaker can create much the same impression by providing what he says are motives for the individual's behavior. *Motives* are inner drives to action.

Motive has the same Latin root as the word motor, and we can think of a motive as the energy source that causes an individual to move and do certain things. We see a person working hard to gain political office and ask, "What makes him tick? Why does he do that? Why does he put up with all the grief of campaigning?" Someone may explain the candidate's actions by supplying a motive, for example: "He is driven by the desire for power. He is power-hungry and is compelled by mastery motivation." A clever person can find some inner drive to account for every behavior. We all play the role of amateur psychologist now and then. Sometimes different people assign different motives to account for the same act. If the question is, "Why does John devote his whole life to making money?" various answers might be, "John is motivated by the need for security and money will provide him with security," "John is motivated by the need for prestige and money will provide him with prestige," or "John craves power and he gets power from his money."

Because we can explain the same actions on the basis of different motives, the skillful persuader searches for good motives to explain what he and his friends do, and for bad motives to explain the acts of his enemies. Most schemes to explain human behavior arrange the motives into higher or lower, good or bad, reasons for doing things. The basic arrangement reminds us of the old religious difference between the drives of the flesh and the aspirations of the spirit, between going down to hell and up to heaven. Generally we consider people who are out for quick satisfaction of fleshly desires less commendable than people who work for some high spiritual ideal. A gourmet, who enjoys elegant food, delightfully prepared, is better than a glutton, who eats anything and everything put in front of him. The physical expression of a deep and lasting love is better than mere sexual lust. We generally feel that unselfish acts are better than selfish ones. The man who is driven to pile up money for the security of his family is a more commendable fellow than the man who wants the money for himself. The advocate of women's liberation who wants to be in the limelight and get a lot of publicity is not as commendable as the woman who is unselfishly dedicated to the whole cause of womankind.

The friends of the evangelist say he does what he does for the purpose of saving human souls and that he works for God's kingdom. He sacrifices his health, they say, and his time and his own pleasure in order to work for the good of others. The enemies of the evangelist explain his behavior by saying that he does it for money, which he uses to buy big cars, fine clothes, and other fleshly comforts.They say he does it to make a big name for himself or to gain power through his control over people. The point is that two people observing a third person's behavior can explain the behavior differently: One can cut the person down by saying his motive was a low, selfish one, and the other can build the person up by saying his motive was a good and unselfish one.

Successful persuasive and propaganda battles among businesses, political parties, governmental agencies, and nations usually need to present the issues in terms of human beings. Real live persons often come to take a part much like an actor in a movie or on TV in the persuasive campaigns to change our attitudes, beliefs, and actions. Persons can come to symbolize ideas or whole movements.

Ralph Nader is proconsumer and actively involved in organizing efforts to help the consumer. We talk of Naderism or Nader's raiders as representing the movement. In the 1950s, Senator Joseph McCarthy of Wisconsin was actively involved in attacking "communists" in the government. His tactics were crude and propagandistic. The attack on individuals as communists or procommunists came to be called McCarthyism.

INDIRECT SUGGESTION AND DRAMATIZING

We come now to the most important way in which indirect suggestion creates attitudes and beliefs. Much has been made of the concept of the *American dream*. The American dream refers to the drama in which a poor but talented, deserving, and hardworking person can climb to success, no matter how humble his beginnings. People who believed the American dream often came from foreign countries to the United States at great sacrifice and hardship and when they arrived in the new country worked hard, often under miserable conditions, to achieve success. Individuals may have personal dreams today much like the widely held American dream of the nineteenth century. You may daydream that you are playing a hero's part and doing interesting and exciting things. All of us want our lives to matter. We want to be appreciated for what we are, for what we can do. The boy who dreams of being a big-league pitcher and sees himself striking out the opponents in an all-star game may practice long hours and live only to achieve his dream. Everyone dreams. And although we may think our own dreams are personal and unlike anyone else's, the fact is that most of us dream similar dreams.

Persuasion often consists of the dramatization of public dreams. The public dramas consist of a cast of characters, some of whom are good guys and some of whom are bad guys, and these characters take part in dramatic situations and do dramatic things. Often the persuasive speaker dramatizes actual events, but the way he depicts the action and the way he discusses the real-life characters (coloring the events with praise or blame, suggesting that the action was good or bad) further suggests that some of the actors were heroes and some were villains.

An important principle of learning is that the more intense the emotional impression something has on a person, the more effective his learning of that thing will be. If something hits us emotionally, we are more likely to recall it. Abstract messages full of statistics, general principles, and words we half understand do not arouse our feelings or emotions. But give us a human-interest story, tell us something about another person so we can sympathize with him, make us happy or sad for him, and we find ourselves reacting with friendly or unfriendly responses to believable people presented in real-life dramas. When a newspaper reports that unemployment has risen by several hundred thousand in the last month, we make a mental note that the rise in unemployment is bad. But what if we then see a television documentary about the unemployment in our own city or town? The program is organized around three families, each from different sections of the area, each from a different socioeconomic level in the community. We meet the jobless father; we see him in the living room of a neat home and hear him tell of his efforts to find employment and his discouragement. We learn that his family may lose its home. We meet the mother who is now working daily as a waitress from 4 PM until midnight to supplement her husband's unemployment compensation. The program narrator interviews the children. We become emotionally involved with the people and thus with the unemployment problem. "There but for the grace of God go I" touches us.

Real people often make the best characters in the public dramas of propaganda and persuasion. Hitler and later Stalin were the villains in many of the international dramas in which the people of the United States participated in the 1930s, 1940s, and 1950s. The character of Hitler, in American and British propaganda and persuasion of the time, bore little resemblance to the real-life man, but that fact was irrelevant to the suggestion involved in the dramas. For their political friends and enemies, American presidents often serve the same function as characters in morality plays. People find it more difficult to hate Nazism than its personification, Adolf Hitler. Heroes and villains in action and conflict arouse our love or hate, fear or joy, admiration or disgust.

Successful persuasion not only relies on real-life people, but also uses fictitious characters who serve as hypothetical examples and who have admirable or hateful characteristics. Superman brings certain qualities to mind. So does Casper Milquetoast. Finally, a persuasive speaker may use the figure of speech called *personification* to create emotional responses to abstract propositions. When a speaker uses personification, he endows an abstract idea, institution, or government with human characteristics so it begins to act like a person in a drama. Mark Twain once suggested that a lie could travel around the world while the truth was still pulling on its boots. Suggesting that truth can pull on its boots gives truth the attributes of a person. In nineteenth-century oratory, the personification of such abstract notions as *truth, virtue, beauty,* and *eloquence* was common.

Persuasive messages may contain personifications of abstractions such as the United States of America in the form of Uncle Sam or of Great Britain in the person of John Bull. Political cartoonists, who often work with suggestion to achieve their persuasive impact, frequently personify John Q. Public or give the atomic bomb the characteristics of a human being.

In addition to characters, a propaganda or persuasive campaign must provide a setting for the drama. Watch several television commercials or clip several advertisements from a magazine. Notice the scene or location of the action. Although only a small number of people still work as cowhands in our country, a high percentage of characters in advertising campaigns ride horses, wear large western hats, and herd and brand cattle. Many commercial advertisements are set in what the wife calls "pluperfect" homes—gorgeous, lovely, and in perfect order. Much political persuasion derives its impact from the particular setting in which the drama takes place. Cesar Chavez battles the grape growers in the fertile valleys of California. The John F. Kennedy drama of Camelot was played out at Hyannisport, Palm Springs, and the White House. Jesse Jackson's Operation Breadbasket is set in the black ghettos of Chicago. Skillful propagandists planning a dramatic action for symbolic effect take pains to select the proper scene for their drama. Do you demonstrate in front of the federal building, or before the main offices of a large ordnance plant? Do you go to Washington, D.C. and march on the Pentagon, or do you go to the state capital? In the 1950s, foes of school integration in the South bombed black churches rather than schools. Friends of integration encouraged black students to enroll at the University of Alabama. In the 1960s, foes of capitalism bombed Bank of America branch offices.

Finally, the characters placed in a scene and situation must participate in a dramatic action that arouses our emotions and causes us to become involved imaginatively in what is happening. Persuaders often can take actual events, and with a bit of imagination remake them into dramatic actions to fit their purposes. For example, in the time of racial strife in the late 1960s and early 1970s, the Black Panthers came into confrontation and conflict with police in major American cities. In Chicago, several Panthers were killed during a police raid on the organization's headquarters. One group of persuaders cast the Panthers in the role of heroes and the police as villains. According to their scenario, the innocent Panthers had been murdered under the pretense of a police raid, and the dramatic action was explained in terms of a conspiracy on the part of policemen and the federal justice department to eliminate the Panthers. Another group of persuaders cast the Panthers in the role of lawbreakers and the police as heroes. The dramatic events lent themselves to two interpretations.

We all have individual dreams that shape our behavior and drive us to certain actions, but when we share a dream with a large group of people, we often share the same emotions, values, and motives because of the powerful suggestive force inherent in the drama. Persuaders and propagandists are in an important sense dream merchants, and to the extent they can catch their audiences up into a dream, they can often persuade them to act and believe in certain ways. One legend has it that in the early days of the automobile, the tendency was to advertise cars in terms of engineering details and facts about their performance. Then an advertising genius developed an ad consisting of a photograph of a handsome young man in his driving togs and goggles, his scarf flying in the wind, a beautiful girl at his side, driving an open car on a road that led across a green valley to the mountains beyond. When asked what in the world he was trying to sell with such a layout, he is alleged to have replied, "A dream"; and modern advertising was on its way.

The heroes of our public dreams are likable and believable and tend to have a good ethos for us. The villains of our dramatization of events can seldom persuade us. Thus the dramatic interpretation of events provides the audience with emotional involvement as well as with credible sources. The positive and negative suggestions inherent in an attractive drama presented as part of a persuasive or propaganda campaign are among the most powerful forces for changing attitudes and behavior.

Some of the dramatizations that compose persuasive campaigns are made up of fictitious materials. The characters are like those in novels or plays, and their actions are made up. The most persuasive dramatizations, however, have solid bases in facts. The persuasive account describes the facts accurately, and the suggestion is a function of how those facts are placed into a dramatic sequence and what characteristics and motives are suggested for the leading characters.

Several different persuasive themes can grow up around the same events, and all can be quite truthful in their descriptions of the actual happenings. The dramas may nonetheless present diametrically opposed suggestions about what to do and believe as a result of the historical event. Cesar Chavez organized Chicano grape pickers in California in the 1960s. The grape growers fought Chavez and his union. In one drama, Chavez was presented as a dedicated and unselfish folk hero fighting against the organized, evil, entrenched wealth of the growers. Against great odds, he fought and won because his side was right. The persuaders who sought support for Chavez and the grape pickers tried to get the American people to refuse to buy table grapes in order to force the growers to heed the pickers' demands. Americans who were caught up in, and who believed, the drama of Chavez the hero fighting the evil capitalists experienced considerable pressure to stop eating grapes. The growers' representatives presented a different drama. They pictured Chavez as a malcontent, a power-hungry demagogue making trouble among contented workers who had no desire to join his union, a man who tyrannized and forced the workers to support him. That one man should keep Americans from eating grapes was a violation of the rights of many by one, according to the growers.

As consumers of persuasion, and as persuaders ourselves, we should be much aware of the importance of public dreams in relation to positive and negative suggestion. We should learn to look for the dreams that seem to be operating currently in our culture, for these dreams change as events around us reshape our priorities. Much of advertising and of the selling of political candidates is shaped by what the dream merchants think the public is buying this year.

This does not mean that dreams are bad and that we should always try to operate on a more realistic level, using our intelligence more than our emotions. Our dreams are important and cannot be entirely separated from our intellectual processing of information. Nor should you fear that you will be manipulated by others who will hook their sales pitch to your private dreams to make you do or believe something you really do not want to do or believe. Even the most skillful dream merchants cannot always predict the public's response to their campaign. Nor is what we see and hear in the mass media necessarily the most persuasive communication we receive.

Sometimes we have a too-simple view of how persuasion and propaganda work in the mass media. Early scholars of radio and television thought mass persuasion flowed directly from the radio or TV receiver to the listener. When, for example, the President went on television and talked directly to the American public, scholars assumed this had a direct and persuasive impact upon the viewer-listener. Subsequent research found that the one-step view of mass persuasion was too simple; it revealed that the persuasive impact of television occurs in at least two steps: The persuasion first affects opinion leaders and then is processed in small group conversations. Thus you are most likely to feel the influence of television at second hand, as the ideas and dreams suggested by the tube are talked about in conversations with family and friends.

Let us say that a group of people are going swimming. They stretch out in the sun and relax, and someone comments about something she heard Mohammed Ali say on television. Her tone of voice indicates she approved of what he said. Someone else in the group picks up the idea, adds a comment, and gets excited about it. Maybe two people sit up and begin to talk excitedly about the event and about what was said, and in the process the whole group becomes involved in dramatizing the event, and each member grows to have a stronger identification with the hero of the drama, the suggestion implied in the dramatization working more strongly on each person in the group.

Professor Robert F. Bales calls such moments of group dramatizing *fantasy chains* and he and others have discovered that fantasy chains greatly influence a group's cohesiveness and the development of a group culture. As important as the mass media are to persuasion in our culture, our peer groups remain powerful forces in molding attitudes and in fashioning action.

In the decade of the 1960s a number of revolutionary and liberation movements grew up rapidly in this country. They were supported by public persuasion transmitted on television shows, particularly the talk shows, newscasts, and documentaries, and by their own underground newspapers, conferences, and conventions. Gradually, the Indian movement, the Chicano movement, and the Black Power movement each came to have a national rhetoric. In much the same fashion, political revolutionaries like the Students for a Democratic Society and social revolutionaries like the Gay Liberation and Women's Liberation movements each developed unique persuasive dramas.

The public dramas of Women's Liberation, however, were not sufficient, in the opinion of some leaders, to excite potential converts to the level of commitment and action required for success; so the activists in the movement turned to the systematic use of small group techniques to indoctrinate and impel members to action. (The same tactics were adopted by other movements such as Gay Liberation and the Weatherman faction of the SDS.) In small group meetings called consciousness-raising sessions the members repeated elements of the public dramas of the national persuasion campaign until some of the fantasies chained out and became intensely personal for individual members; then the group became excited and emotional and talked about identity and the nature of the oppressive forces in society. When the public dramas were re-created in the small face-to-face interacting groups, they acquired the reinforcement of personal involvement, and group pressure for conformity worked on individual members to achieve greater commitment to the cause and increased action for the movement's goals.

The small group is important not only because it is a consumer of persuasion, but because the dramatic themes that become public are often first created within a small group. People of like interests, meeting together for some purpose or just casually, sometimes chain out a fantasy. A participant presents a dramatic situation in which a person not present at the meeting is an active character. Another participant responds; another enters the drama and reacts or modifies the conversations; soon most of the group members are involved, excited, and emotional in their interaction. They are so taken with their experience that they repeat the dramatic theme in other groups, and if the appeal of the drama is strong enough, it catches on at a grass-roots level in many such groups. Gradually these successful group fantasies are worked into the mass media, are broadcast, and are again processed and vitalized in other groups.

The suggestion inherent in a small group fantasy is a powerful force of persuasion for all of us, in our many relatively private dreams that never reach the mass media, as well as in those dreams we share with much of mankind. We all belong to many small groups, and we are much committed to them—our families, friends, and the people we work with every day. The powerful persuasive suggestion that comes from the fantasies generated by our own groups influences our life styles, our goals, and our commitments. One family dreams that its children will have more education than the parents could have and that they will lead richer lives; this dream sustains the family to a great extent. Perhaps you grew up in a large city in an area jammed with apartment buildings filled to overflowing with people. Perhaps you were part of a gang that sustained itself for years with the fantasy of overthrowing the larger gang that ruled your street, bullied your friends, and made life miserable for you.

Much of our motivation to be and to do is contained within the dreams that become real and exciting to us. Our personal dreams often are shaped by the positive and negative suggestion inherent in the messages of the mass media; many of our dreams are these messages after they have been discussed, re-created, re-shaped in our talk with other people we like and enjoy; some of our dreams are the product of fantasy chains made up by the groups we belong to, and we become part of a dream that others share.

We are not necessarily persuaded by reason. We are often persuaded by suggestion that ties in with our dreams. To limit communication to factual information is to deny the powerful influence we all feel when those things we hold most dear, our innermost hopes and dreams, are involved.

the key ideas

The principle of aping behavior is simple; what one person starts, others tend to follow.

A propaganda technique based upon aping behavior is called the bandwagon appeal.

People tend to do and believe as they are told.

Suggestions recommend a belief or action, but their style is soft sell compared with directions.

Suggestion puts positions or points into the mind so they are hard to attack logically.

Suggestion is one of the most commonly used persuasive devices in advertising and propaganda.

Whereas direct suggestion tells the listener clearly what he is to do or believe, indirect suggestion only hints at it.

A persuader may suggest or direct a belief or course of action in either positive or negative form.

Negative forms of persuasion sometimes backfire because the listener may be tempted to do what he is told not to do.

Selecting names for people and events that carry positive or negative connotations is an important technique of persuasion.

Because the same action can be explained by several different motives, a skillful persuader selects an explanation that suits his purpose for a given message.

Because we are more interested in people than in abstract ideas or faceless organizations and corporations, persons can come to symbolize ideas or entire movements.

SUGGESTED PROJECTS

1 / Write a short paper in which you describe and discuss six techniques of indirect suggestion that you have noticed in current television ads or in magazines and newspapers.

2 / Select a persuasive drama or public dream from a recent speech, magazine article, book, or television program. (If you wish

in chapter 9

Persuasion often contains the dramatization of public dreams.

Real people often make the best characters in the public dramas of propaganda and persuasion.

American presidents often serve the same function for their political friends and enemies as characters in morality plays.

When a speaker uses the figure of speech called personification, he endows an abstract idea or institution with human characteristics.

Persuasive dramas gain part of their suggestive force from the location or setting of the play.

Persuaders often use actual events as the basis for the dramatic action of their messages.

Persuaders are in an important sense dream merchants, and to the extent they can propagate a certain dream, can sell products and ideas that promise to fulfill the dream.

Several quite different persuasive themes can use the same events and be quite truthful in their description.

Mass-media persuasion has its impact first on opinion leaders and through them on the general public by means of small group conversations.

When public dramas are repeated in small face-to-face groups, they are reinforced and the participants gain a sense of involvement that persuades them to change belief and take action.

The small group is not only a consumer of public dramas but a generator of small group fantasy chains which become public dreams.

---

to piece the drama together from several sources you may do so.) Write an analysis of the persuasive power of the dream. Who are the heroes and who are the villains? What rewards does the dream promise that will move people to action? How would you predict that people who believe the drama or dream would act in some given situations? Be specific.

3 / Write a short paper in which you discuss the "ethics of persuasion."

SUGGESTED READINGS

Bales, Robert F. *Personality and Interpersonal Behavior*. New York: Holt, Rinehart and Winston, 1970.

Bormann, Ernest G., William S. Howell, Ralph G. Nichols, and George L. Shapiro. *Interpersonal Communication in the Modern Organization*. Englewood Cliffs, N.J.: Prentice-Hall, 1969. "Logical and Nonlogical Persuasion," pp. 242–259.

Brembeck, Winston, and William S. Howell. *Persuasion*. Englewood Cliffs, N.J.: Prentice-Hall, 1952.

Cronkhite, Gary. *Persuasion: Speech and Behavioral Change*. Indianapolis: Bobbs-Merrill, 1966.

Minnick, Wayne C. *The Art of Persuasion*, 2nd ed. Boston: Houghton Mifflin, 1968.

Scheidel, Thomas M. *Persuasive Speaking*. Glenview, Ill.: Scott, Foresman, 1967.

10 how to persuade: the persuasive power of evidence and reasoning

For many years a basic assumption of communication theory was that argument was different from persuasion because man is a creature of reason and of will. Argument appealed to the mind, and successful argument resulted in convincing the listener. Persuasion appealed to the nonrational faculties, and successful persuasion resulted in the movement of the will. Subsequent research has indicated that the separation of head and heart, of reason from emotion, is artificial. Human beings tend to react as total organisms. We have divided the material on persuasion into three divisions for the purpose of emphasizing various aspects of the process, but all are closely related. To be a successful persuader you must use all three components, and to be a good critic of communication you must be aware of all elements.

As consumers of persuasion, we must learn to separate the personality from the drama and the drama from the evidence and reasoning; we must demand a direct and realistic link between the dramas presented to us in a persuasive campaign and the actual events. In other words, although we can expect that reasonable men will disagree about what an event means, we still must demand that all men provide a complete and accurate description of the event. We call this connection between the public dramas and the facts, *reality links*.

The reality links in a persuasive message consist of those parts that describe things along the lines discussed in Chapter 3. Naming objects and ascribing properties and relations accurately provides a persuasive message with its reality links. We can think of the relationship between the suggestion in a message and the reality of a given situation as the reasonable or logical portion of a communication. The reasoned elements of the persuasive effort consist of proving the points that make up a case and fitting the individual points into a logical pattern. What we hope to emphasize is the uncommon use of common sense.

The dramas of persuasive messages can be attractive and interesting, but if they are false or unrelated to the facts, they should not move us to action simply because we like them. Monitor your TV set and count the number of dramas that relate to the simple matter of washing clothes. Attractive, sometimes funny, sometimes folksy people are involved in some problem in the laundry room. Even more attractive and pleasant people come to their rescue, bringing a laundry product with them. The dramatic action is simple: The unhappy heroine with a laundry problem washes the clothes with the product, waits eagerly for the result, discovers the clothes are brighter-and-whiter-and-cleaner-than-ever, and is happy once more. For the consumer of these dramas, the problem is that five different manufacturers use essentially the same drama to suggest that the viewer buy their respective products. If in fact there is no difference in the way a given washer will perform with any of the five laundry products, the decision to buy one or another is made, not on the basis of facts, but on the basis of name identification or the attractiveness of the commercial. In this case, the advertisers have no facts that could be used in the persuasive message; we, as consumers of the persuasion, should be aware that no facts are presented to us in the message. This is persuasion with a key element missing.

A powerful factor for persuasion is evidence in support of an idea or product or course of action. For many years the public dramas suggesting that we buy a given brand of toothpaste were similar to those selling laundry products. The situations in the dramas varied, but the plot was generally that an attractive hero could not get his teeth clean and thus had dingy teeth and bad breath, making him unpopular. Every toothpaste advertised could, of course, give the hero sweet breath, shining teeth, and popularity. Then the American Dental Association tested a new product ingredient and found that it reduced tooth decay. Controlled experimental conditions provided evidence that one product was better than the others, and immediately the advertising campaign for that toothpaste switched to extensive reports of these tests, long quotes about the results, personal testimonies from participants in the experiments, and heavy emphasis on the endorsement by the American Dental Association. When facts are added to the persuasive impact of personality and drama, the strength of the message is greatly increased.

PROVING A POINT

When we discuss proving a point for an audience, we must remember that we cannot tell whether a given piece of information is proof until we look at it in relation to the point to be proved. The best way to prepare or evaluate the reasoned part of a persuasive message, therefore, is to look at message units. Each unit, to be complete, must contain a point to be proved, worded in a clear way, and the material that supports the point. Information that may be excellent proof for one point may not be logically related to another. We will not always mention the point being proved in our explanations of evidence, but you should keep in mind the idea of a message unit as you study the art of proving a position. Refer back to the section, "A Basic Message Unit," in Chapter 7, if you want to refresh your understanding.

Evidence is material that furnishes grounds for belief or makes evident the truth or falsity, rightness or wrongness, wisdom or folly of a proposition. It is a technical legal term that refers to material supplied by lawyers in support of their arguments in court. Legal evidence may include testimony of witnesses, written documents, actual items such as pistols, knives, or clothing.

Proof is the process of gathering together, ordering, and presenting enough evidence to convince the judge or jury (or us, the listener-consumers) to accept a given proposition.

Although we can look at evidence and make some decision about how good or bad it might be in terms of general rules about evidence, we must look at proof in terms of the audience. We can evaluate evidence against some absolute and general standards of excellence, but proof has to convince somebody. A given message unit, consisting of a proposition and supporting evidence, may convince one individual but not another. An old folk saying claims that "the proof of the pudding is in the eating." Even though the cook thinks the ingredients are good and his recipe interesting, if the people eating the pudding do not like it, for them anyway, the pudding is no good. No matter how good the speaker thinks his evidence is, no matter how sound his reasoning, if the listener is not persuaded, his proof is no good.

In Chapter 7 we talked about the basic message unit and described the way to phrase a point to be made clear. We also discussed the ways the components of the basic unit (the point and the supporting material) can be arranged in relation to each other. The message unit containing a point to be proved is developed in the same way as a unit containing a point to be made clear.

The three major forms of evidence used as proof for persuasive messages are statistical descriptions of facts, real examples, and testimony. A speaker uses evidence for two main functions: to describe and to evaluate the facts. The first and most important use of evidence is to describe what is the case. Factual information consists of statistics, real examples, and eyewitness accounts of what happened. The second use of evidence is to present expert opinion about what the facts mean. The testimony of authorities provides expert interpretation.

STATISTICS

Statistics are numerical comments about facts. A person may comment that Bill is tall. This is a simple descriptive statement. A similar statement may say that Bill is 6 feet 6 inches tall. This last statement includes numbers and is thus a statistical comment. When the statistics are true, they give us more precise information about facts than can most other forms of description. When a speaker wants to talk about many things and has only a short interview or conference in which to make his statement, his use of statistical description enables him to pack a lot of information into a few sentences.

Suppose a student asks the dean, "What are my chances of going on to the university if I enroll at Pleasant Hills Community College?" If the dean answers, "Of every 1000 freshmen who start at Pleasant Hills, 300 go on to the university," he covers a large number of facts (he is talking about 1000 individuals because implicit in his answer is the information that while 300 go on, 700 do not), and he has given this information in a short sentence.

However, because the answer provides only a little information about a lot of students, we may get an incomplete picture. How many of the 700 who do not go on for further education wanted to or planned to? Many community and junior college programs are designed as 2-year programs and are complete in themselves. How many of the 300 who go on for more education finish with university or 4-year college degrees? In other words, many things are left unsaid by the dean's initial statistical statement. Many persuaders and pressure groups use figures to fool the public as well as to inform people. Even when used carefully and honestly, as in the dean's statement, the statistics are abstract and present only a part of a larger picture. Particularly in our discussion of statistics, we will look at both the sound use of statistics and the dangers of presenting factual information in the form of figures without explaining exactly what these figures mean or, almost more important, without explaining what the figures do *not* mean.

Numbers suggest precision and accuracy. Most of us think of figures as being factual and scientific. We do not know how to answer a statement such as, "Twenty percent of the American troops in Southeast Asia used heroin," unless we have some statistical information of our own. We may say, "I find that hard to believe," or, "That figure seems awfully high," but if the other person repeats the statement, the suggestive power of the number itself, "20 percent," is persuasive and is difficult for us to answer.

We all use numbers to talk about such things as our age, height, and weight. We count things like apples, pennies, and oranges, and we know how useful counting and measuring can be. One important way to reason is to count things and then, applying addition, subtraction, multiplication, and division to the numbers we have, compute further answers for ourselves. If I compute my salary on the basis that I make $50 a week, and $11 is deducted in taxes and insurance, I figure that I will have $39 in my weekly pay check. As long as my basic premises are right (I make $50 and $11 is deducted), then when I make my mathematical computations, my experience will agree with my predicted outcome. I calculated that I will have a $39 pay check, and when payday arrives, I *do* have a check for $39.

All this seems somewhat obvious to us at this stage in our lives. We have no difficulty counting apples or people, because we can tell one apple from another and we can differentiate people. But the use of numbers becomes much more complicated as soon as we leave individual, single items. Counting the length of a table, for example, is more difficult than counting the number of tables in a room. A table is one long uninterrupted length .We have, then, to make arbitrary divisions or units along the length of the table so that we can count each division just as we counted the apples. The unit we set up for counting the length of the table is, of course, an inch. Each inch is the same size as every other inch. We mark off the inches along the length of the table and add them up. Our hypothetical table, however, does not consist of an exactly even number of inches; when we mark off the last full inch, we find that the table extends a little further, but less than 1 inch. Then we have to break up that final inch into fractions, or parts, of the inch. In spite of the complications of measuring and counting, however, we can achieve fairly accurate results when we measure a table or count apples. We can compare lengths of various tables, and we can compare the total number of apples in one box with the total number of apples in another.

Because numbers are such useful labels, we tend to use numbers for many things that cannot be counted in the simple way apples and inches can. When we do this, the accuracy with which the numbers represent the real world is decreased. You have all taken essay-type tests in which the instructor assigns points for each answer. Question 1, you are told, is worth 25 points. The instructor then has the job of deciding whether the answer given by a particular student is worth all 25 points, or only 20 points, or 10, and so on. What can the instructor count to arrive at a conclusion that the answer is worth 20 points? Nothing, really. The number 20 is a number evaluation which corresponds to a word evaluation of the answer, such as "good" or "fair," and the instructor is simply using the convenience of a number to stand for his general evaluation of one answer to one question.

If you say that Mary is 5 feet tall and weighs 100 pounds, you have made a measurable, accurate statistical statement. Suppose you are told that Mary has an IQ of 140. Is this an accurate, dependable statistical statement? Not so much so. We are impressed that Mary's IQ is 140 because we know that this value borders on the genius range of human intelligence, but what have the testers counted to arrive at the number 140? They have certainly not been able to count anything like apples or inches or pounds. Mary has done certain tasks, and the tester has assigned number values to them. He has added up the number values of the tasks Mary completed correctly (her score) and has compared her score with those of others her age who have taken similar tests, and on that basis assigned the number 140 as a measure of Mary's intelligence. To say Mary has an IQ of 140 is a less valid statistic than to say Mary is 5 feet tall and weighs 100 pounds.

When we use or listen to statistics, we must make sure we know how the people who observed the facts picked the numbers they assign to the facts as statistics about them. Did the person gathering the statistics count something that could easily be counted by you or by anyone else, so that several people would come up with the same numbers, or did he use the number as an evaluation or a name? Numbers that come from counting tend to be more useful and accurate than numbers used as names or evaluations.

Many people and organizations are engaged in counting and evaluating things and publishing statistics. Today's student acquires facts and figures from many different sources. In organizing communication messages, we seldom have any trouble finding statistics; the newsstands are full of magazines that are, in turn, full of statistics we can repeat in a communication class. Our trouble comes when we begin to puzzle out what the numbers we find actually mean. The basic information we need to understand something or to make a wise decision is often a comparison of how two things are similar, how they are changing, or how they are different. The things we want to know can often be described by such terms as *enough, too much, on time, gaining, out of reach, leveling off, losing ground, the weakest regions, the strongest area, ahead of schedule, above average,* and *less than we expected.*

One of the most important ways people use figures is to make comparisons. Basically, we compare figures to get a clear indication of *more* or *less.* We can use figures to find out about more or less by looking at two things at about the same point in time (we measure Joe's height and Harry's height and say that Joe is at this moment 2 inches taller than Harry) and by looking at the same thing at different times (Metropolitan Junior College had an enrollment of 1500 in 1965, 2200 in 1970, and currently has 3100).

When we compare figures we must be sure not only that the numbers are a result of counting and not of naming or evaluating, but also that the units counted are comparable in terms of the point we wish to prove. The most common thing people try to count, which is not comparable from time to time, is the dollar. Usually the dollar buys less this year than last, although in some periods of American history the reverse was true. Suppose an older person says to a high-school student, "When I started my first job I made only $1 an hour and here you are beginning at $2. Are you lucky! You're making twice what I made then." The idea that a student making $2 an hour today is earning twice as much as a man making $1 an hour in 1945 is wrong, because the value of a dollar depends on its buying power—how many hours a person has to work to buy a good dinner in a restaurant, or a car, or a bag of groceries. Someone making $2 an hour today can buy little, if anything, more than a person making $1 an hour in 1945.

Even on the same day in different parts of the country, the dollar is not comparable in terms of buying power. If someone says welfare payments are much higher in New York City than in Jackson, Mississippi, what are they saying? Maybe the dollars paid in New York City buy less than the dollars in Jackson. What you buy for a dollar in one part of the country often costs more, or less, in another part of the country. This is even more true in various cities around the world.

Even when the things compared are the same size, or are corrected to make them comparable, the people who compare figures for today with statistics from the past often ignore the effect of the increasing or decreasing numbers of people in a given city or region. For example, the latest figures regarding deaths in automobile accidents, arrests for using illegal drugs, or the occurrence of venereal disease are usually larger than the same statistics from 10 or 20 years ago simply because the population of the United States has increased in the last 20 years. Comparisons of absolute numbers are poor evidence to prove a trend toward better or worse. Comparing the total number of deaths on the highways 10 years ago with the total number this year is not as valid a statistic for proving the increased rate of automobile-related deaths as is the number of deaths per every 1000 cars in those years or, better yet, the number of deaths per every 100,000 automobile-miles driven in those years. Because some cars are driven so much more every year than others, a comparison of car-miles driven is more meaningful than a comparison of deaths per so many automobiles. Airlines usually present safety statistics in terms of passenger-miles rather than number of flights or length of flights.

To this point we have assumed that the figures under discussion were the result of observing everything we want to know about. That is, if we want to know how many students are enrolled at our college, we find out the number by tabulating every student. Many important statistics are the result of such complete counts. If the counting is complete and no item is overlooked, the numbers that result are most useful. Much statistical information, however, comes from observing only part of the total and then trying to figure out what the whole picture looks like by making educated guesses about the whole from the part actually counted. The argument is that you do not have to drink the whole glassful to know the milk is sour.

Statisticians often take a sample from the population they are studying and then count the occurrence of some important feature in the sample. If they are careful and follow the formulas of statistics, they can usually figure out, with a rather small margin of error, the occurrence of that feature in the entire population. Taking a sample saves counting and thus time and money. A good sample must be large enough and selected in such a way as to be representative of the total population. A good way to acquire a sample that is representative of the total population is to select it in such a way that every member of the total population has an equal chance of being picked for the sample. Suppose you want to know how the students at your school feel about the library hours. You can ask 20 people in your English course, but since people in an English class might use the library differently from people in another class, you would know about the students in your English class but not about all the students in your school. If you obtain a list of all the students in the school, assign a number to each name on the list, and then pick 20 names by using a table of random numbers, you will have a more representative sample for determining what the whole student body thinks about the library hours.

Many of the figures we hear and use come from sampling events and are thus less accurate than those resulting from counting every item under study. Still, if we are careful how we study and evaluate statistics, we can learn a great deal about factual matters by the sampling procedure.

Most polls of public opinion are based on the answers of several hundred or perhaps several thousand people to various questions. Surveys of television viewers also record the responses of a sample of the total viewing audience. Often surveyors report their results in specific figures. One may read that the most recent poll shows that 53 percent of the American people approve the way the President is doing his job. These same polls seldom also indicate that, given the number of people polled and the error that creeps into such sampling, the results are accurate only within 2 or 3 percentage points.

In addition to describing numerically the whole or a group, statistics can be used to describe the average of a group. For instance, the average student at a state college is 21 years old. We often want to know what is typical, and averages help us find out. But an average can be misleading as well as useful. For example, if all 20 members of a class in interpersonal communication have part-time or full-time jobs, we may not discover the typical salary if we add all the salaries and divide by 20 because, for one thing, those with full-time jobs probably earn more than those with part-time work. Even if we limit our group to 10 students with full-time jobs, averaging may be misleading. For example, if 1 student is a highly successful door-to-door salesman who makes $20,000 per year, including this high salary in the averaging gives us a misleading figure. If the 9 remaining students have salaries between $6000 and $8000 a year, averaging for the 9 people about $7000 per year, including the single $20,000 salary produces an average of $8300 per year, which is higher than the earnings of 9 members of the sample and lower than the earnings of 1.

All numerical statistical evidence must be carefully examined when you use it or hear it as part of a persuasive campaign to prove a point.

REAL EXAMPLES

In Chapter 7 we discussed real examples as ways to make a point clear. Examples that are factual can also support a point as evidence of its truth or wisdom. A person trying to find out the truth about a particular problem must weigh the real examples carefully to be sure they are factually accurate and typical of the things they are supposed to illustrate or represent. We take one or two examples as being representative of a class of people or events. We imply that the examples are able to stand for a great many more just like them that we could use if we had the time to discuss them all. The danger, therefore; is that we may, in the interest of proving a point, use an extreme example. In the early 1970s, two dramatic and compelling events caught the imagination of the American public. The first was a series of bloody murders of Hollywood personalities, for which a long-haired commune leader named Charles Manson and several of the women in his "family" were convicted. The second was a war atrocity in which a number of Vietnamese women and children were killed at a village called My Lai, for which an infantry lieutenant named Calley was convicted. Some people argued that the hippy culture was morally bankrupt and vicious and submitted the Manson murders as an example to prove their point. Other people argued that the military-industrial complex was morally bankrupt and vicious and submitted the My Lai massacre as an example to prove their point. Both groups were guilty of using extreme, rather than typical, examples.

The use of extreme examples as proof is characteristic of popular magazine articles. A writer in search of an attention-catching device for his opening paragraph often describes a dramatic, but unusual case and implies that it is typical.

Students of straight thinking have found so many instances of the use of a few extreme examples to prove points that they call such errors of thinking the fallacy of *hasty generalization*. If one of your friends did something your parents thought was out of line, they may have made a hasty generalization about your whole group of acquaintances. When someone submits an extreme example to another person in a conversation or discussion, and then jumps to the conclusion that the example is typical, both speaker and listener may be misled about the facts of the case. When we make mistakes about the way the world really is, we can usually expect a rude awakening sooner or later.

The notion of typicality ties together the use of statistics and examples. An important part of statistical analysis is the discovery of the fact or facts that are the most usual or that are in the middle of a range. We have mentioned the average—the sum of all the numbers divided by the frequency of their occurrence—which is often an appropriate device for indicating what is typical. If we take the weight of each of the 11 players on a football team, add them to find the total weight of all players, and divide by 11, we have the average weight of a player on the team. If the average turns out to be 220 pounds, that statistic gives us a better impression of how heavy the players are than would an extreme example of Harry Potter, a 180-pound quarterback, or William Jones, a 167-pound scatback. As the two lightest-weight players on the team, Harry and William would be poor examples of the weight of the team as a whole. There may not even be a player who weighs the exact average, 220 pounds, but if we use Fred Smith, a 223-pound end, or Elbert Reed, a 217-pound running back, for our example, we have selected an example close to the actual average weight.

Another way statisticians discover the typical is by arranging all the facts in order from larger to smaller, and then picking the fact at the middle point and using this statistic to show what is the usual. If we made a list of the incomes of all the families on the Red Lake Indian Reservation and arranged the incomes in order from the highest to the lowest, we could count halfway down (or up) and consider the income in the middle of the list to be the typical example of the income of these families. In the discussion of salaries used earlier to illustrate the pitfalls of averaging, a midpoint or median example would give a more accurate indication of what was typical than would a numerical average. The median example is often a good statistic to use when the figures you are discussing range from unusually high to unusually low. These extremes are accounted for when you pick the point in the middle.

Real examples add interest to statistics because they relate the dry figures to the human world. Statistics can express many facts in a short statement, but without examples, they often seem dull and boring. As we saw in Chapter 9, facts presented in terms of people who are heroes or villains, who suffer and have moments of joy and happiness, are more interesting and more understandable. Real examples are vital also because they serve as reality links to the highly persuasive dramas we discussed in Chapter 9. Because examples can contain characters in action, they can be persuasive as evidence and as *indirect suggestion*. As a student of persuasion, you should watch how skillful speakers use examples for maximum effect. Try this exercise: Present the same real example in several different ways to achieve different impressions. Make your real example on one occasion have the main character as the good guy. In another version, let the main character be the bad guy. Make us sympathetic with your example; then make us detest him. Learn to think of examples as highly effective tools in persuasive communication and practice using them.

TESTIMONY

"When in doubt, go see for yourself," is generally good advice. In other words, if you don't believe me, go find out with your own two eyes and ears. We depend upon the evidence of our senses in deciding many factual questions. If you want to know if it is raining, you go to the window and look outside. Say that a fight breaks out in the hallway. You run to see what is going on. Someone else runs up after the fight is over and asks, "What happened?" You describe the fight. This other person says, "I don't believe you." You shrug your shoulders and say, "Suit yourself. But that is what happened." You believe the evidence of your own senses.

Many times in our communications with others we want to prove a point about some facts, but have not had the time or the chance to see the particular facts for ourselves. Maybe the facts, such as what happened in the fight in the hallway, occurred at only one place in time, so that unless we happened to be there, we have to depend for information on the story of a person who did see the event. Some facts are complicated and occur over a period of time or at a considerable distance, so that we would need much time to observe them all. During the years the United States did not have diplomatic relations with Communist China, the facts about what was going on in China existed, but could not be observed by Americans. If we wanted to know how things were going in China during those years, we had to rely on the testimony of people who were there—foreign correspondents from countries that did have diplomatic exchanges with China; we often read reports about China that were written, for example, by Canadians, who were there to observe at first hand.

Thus an important source of evidence is the testimony or word of an eyewitness. In a court of law, the only testimony about facts allowed is that of an eyewitness. Sometimes, in everyday living, we are willing to depend upon what the law terms *hearsay* (second-hand information, gossip, or rumor; the word of somebody who got the story from someone else), but when we are trying to prove something, rumor is a shaky substitute for eyewitness accounts. Think of several rumors you have heard recently. How many turned out to be entirely accurate?

Many times we quote testimony from a witness who has written up an account of what he saw in a newspaper or magazine. Sometimes we refer to a statement made on radio or television by an alleged eyewitness. When using the testimony of a witness to prove a point, we ought not to assume that just because the person saw the event he is necessarily telling the truth about it or giving a good picture of what happened.

Suppose we ask a friend of Bill's what happened in the hallway fight between Bill and Harry. Bill's friend may well say that Harry did not knock Bill down, that Bill slipped. Another eyewitness who has no stake in the matter such as friendship with one of the participants, may say that Bill provoked Harry, Harry hit Bill a solid blow to the jaw and knocked him down. Which eyewitness do you believe? How do you decide which reporter is the more reliable witness to what actually happened?

When trying to decide what happened in any given instance, we have to examine the testimony of eyewitnesses carefully. You should ask yourself such questions as:

What exactly did the witness intend to say?

Was the story a put-on? Was it supposed to be funny?

Was the person able to make a good report? Was he in a position to see? Did he have the training that would make him better able to keep track of what was going on? Is he a reliable person?

Was the person willing and able to tell the truth?

Was there any reason for the witness to lie or distort the truth?

Did the witness have a bias? What did the witness expect to see? (We all have a tendency to see what we expect to see. Each of us has a personal bias built in when we view or hear an event.)

An important additional way speakers use testimony is in interpreting the facts. Usually we use *expert* witnesses to testify about what the facts mean. If we go to a doctor and he shows us our x-rays, we may still ask, "What does it mean?" He could then tell us that the facts indicate there is a fracture of a small bone in the right foot. Many facts are difficult to interpret, and people who specialize in a given area can often help us decide what the facts mean. An expert in foods may testify that the diet of the poor people in an area is not good enough to keep them healthy; he may testify, further, that studies have shown a direct relationship between diet and intelligence in young children. Another expert on drug usage may testify that the facts indicate that the use of marijuana does not affect a person's physical ability to drive a car as much as does the use of alcohol in comparable amounts.

A final way in which we may use testimony to prove a point is to ask someone what we ought to do in a given case. We might ask the doctor who told us we have a fractured bone in the foot, "What shall I do?" He might advise us to have the foot put into a cast to keep it immobilized for 6 weeks while it heals. We often depend upon an expert's advice; in the case of the doctor, his advice is evidence for you to consider as you decide what to do about the facts. Obviously, when you want advice to use as evidence, you must ask the right expert. Suppose an unmarried pregnant girl asks her mother, "What should I do?" Suppose she asks her boy friend, a girl friend, or her doctor the same question. Her mother might say, "Get married." The boy might say, "Have an abortion." The girl friend might say, "Keep the baby." The doctor might say, "Take these pills, they're vitamins; don't gain too much weight, and come back to see me in a month." The girl has received testimony from four sources. Whose testimony is more persuasive? Whose testimony ought to be more persuasive? Has the girl perhaps not asked the right expert or the right questions yet? Consider the involved interests of her sources.

One widely used propaganda technique cites the testimony of glamorous and famous people telling us we ought to buy or do something. We often see baseball or basketball or football players advising us to buy a certain kind of shaving cream, cologne, or breakfast food. Movie stars advise us what political candidates to vote for. The trick is that, supposedly, if we admire and value the opinions of a sports or television star, we will transfer our liking to the product he tells us to use and will buy it.

When an expert tells us what to do about a health problem, or getting an education, or voting for or against a tax increase or school bond, or to support an antiwar position or candidate, or to support a disarmament conference or an antipollution effort, we should be sure that the person is an expert *in the field* he is talking about. We should not follow a person's advice just because he is likable or glamorous. If the person talking about facts has a vested interest in how he interprets the facts to us, we must keep that in mind when we consider his testimony.

MAKING A PERSUASIVE LOGICAL CASE

Most people find good evidence and sound reasoning persuasive. One of the most effective ways to persuade others about what they should believe or do is to give them good reasons, well supported with evidence.

We have seen that the clear statement of a point to be proved and the evidence that supports that point are the basic building blocks for a logical argument. We now turn to how the basic building blocks can be fitted together to form a strong case for a particular position.

For our purposes we will define *logic* as the process of drawing a conclusion from one or more points that need to be proved with evidence. When we present the results of straight thinking to a listener or an audience, we can begin with the conclusion and then give the reasons for believing the conclusion, or we can begin with the reasons and draw the conclusion at the end of our message. An audience generally requires proof composed of both logic and evidence.

In an interview or conference between two people, the give-and-take of question and answer, statement and answering statement tends to break up the connections between evidence and point and general conclusion. Even so, many interviews contain chains of hard logical thought. In an interview, a person may present a conclusion and have it accepted without further proof. He may present another conclusion and have it challenged, then submit a reason to support the conclusion and have it challenged, then present evidence to prove the point until the other person accepts the argument. In a two-person conversation, the possibility for source and receiver to interact and to thus indicate when evidence is understood or misunderstood, or when a person is convinced or is skeptical about a point, allows them to think together in a productive fashion.

Much the same opportunity for give-and-take and for discovering when members are convinced of a point exists in the small group discussion; in this regard the interaction is much the same as in a two-person situation. For larger groups, however, the speaker often plans the logic of the case ahead of time, structures the message with the audience in mind, and presents larger chunks of proof and logic without interruption. The pressure of arguing in persuasive fashion before large audiences often makes a speaker examine the reasons behind his conclusions and analyze the way the parts of his arguments hang together. We too should plan for the interview, conference, or meeting by thinking through the logic of our argument beforehand. We have more difficulty keeping arguments in mind when they can be questioned or challenged as we go along. All of us have a tendency to underestimate the need for ordering our evidence when we hope to be persuasive in informal communication.

Lawyers call the paper they write that contains the logic of an argument a *brief*. Someone working on an important persuasive project might well outline the main conclusion and the points that support it, much as a lawyer briefs a case. By following an outline, a person can see the connections from reasons to conclusions clearly and decide whether they fit together logically.

When someone questions our logic, he often asks the short but troublesome question, "Why?" When we answer a *why* question, we usually provide a *because* response. One good way to check the logic of a conclusion following from reasons is to write the conclusion clearly at the top of a sheet of paper and then indent a list of the reasons supporting the conclusion under it, beginning each reason with *because*. If the outline—keeping in mind our common-sense meaning of *because*—makes good sense, the logic is probably all right.

For instance, here is a conclusion with its supporting reasons, using *because* to indicate logical connections:

Black English is a good legitimate language dialect *because* Black English is not a substandard dialect *because* Black English is not a deprived language.

One can also test the logic of conclusions drawn from a set of reasons by listing first the reasons, and then the conclusions introduced by the logical word *therefore,* as in the following example:

> Many teachers believe in the cultural deprivation idea that blacks fail to use standard English because of a cultural deficiency; *therefore,* many teachers refer thousands of black students to speech correctionists to bring their speech up to standard; *therefore,* many black students are being destroyed psychologically in our schools.

When checking your own logic, keep in mind that the evidence must relate to the point you want to prove and the reasons you present must support your conclusion. One of the most difficult things to do when trying to think clearly and logically is to make sure that every step of the argument is to the point. Here is an example of an argument that makes a mistake by trying to fit two related reasons together, one as the support of the other, when they do not logically fit as reason and conclusion:

> Many black students are being destroyed psychologically in our schools *because* many blacks get a psychologically damaging image of blacks from motion pictures and television.

The point to be proved relates to the effect of schools and the reason supplied to prove the point says something about motion pictures and television. Although both ideas are related to the general topic of the psychologic effect of certain experiences on black students, they do not fit together as main point and supporting reason.

When we prove to someone the wisdom of acting, believing, or thinking in a certain way by means of evidence and logic, we have used one of the most powerful means of persuasion. Often the decision based upon facts and careful inferences from evidence is better than the decision made solely on the basis of the advice of a person we like and trust or on the basis of suggestion. We all need to know the methods of straight thinking not only for our formal communications but also for group discussions, interviews, and other two-person conversations. Most importantly, as consumers of persuasion, we need to be skillful in testing messages for their factual content and the soundness of their logic.

the key ideas

Reasonable people may properly disagree about what events mean, but before differing, they should agree about the facts.

The dramas in persuasive messages can be attractive and interesting and still be false.

Evidence is material that furnishes grounds for belief in the truth or falsity, rightness or wrongness, wisdom or folly, of a proposition.

An important use of evidence is to describe what is the case.

Expert interpretation of facts is a form of evidence.

Statistical descriptions of factual material often contain much information in a few words.

Skillful charlatans can juggle statistics to fool the listener by distorting or misrepresenting the facts.

Even when carefully and honestly presented, statistics often give the listener an incomplete picture.

Numbers that come from counting tend to be more useful in learning about the world than figures used as names or as evaluations.

The most common unit that is not comparable from time to time is the American dollar.

The latest figures regarding any vital statistic are usually larger than the same figures for several years ago simply because the population has increased.

Much statistical information comes from observing a sample of the total population and making an educated guess about the whole on that basis.

A random sample allows a more precise guess about the total population than most other kinds of samples.

SUGGESTED PROJECTS

1 / This is a project in proving a point. Select a controversial point, phrase it in suitable form, and then, using only statistical information, support the point for 2 minutes.

2 / Select an argument presented in newspapers, magazines, or on television. Note the point to be proved and then analyze the sup-

in chapter 10

Hypothetical examples are useful in clarifying ideas, but only real examples can be used as evidence to prove a point.

Extreme examples are poor evidence.

The fallacy of hasty generalization results from jumping to a conclusion on the basis of a few extreme examples.

An important part of statistical analysis is the discovery of facts that are usual or typical of a wide range of things.

Real examples are a good way to add interest to statistics, and statistics provide a good guide to typical examples.

Real examples serve as reality links to the persuasive dramas that are part of many messages.

We depend upon the evidence of our senses in deciding many factual questions.

The testimony of eyewitnesses is an important source of evidence about factual matters.

In an age of specialization, expert testimony interpreting complicated factual matters is often an important part of persuasion.

A widely used propaganda technique is to cite the testimonial of a famous and glamorous person in behalf of a product or service.

If someone testifies that we ought to do or believe something, we should examine that person's authority carefully.

Logic is the process of drawing conclusions from one or more points.

Decisions based upon careful inferences from evidence are often better than those made solely on the basis of the persuasive power of personality and suggestion.

porting material critically. How could the argument have been better supported, in your estimation?

3 / Although it is seldom possible to ignore your emotional reactions to the personalities and suggestions, direct and indirect, involved in decision-making, it is always good practice to work toward making decisions as much as possible on the basis of

evidence and reasoning. Consider a recent decision of some importance to you that you had to make. It could have been a decision about what course of study to take at school, what career to prepare for, a decision to participate more fully in your religious group or to cease your participation completely, to move into an apartment with friends—something you had to think about quite a while. Now, looking back, list in the order of their importance in influencing your final decision, the evidence and reasoning you considered.

SUGGESTED READINGS

Bettinghaus, Erwin P. *Message Preparation: The Nature of Proof.* Indianapolis: Bobbs-Merrill, 1966.

Huff, Darrell, *How To Lie with Statistics.* New York: Norton, 1954.

Miller, Gerald R., and Thomas R. Nilsen (eds.). *Perspectives on Argument.* Glenview, Ill.: Scott, Foresman, 1966.

Mills, Glen E. *Message Preparation.* Indianapolis: Bobbs-Merrill, 1966.

Newman, Robert P., and Dale R. Newman. *Evidence.* Boston: Houghton Mifflin, 1969.

Walter, Otis M., and Robert L. Scott. *Thinking and Speaking,* 2nd ed. New York: Macmillan, 1969.

11 how to communicate in group discussions

College students attend as many meetings as any group in our society. A student may be a member of an athletic team or club, a street gang, a fraternity or sorority, a black student union, a Young Americans for Freedom club, a Students for a Democratic Society chapter, a Young Republican or Democrat club. Students also attend meetings of committees related to student government, departmental clubs, dormitory groups, student unions, religious foundations, and increasingly, to prepare projects for classes.

In addition to performing his duties with his immediate work group on the job, the person who works for a store, a factory, a service industry, a government agency such as a police force or fire department, attends committee meetings, training groups, and union meetings. Off the job, a typical citizen takes part in discussions at church, for political organizations, for other community and voluntary purposes.

Every project to get things done requires working with small groups. If we wish to change our neighborhoods, organize for community power or political power, or establish a cooperative, we must work productively in groups.

Despite the importance of working with small groups of people, most of us take for granted our role in a discussion. Few people have a chance to study group discussion or drill in the techniques of group work in order to become more professional in their leadership and participation in meetings. One of the best ways to ensure that the group meetings you attend in the future will be useful and that you will feel satisfied about your contribution to them is to study small group communication and to critically evaluate the dynamics of the meetings you attend.

GROUP DISCUSSION

Group discussion refers to one or more meetings of a small number of people who communicate face to face in order to fulfill a common purpose and achieve a common goal.

The small group is an identifiable social entity. Authorities differ on details relating to the size of a small group, but the general features are agreed upon. The communication networks and personal relationships that develop while people hold a discussion change when the size of the group is increased, and these changes can be used to describe the "small" group. When a third person is added to a two-person interview, the nature of the working relationships and the flow of communication changes; thus a small group is composed of at least three people. The upper size limit of the small group is more difficult to specify. However, when the group becomes so large that it begins to change its patterns of communication, it should no longer be considered a small group. In groups of five or less, all members speak to one another. Even those who speak little talk to all the others. In groups of seven or more, the quiet members often cease to talk to any but the top people in the group. As groups become even larger, the talk centralizes more and more around a few people; group interaction falls off. In groups of thirteen or more, from five to seven people hold the discussion while the others watch and listen.

The best size for a group discussion is probably five. Members of groups with fewer than five people complain that their groups are too small and suffer from a lack of diversity of opinion and skill. Groups composed of even numbers of people tend to be less stable and rewarding than groups of odd numbers. A group of five or seven works better than a group of four, six, or eight. On learning this, many people have said, when analyzing unproductive groups they have been in, "Well, that was our first mistake! There were ten of us."

A discussion group is a special form of the work group. Work groups use several different sorts of meetings. If the members come to the meeting with the wrong idea about what the meeting is supposed to do and what it will be like, they may be frustrated. For example, if the meeting is just a ceremony to rubber-stamp decisions already made, and a member comes expecting to change the decision, he feels cheated.

Every organization has some meetings that are rituals. A ritual is a set ceremony that has come to be expected at certain times to celebrate the organization or group. In a meeting that is a ritual people may say one thing and mean another. Some religious rituals contain prayers which the worshippers repeat over and over again, and the meaning of the prayers as expressed in the words is not as important to the worshippers or to the ritual as the act of saying the words over and over again. The ritual meetings of an organization may aid its cohesiveness, or its ability to stick together, and ensure that people in authority are recognized. For example, the department heads of a business organization may make an oral presentation of their yearly budgets at a meeting of all the vice-presidents. The meeting is really meant only to rubber-stamp decisions already made. Yet the meeting is important to the others in the business. The newcomer who says the meeting accomplishes nothing and is therefore a waste of time is judging it on the wrong grounds.

Another kind of meeting is the briefing session, used to give members information they need to carry through on plans already made. The objective of the group is clear: The members know what they want to do and need only find out who is to do what, when and where.

A group discussion may also have the purpose of instructing participants in some concepts or skills they can use in the future. Teachers may use small discussion groups to teach a course in English literature, for example, by dividing up the class and having each group discuss a novel.

A small discussion group may meet to advise the person or persons empowered to make decisions. We can say that the person in charge consults or asks the advice of the people in the meeting. A department head at a college or university might consult a committee of students and faculty about changes in course requirements. If the meeting is consultative, the department chairman does not promise to abide by the advice, but does ask for and consider it. The danger in an advice-giving discussion is that if the people who attend do not understand its purposes, they may expect their advice to be accepted and feel cheated when it is not. "We spent all that time making that decision and then they ignored it."

Finally, an extremely important kind of meeting is one called actually to make the decision. Members of decision-making groups often are more fully committed to their decisions and usually work harder to implement them than do the participants in other kinds of groups. One of the most important functions of small groups in many organizations is to provide a way for people to participate in management decisions and to exercise some of the power relating to the use of the organization's resources.

Students of small group communication must understand not only that a discussion meeting may serve different functions but also that groups differ in other significant ways. In a group that meets only once, the dynamics of the communication are quite different from those that operate in a group that meets several times. Groups also differ depending on how closely they relate to an organization. A group of students from a speech class is different from a standing committee of the speech department composed of students, teaching assistants, and faculty members.

The one-time discussion group is such an important communication event that it deserves some special attention. The people in a one-time discussion group have not worked together before and are not likely to do so again for the purposes under discussion. Some may have worked with others in similar groups and some may know one another socially, but the particular grouping of these five or six people for this particular purpose has not happened before.

The one-time discussion meeting is different from an *ad hoc* committee. *Ad hoc* is a Latin term meaning "for this special purpose." An *ad hoc* committee thus is formed for a special purpose important enough to cause the group to meet for several sessions over a period of weeks or months before it makes its final report. An *ad hoc* committee is different from the standing (permanent) committees of an organization, which continue for as long as the organization exists. For example, if a political action group such as the Black Panthers has a ministry of information, the ministry will continue to function as long as the Panthers continue. However, if an individual Panther gets in trouble with the law and a group of people organize a committee to meet and work for several months for the specific purpose of freeing that individual, that committee is *ad hoc*.

The one-time meeting is held by people who expect to achieve their purposes in a single meeting. Since its composition is unique, the discussion group has no history, and the people who come to the meeting cannot be guided by past experience with one another in such a discussion. The group holding a one-time meeting has no team spirit, no usual way of doing things, no idea about how the communication and social interaction will proceed.

The *ad hoc* committee is like the one-time meeting in that its members have not previously met together for this particular purpose. But although the *ad hoc* committee has no history, it does have a future. The members will be meeting together for a considerable period of time, and the influence of the future expectations produces some important differences between the first session of an *ad hoc* committee and a one-time meeting.

The group without a history but with a future is under pressure to test potential leaders and other possibly important members, to develop a common way of doing things, to take nothing at face value, and to check reputations, formal status, and assigned structures before accepting them.

One of the most important things about the one-time meeting is the willingness of the participants to accept leadership. Whether the person calling the meeting is a self-appointed moderator or has been assigned to lead the meeting by some organizational unit, the members are likely to accept and appreciate guidance from that individual. The group needs quick help in getting started. Members realize they have little time to waste and tend to accept with little argument the leader's description of goals and his method of getting on with the meeting.

Participants in one-time meetings tend to use any information they have to help form an impression of their fellow committeemen. If students in a speech-communication class meet to plan something and discover that one member is majoring in elementary education, another is the president of the freshman class, a third was a beauty-contest winner, and so on, they use such information to help them structure their meeting.

Once the discussion is under way, those members who do not hold positions of stature, or who are not known by reputation, tend to be quickly stereotyped. The stereotyping that takes place in the one-time meeting comes from first impressions. Each person makes a quick judgment about every other member and, thus, a person who does not speak for 15 or 20 minutes may be stereotyped as quiet, shy, apathetic, or uninterested and be dismissed as unimportant. Another, who speaks loudly, expresses strong opinions, and makes flat judgments may be stereotyped as bossy or pushy.

The people in a one-time meeting take short cuts to structure their group into a pecking order so they can get on with the business at hand. They are willing to risk getting a wrong impression because they are pressed for time and often because they think the purpose of the one-time meeting is less important than that of a discussion group that meets repeatedly.

Members of one-time meetings tend to accept a stereotyped picture of how a meeting should be run. A newly formed group that plans to meet for many sessions works out its own unique ways of getting the job done, but the one-time meeting does not allow enough time to do this. The accepted picture of how a small group meeting should be conducted—the stereotype which most North Americans come to accept by the time they reach college—includes the idea that there should be a moderator, leader, or chairman (depending upon how authoritarian the leadership style is to be) and a secretary or recorder.

The moderator, leader, or chairman of a one-time meeting is expected to attend to the administrative details of setting up the meeting place, planning the agenda, sending out preliminary information, and scheduling the meeting.

PLANNING THE ONE-TIME MEETING

If you are assigned the duty of moderating, leading, or chairing a one-time meeting, you ought to do the following things in the planning stage:

1 / Determine the purpose of the meeting. Every one-time meeting should have a clear and specific purpose. Make sure the other members know the purpose of the meeting either before it starts or early in the session. You should also make the type of meeting clear to the members. Is the meeting for briefing, instructing, consulting, or decision-making? In addition to that general information, you should tell the others the specific purpose of the meeting.

2 / Plan the meeting to achieve the purpose. You should ask such questions as: Where is the best place to hold the meeting? What format will best achieve the purpose? Who should take part in the meeting? Should people with special knowledge be invited? Should some high-status people be invited?

3 / Plan the little details. A successful one-time meeting requires time and effort in the planning stages. Do not neglect the small details. If you do, you may save a bit of your own time, but wasting the time of your colleagues in a useless meeting is not wise. Little things such as providing pads and pencils, refreshments, properly arranged (and enough) seating all contribute to the success of the meeting. When minor details of administration are handled smoothly, people feel the meeting is important and is going to do significant work.

4 / Specify the outcomes of the meeting. Making the outcomes clear is not the same as deciding on the purposes. If plans are to be made, how will they be developed? In detail? In general outline? Decide what decisions can be made in such a meeting and in what form they should be made.

5 / Utilize the results of the meeting. What can be done to follow up and apply the results? Do not let important leads drop at the end of the meeting.

LEADING THE ONE-TIME MEETING

During the course of the meeting the assigned (or elected) chairman is expected to lead the discussion. The chairman's duties are commonly understood to include the following:

A. Chairman's duties in regard to the task
1. Start the meeting
2. Act as pilot to keep the group on course, remind members of the discussion outline, cut short those who wander too far from the outline
3. Help the group arrive at decisions (take votes when necessary)
4. Provide transitions from topic to topic
5. Summarize what the group has accomplished
6. Control the channels of communication to ensure that everybody has a chance to talk and that all sides get a fair hearing; encourage the quiet members to take part and discourage the too-talkative ones
B. Chairman's duties in regard to human relations
1. Introduce members to one another
2. Help break the ice at the start and relax people so they can get down to business
3. Release tensions and bad feelings that come from disagreements and conflicts of personality or opinion

TECHNIQUES FOR LEADING THE ONE-TIME MEETING

Assuming a willingness to follow his direction, the leader still needs certain basic skills to conduct an efficient meeting. The three basic techniques for this purpose are the question, the summary, and the directive. Summaries are always useful to indicate progress and to orient the group. The democratic style requires more questions than directives; the authoritarian style, more directives than questions.

The first task is to get the group down to business. A certain amount of time should be devoted to getting acquainted, but then the group must go to work. Questions are useful. Open-ended questions are asked in such a way that they cannot be answered with a simple "yes" or "no." An open-ended question can get things started. Early in the meeting, the leader should set the mood for short, to-the-point comments. If the first comment runs too long, the leader may have to interrupt with a question directed to someone else.

The leader needs to watch carefully and make running choices about the drift of the discussion. Is it part of the necessary kicking around of an idea? He should not take the easy way out and make the choice on the letter of the agenda. When he decides the discussion is wasting time, he should bring the meeting back to the agenda. Questions are most useful for this: "Can we tie this in with the point about rules in the student union?" "Just a minute; how does this relate to grading procedures?" Summaries can give an overview of the last few minutes of the meeting and bring the group back to the agenda. Finally, a leader may simply assert that they are off the track and direct that they get back. "We seem to be getting off the subject. Let's get back to Bill's point."

The moderator should not push the group too fast; on the other hand, devoting 20 minutes to material that deserves only 5 produces restlessness and frustration. The leader should watch for signs that a topic has been exhausted. If members begin to repeat themselves, fidget, pause for a lack of something to say, the leader should move to the next item. The summary is the best way to do so. A summary rounds off the discussion of one point and leads naturally to a new one. It also gives the group a feeling of accomplishment.

From time to time the group needs to make decisions. The leader can help if he steps in at those times and asks, "Are we in substantial agreement on this point?" If the question is important, he may call for a vote.

Often some tension-producing behavior creates an awkward moment for the leader and the participants. What we offer here are some hints about how to handle the awkward situation immediately when it crops up in a meeting. One common difficulty for the moderator is the member who talks too much. The leader may break into a long comment by an overtalkative person with a yes-no question and then quickly direct another question to someone else:

Leader: Just a minute, Joe; would you be willing to drop that course from the requirements for a major?

Joe: Now, I didn't say . . .

Leader: I just want to be clear on this. Would you be in favor of that?

Joe: Well, no, but . . .

Leader: Bill, I wonder how you feel about this?

Sometimes he can stop the talkative member by asking for specific information. Interrupting him for a summary is another technique. He can conclude the summary by directing a question to someone else. People usually sit back for a summary. Sometimes he simply has to say, "I'm going to ask you to stop there for a minute and hold your next comment. Everyone has not had a chance to be heard on this point."

The member who is too quiet also poses problems. The leader should use questions to draw out the quiet members. He should ask the nonparticipating person a direct open-ended question, by name, so that only he can answer. Do not ask a question that can be answered with a "yes" or "no," and, of course, do not ask a question that he might be unable to answer for lack of information. Once he answers, encourage him to elaborate.

PARTICIPATING IN THE ONE-TIME MEETING

The stereotype of a one-time meeting does not assign specific roles to any group member except the chairman. All leadership functions are assigned to the moderator, and other members are expected to follow his lead and accept his directions. When the chairman recognizes a person, the others are supposed to respect that decision and not interrupt. When the chairman cuts off discussion on a topic, the others are supposed to accept that decision.

The duties of the participant include the following:

A. Participant's duties in regard to the task
   1. Enter into the discussion with enthusiasm
   2. Have an open-minded, objective attitude
   3. Keep contributions short and to the point
   4. Talk enough but not too much
   5. Speak clearly and listen carefully
B. Participant's duties in regard to social and human relations
   1. Respect the other person
   2. Be well mannered

3. Try to understand the other person's position

4. Do not manipulate or exploit the other person

Of course, the picture of how a good one-time meeting should proceed differs considerably from the realities of even a short session. Participants do not all willingly follow the assigned moderator even when they know they should. They are, however, much more likely to do so in a one-time meeting than in the first session of a group that will meet a number of times. People in the more permanent group move strongly in the first meeting to test the assigned leader's abilities.

Even in a short meeting, role differences take place. A few people speak more than the others despite the best efforts of the chairman. Some people are silent. Others are humorous and friendly. The generalized picture of a meeting composed of a chairman and a group of indistinguishable followers soon changes under the pressure of discussion with a common purpose.

The group discussion, even a short one-time meeting, is an extremely complicated event. The addition of a third person (or several more) to the two-person communication situation adds a good deal more than one-third in additional complexity. The general discussion above of how to prepare for, moderate, and participate in the discussion should be viewed in terms of our knowledge of group dynamics.

If, indeed, a small group meeting is such a complicated thing, why do most people think it is easy to assemble a few people, and, in the course of an hour or two, discuss a series of important topics, make a couple of vital decisions, and adjourn in time for the next class?

The main reason for our too-simple approach to groups is that we have what we think is a rather clear idea of what a meeting ought to be like, and this acts as a substitute for what a group, in fact, *can* be like. Many people think a business or committee meeting should be an efficient, no-nonsense affair. The meeting should be well planned. The discussion should follow the agenda. Everybody should say about the same amount and everything they say should be to the point and helpful. The members ought to be involved, eager to participate, good listeners and speakers.

The ideal discussion is largely a fiction seldom encountered in real life. Lest you think our treatment of the one-time discussion reflects the common stereotype of an ideal discussion, we hasten here to set the record straight. What we have described above are the expectations people commonly have about what moderators and participants should do in preparation for and during a discussion. Below, we describe what, in fact, tends to happen in a discussion.

Committee meetings and discussion groups rarely conduct business along the lines indicated above. The reason is not just lack of skill on the part of the people in the meeting but more importantly that the ideal is unrealistic. About the only way a group of people can talk with one another, participate equally, keep to an outline, and stick to business is to prepare a playscript and act it out in a public performance. (Even when they prepare such a public production, they do so in a meeting that is filled with false starts, stops, moments of confusion, disagreements, monologues, withdrawal of some members, and other earmarks of groups at work that are contrary to the ideal.)

We would be happier and more productive in group discussions if we replaced the impossible ideal of what a business meeting ought to be like with a truer picture based on the way people really do communicate in small groups when they are working at peak efficiency.

A REALISTIC PICTURE
OF SMALL-GROUP COMMUNICATION

What is a realistic picture of how a good group communicates? Good group communication takes time. Given the complicated communication network that must be developed in a work meeting, we should not expect a group to cover more topics in a 2-hour meeting than one person could study and decide about in 1 hour if he were working alone. Yet we often expect a group to cover as much work in a few hours as one person would be hard-pushed to accomplish in a day. When we ask a group to do more than it can, it either gets bogged down on the first part of the agenda and leaves some business undone or races through the meeting without dealing adequately with anything. As a result, the people who attend come away feeling the meeting was a failure.

Also unrealistic is the notion that a group can organize its discussion so it keeps to the main ideas and moves in a logical, step-by-step way through a series of topics. Individuals have attention spans measured in minutes and sometimes in seconds. When we listen, read, or think about something in a logical, step-by-step way, we often find our attention wandering. You may read a paragraph and understand it quite well; then halfway down the next page you realize that while your eyes are moving, your thoughts are on getting a drink or on the date you are going out with later. People who listen to a speech may attend closely to the speaker for a minute or so and then begin to daydream about something else. Even when people puzzle about an important problem or decision, they often find their attention drifting to other subjects.

Groups, like individuals, have short attention spans. Most groups cannot talk about a topic for much more than a minute before someone changes the subject. Sometimes the group wants to change the subject because it has finished talking about one topic and should move on to another, but quite often the person who changes the topic does so while others still want to consider the original subject. Sometimes the new topic is not relevant to the matter under discussion. A short attention span for a group meeting is natural and inevitable and we must work within the limitations it imposes.

Most of what we have said about a group's short attention span comes from research on what members said during the meetings. Investigators studied the group's communication and noted when the group changed topics. Of course during any given period of time during the meeting, people may or may not be listening to what is being said. Thus the job of holding everybody's attention is probably even more difficult than the evidence, gathered by looking at the content of the messages, indicates.

When several people are fighting for control of the channels of communication or trying to take over the meeting as message sources, they often do not listen to others. Early in a meeting whose participants do not know each other well, a member who wants to make a good impression may try to make a brilliant comment or say something funny. When he has to move out of the limelight he often does not listen to the next person but thinks about what he will say next.

Clearly, people in small groups have difficulty keeping their attention on an idea so they all can understand it and give their opinions about it. They have trouble chaining together several ideas to get the big picture or see how things relate to one another. Yet if the meeting has work to do, they feel pressure to get on with the job. Participants in a discussion with a purpose do not like the aimless skipping from idea to idea that is common in social conversations. If the group has an outline or an agenda for the meeting, the members will keep looking at the plan and using it to measure how well they are doing. When the discussion leaves the agenda, they often comment that they are getting off the topic or that much still should be done.

People vary as to how much fooling around they can stand in a meeting. Some are uncomfortable unless the point of the meeting is clear and the outline of topics is specific. They want the group to stick to business. Others feel hemmed in by a sticking-to-business approach. They have what seems to them an important or exciting comment and they want to say it even if it does not relate directly to the topic under discussion.

How does a person organize a discussion in a realistic and yet productive way? At times participants want and need the freedom to suggest ideas and mull them over without worrying too much about how they hang together or how they fit into the agenda. At other times, a group needs and wants to get on with the job and to get things organized. At this point, group members seem to feel they know what they want to do and they are tired of rehashing things that are clear or decided. You should be alert to the alternate needs for free-wheeling and for structure. Most groups develop a rhythm in regard to when they want to be loose and easy and when they want to get things organized. Careful attention to verbal and nonverbal cues can help you decide about any given group. For example, members of a group may display frustration when the chairman reminds them their discussion is off the topic. A person may accept the suggestion that his comment is out of order in a grumpy fashion, sitting back in his chair and frowning. Another person may say, "I don't want to make a motion or ask for a decision but I would like to throw out a few ideas and see what you think of them before we get down to business." When you see gestures or hear comments expressing the desire for less concern with the agenda or with structure, you should go along with the group members and give them a chance to kick the ideas around.

Other verbal and nonverbal cues indicate that the group wants more structure. A member might look at his watch, shift in his seat, and let his attention wander. When several people seem to be saying, "Let's cut out the talk and get down to business," or "What should we do to get rolling?" the chairman or someone else in the meeting may suggest that they divide up some work or follow an outline, and the group will accept the suggestion and stay with an outline. When they wish to have a more tightly organized meeting, their attention span will continue to be short but they will welcome the attempts to get them back to the business at hand and willingly follow such suggestions.

A realistic picture of how groups work includes the notion that groups do not systematically pick the best solution from a

the key ideas

Every organized attempt to get things done in our society requires working with discussion groups.

The small group is an identifiable social entity.

The best size for a group discussion is probably five members.

Groups composed of even numbers of people tend to be less stable and rewarding than groups of odd numbers.

Every organization has some meetings that are rituals.

Discussions may be used to brief or instruct the participants.

Some group meetings advise the person or persons with the authority to make decisions.

An extremely important kind of meeting is one called actually to make a decision.

People in a group without a history but which is expected to meet again size up each other very carefully.

The participants in a one-time meeting with no history and no future are generally willing to accept assigned leadership.

The people in a one-time meeting take short cuts to structure their group so they can get on with the business.

The moderator of a one-time meeting is expected to attend to the administrative details of setting up the discussion.

---

carefully drawn list of possible solutions; rather, they tend to throw out the worst, the not so good, and the fair, until they are left with several good answers which they mull over until the final decision emerges. The group circles problems rather than dealing with them in a straight line. Thus, a sensible agenda might well suggest a run at topics A, B, and C in about 30 minutes and then a return to the total agenda for a more penetrating discussion. The group needs to find the areas of quick agreement and the points of minor and of serious conflict.

Groups tend to approach the total problem, grabbing hold of it almost any place in order to get started. Their first pass at the

in chapter 11

During the course of a one-time discussion the moderator is expected to start the meeting, make transitions, summarize, take votes, and generally guide the group.

The participant in a discussion is expected to follow the moderator's lead, enter into the discussion with enthusiasm, and stick to the point.

The main reason many people get upset with meetings is that they have a clear, simple, and impossible ideal for a good discussion.

The ideal discussion is seldom encountered in real life.

Groups, like individuals, have short attention spans.

When several people are fighting for control of the channels of communication, they often do not listen to one another.

Members in discussions have trouble chaining ideas together and getting an over-all picture of the topic they are discussing.

People vary as to how much fooling around they can tolerate in a meeting.

At times, particularly early in a discussion, participants want and need the freedom to introduce ideas and mull them over without worrying too much about sticking to an agenda.

Later in a discussion, participants want some structure to organize their work.

Decisions tend to emerge from group discussions rather than being carefully discussed, and voted upon.

---

topic results in a rather simple approach. They return again, dig more deeply, and begin to cut closer to the important difficulties. When people start to argue and disagree they feel social tension and become uncomfortable, so they pull back and turn to less painful matters. After a time they return to the central issue and drive still closer to a solution. The approach-withdrawal action is typical of groups making tough decisions.

A group often appreciates a relatively free and unstructured period early in the meeting to allow a quick survey of all the business and get some idea of how people feel about things. Some members will need to prod the others to get down to the important arguments, because groups do not like to discuss touchy subjects. If you watch for the tendency to take flight, you can often help the group by pushing for a discussion of the tough issues. Once a decision has emerged, the group ought to state formally, confirm, and plan details to implement the decision. At the point of getting things in order to carry out a decision, the members are usually pleased to have an outline or an agenda and work through these items with fewer digressions during the last stages of the problem-solving process.

SUGGESTED PROJECTS

1 / The class is divided into one-time meeting discussion groups of five or six, and the instructor provides each group with a timely community or campus topic to discuss. A moderator is appointed and the group plans a brief agenda. The group tries to have a good discussion and, at the same time, to let everybody participate equally. To aid in this equal participation, each group member is given the same number of poker chips or tokens of some sort. Each time a member speaks, he has to "spend" a token. When all his tokens are spent, he can no longer participate. Each group should devote 10 minutes after the discussion to evaluating the effect of striving for absolutely equal participation during the meeting.

2 / Attend a one-time meeting of a real-life campus group. Write a short paper describing and evaluating the leadership of the meeting. List the specific techniques used by the leader to keep the discussion moving, on the track, and with maximum involvement of the group members.

3 / Find three real examples that have occurred in the last month in your community of each of the following kinds of group discussion meetings: (1) ritualistic, (2) briefing sessions, (3) instructional meeting, (4) consultative meeting, (5) decision-making meeting.

SUGGESTED READINGS

Bormann, Ernest G., and Nancy C. Bormann. *Effective Small Group Communication.* Minneapolis: Burgess, 1972.

Brilhart, John K. *Effective Group Discussion.* Dubuque, Iowa: William C. Brown, 1967.

Phillips, Gerald M. *Communication and the Small Group.* Indianapolis: Bobbs-Merrill, 1966.

12 how to communicate in work groups

Many of the same basic communication skills that are important in the one-time meeting can be used in communicating in continuing groups. The essential difference between the one-time meeting and the meetings of groups that work together over a period of time is that the work group's history influences the participants' thoughts about the future, and the future hopes and plans influence the present. A basketball player can learn some important skills in a pick-up game with two or three other players on a side using half a basketball court. You can learn important communication skills in a one-time meeting in much the same way as the player learns in the simpler game situation. When a basketball player takes part in a full-dress game, however, with five players on each side and the entire court in use, he acquires a whole new set of skills relating to the teamwork involved, the potential for more complicated plays, and the psychological momentum of the real game. In this chapter we will take the principles and skills of the one-time meeting and build upon that foundation the small group theory that has to do with continuing groups. We will start with the *ad hoc,* or standing, committee and then examine the effect of an organizational structure on the work groups that do the organization's tasks.

The work group is a social event. When several people share ideas or produce a product, a whole new social dimension is added. The first question in the mind of every person in a new work group is: *How do I relate to these other people as a human being?* Every member wants this question answered and he wants it answered early. Even after he has been in the group for months or years, he wants the answer repeated from time to time.

If a person feels that the others like, admire, and respect him, enjoy his company, and consider his ideas important, he can relax and turn his full attention to doing the job. Such an atmosphere of trust and understanding should be the goal of every participant, and *particularly* of every manager, chairman, moderator, or leader of a work group.

We are discussing only those groups that have a job to do. Inevitably the members expect to, and usually want to, concentrate on the job. If the group is a discussion meeting or conference, they want to start talking about the agenda. If the group is working in an office, the members want to start reading the mail, filing papers, drafting letters, holding conferences. If it is a production group, the workers need to get the machines rolling. The family too is a working group; its job is to maintain the living arrangements of its members and manage their day-to-day existence. Many studies have been made on "the family as a group." The group's work is hampered by poor plans, misunderstandings, faulty reasoning, inadequate concepts, bad information, and most importantly, the way directions and orders are given and received. *A whole book could be devoted to the subject of giving and receiving orders.* Orders must be given, but when you give another person an order, the task and social areas come into conflict. If the group member thinks the direction indicates that the leader feels superior to him or is using the group for his own purposes, the order may be misunderstood or disobeyed even though it is a good order.

A good work group has high morale. The members are happy with the group; they enjoy working with the others on the job and are pleased with their place in the group. They receive a sense of belonging and a feeling of personal satisfaction from their role.

A good group gets things done. It reaches its goals with a minimum of wasted motion. It turns out a large quantity of a high-quality product, wins games, solves problems, makes good decisions.

Some people think productivity is all that counts, but the individual should gain a sense of satisfaction and worth from his participation in the group. We do not believe that the individual exists solely for the group. The group has certain duties and responsibilities to the individual.

Cohesiveness is the key to successful work groups. *Cohesiveness* refers to the ability of the group to stick together. Another term for the same quality is *group loyalty*. A highly cohesive group is one in which the members work for the good of the group. They form a tightly knit unit and they help one another. They exhibit team spirit. They reflect the motto of Alexander Dumas' *Three Musketeers*, "All for one and one for all."

Cohesiveness encourages increased and improved communication, morale, and productivity. Cohesive groups do more work because members take the *initiative* and help one another. They distribute the work load among themselves, and take up the slack in times of stress. People in groups with little cohesiveness tend to stand around and wait for assignments. They do what they are told to do and no more. They do not care about the work of others. While members of cohesive groups volunteer to help one another, people in groups with little cohesiveness look out primarily for themselves.

The more cohesive the group, the more efficient the communication within the group. Cohesiveness encourages disagreement and questions. Both are necessary to communication. Highly cohesive groups disagree among themselves. A member of such a group cannot stand by and watch the others do a shoddy job or make a wrong decision. His group is at stake. He must speak up and do what he can to assure its success. Such disagreements improve the quality and quantity of the work by assuring a high level of communication. Cohesiveness encourages questions because in the cohesive group, every member knows his place and is secure. His position is not threatened if he admits he does not know something. Indeed, the welfare of the group requires that each member have adequate information. The group rewards questions that help it achieve its goals. Likewise, the important member does not feel insulted when people demand more information. He is more interested in the welfare of the group than in his own personal feelings. Since the group largely succeeds or fails depending upon the efficiency of its communication, the cohesive group encourages its members to work cooperatively to achieve understanding.

To build cohesiveness for your group, you need to know some of the dynamics of group process. Every member of the work group is constantly experiencing pushes into and pulls away from the group. The cohesiveness of the group changes from day to day. A unit that is highly cohesive this year—an effective, hard-hitting group—may next year suffer a series of reverses or a change of personnel that causes it to lose cohesiveness and be less effective. If the group comes in competition with similar groups, cohesiveness is usually increased. Athletic teams develop high levels of team spirit and will to win because they compete with other teams in a win-or-lose situation. Coaches know the importance of cohesiveness and how to build it. On the other hand, a *competing* group may try to lure a member away from his group and thus decrease his feeling of commitment. If you wish to examine the cohesiveness of your group, you must look to the other groups that are competing for the loyalty of the members. The attractiveness of his group for a given member is partly dependent on the character of the *next best group* he could join. If the next best group becomes more attractive, a person may leave his original group.

If you want to know how attractive your group is to a member, total the rewards it furnishes him and subtract the costs; the remainder is an index of group attractiveness. At any given moment, an individual feels the pull of his group because it satisfies one or more of his basic needs.

If you understand how a group can satisfy the needs of its members, you are well on the way to understanding how to make a group more cohesive. A group can provide its members with material rewards such as money, with social rewards such as the sense of belonging, with prestige rewards that come from being part of a respected group, with an opportunity to do good work and to achieve, with the chance to fight for a good cause, and with a sense of individual significance and worth. Think of a group you are working with and ask of each member: What is this person getting out of the group? Run down the list. Does the group give the person material rewards or does it cost him money to belong? Does the group give the person social rewards? If you wish to improve the group, the next step is to see if changes can increase the rewards the group furnishes for the individuals who are not committed to the group.

BUILDING A POSITIVE SOCIAL CLIMATE

One way to increase the attractiveness of a group is to build a social climate that is rewarding and fun for all members. When the members of a new work group meet for the first time they begin to interact socially. They nod or talk to one another. They smile, frown, and laugh. All these things help build a climate that is pleasant, congenial, and relaxed, or one that is stiff and tense. A positive social climate makes the group attractive, builds cohesiveness, and encourages people to speak up and say what they really mean.

Investigations of the social dimension of groups indicate three kinds of verbal and nonverbal communication that build good social feelings among group members, and three that build a stiff and negative social setting. The positive communications are shows of solidarity, of tension release, and of agreement. The negative messages are shows of antagonism, of tension, and of disagreement.

Any action or statement that indicates to the others that the new group is important is a show of solidarity. Raising another's status, offering to help do something for the group, volunteering, or indicating you are willing to make a personal sacrifice for the group shows solidarity.

The opposite of showing solidarity is showing antagonism to the group or to another person. While shows of solidarity build a pleasant spirit and rapport, shows of antagonism make the others uncomfortable.

People in new groups always feel a certain amount of tension. Embarrassment, shyness, and uneasiness when meeting with strangers are shows of social tension. When a discussion group first meets, everyone experiences *primary* tensions. They feel ill at ease. They do not know what to say or how to begin. The first meeting is tense and cold and must be warmed up. When groups experience primary tension, the people speak softly; they sigh, and they are polite. They seem bored and uninterested. No person is really bored when he has an opportunity to speak up and make a name for himself. Every individual, however, gambles a great deal by plunging into the meeting, by taking an active part. He may make a good showing. A person who has had success in similar situations in the past may be more willing than others to take this chance. The others may be impressed by his ability and decide they like him as a person; on the other hand, they may be irritated by him, decide he is stupid and uninformed, reject him. This gamble makes a person feel nervous and tense, and he may take flight from the situation by pretending he is not interested. Do not be misled. The person who seems bored and uninterested is really tense and most interested, particularly in the social dimension of the group. If the meeting never releases the primary tension, the whole style of future meetings may be set in this uncomfortable mold. It is vital that the primary tension be released early! Tension is released through indications of pleasure such as smiles, chuckles, and laughs. Spend some time joking and socializing before getting down to business. Judiciously used, socializing is time wisely spent. Once the primary tension is released, however, the group should go to work.

Once people relax and get down to work, new and different social tensions are generated by disagreements over ideas and by personality conflicts. Secondary tensions are louder than primary ones. People speak rapidly, interrupt one another, are impatient to get the floor and have their say; they may get up and pace the room or pound the table. When secondary tensions reach a certain level, the group finds it difficult to concentrate on its job. When that point is reached, the tensions should be released by humor, direct comment, or conciliation. Secondary tensions are more difficult to bleed off than primary ones. There are no easy solutions, but the tensions should not be ignored. By all means, bring them out into the open and talk them over.

Agreement is one of the basic social rewards. When the group members agree with a person, they say, "We value you." When the others agree with us, we lose our primary tension; we loosen up; we get excited; we take a more active part in the meeting. The more people agree, the more they communicate with one another.

Disagreements serve as negative-climate builders. When people disagree, they grow cautious and tense. *Disagreements are socially punishing but absolutely essential to good group work.* They are double-edged. They are necessary to sound thinking. Yet, disagreements always contain an element of personal attack. The person who finds his ideas subjected to rigorous testing and disagreement feels as though he is being shot down.

One of the reasons that the number of disagreements increases with a rise in cohesiveness is that groups must develop enough cohesiveness to afford disagreements and still not break up. The rate of disagreements is often highest in the family—the most cohesive unit in our society. How often someone complains, "You're so much nicer with strangers than with the members of your own family!"

Some people try to cushion the hurt in a disagreement by saying things such as, "That's a good idea, *but . . .*" or "That's right. I agree with you, *but. . . .*" Eventually the others discover that these prefatory agreements or compliments are just ways of setting them up for the knife. They begin to cringe as the " . . . *but* I think we ought to look at the other side of it" hits them. The fact is, disagreements must be understood to mean: Stop, this will not do. When they are thus understood, no amount of kind words of introduction serves to sugar-coat them.

An important way to resolve conflicts is by building group cohesiveness. Another way to help in conflict situations is to do things to knit the group back together after a period of heavy disagreement. Often disagreements increase as the group moves toward a decision. Good groups use the positive-climate builders after the decision is reached. They joke and laugh. They show solidarity. They say, "It was a good meeting." "It accomplished something." "Let's all get behind this decision." They compliment the persons who advocated the rejected plan. They tell them they are needed, that the group cannot succeed without their help. Another technique sometimes used by successful work groups is to allow one person to become the "disagreer." He tests most of the ideas and the group expects him to do so. Whenever they feel the need for disagreements they turn to him. They reward him by giving him a nickname or by joshing him about how disagreeable he is. Since he plays the role of critical thinker, other members are less hurt by his criticisms because, "After all, he disagrees with everybody."

GROUP ROLES

In Chapter 11 we described the one-time meeting. Here we analyze the dynamics of an *ad hoc* group that starts without a history but continues to meet over a period of time until it develops a group culture and the members get to know one another well enough to form friendships, animosities, and opinions of one another.

The first important discovery from research into zero-history groups is that after several hours the members begin to specialize. That is, not every member does an equal amount of the same thing. If we analyze the content of the typical group's communication, we find that some members talk more than others and that members tend to say different kinds of things. Some give more information along the lines discussed in Chapter 7; some talk more about personal characteristics and social relationships; some make more suggestions about doing the work of the group.

When it becomes clear to a person that he is specializing and when the group discovers he is doing so, he takes a *place* in the group. He has his particular *role*. Individuals change "personality" as they go from group to group. The buxom college woman who has such a sparkling personality in class and enjoys flirting with the men may be quiet, devout, and reserved with her church circle. She may be ill-tempered and bossy with her family. Think of yourself. In one group you may be a take-charge person who gets things rolling. In another you are likable, joshing, and fun-loving, but not a leader at all. In a third group you are quiet, steady, and a responsible worker.

A member's role is worked out jointly by the person and the group. This is the basic principle. We should not blame the group's problems on innate unchangeable personality traits inherent in a troublesome person. Groups can be more neurotic than individuals and they love to blame their troubles on one member—make him the scapegoat for their failure. If we understand the nature of roles, we will no longer make that mistake. Instead of wishing we could get rid of Bill so we could have a productive group, we ask what the group is doing to Bill to make him act as he does.

Once everyone has found a place, a second important thing happens. The group judges the relative worth of each role. It gives the roles it judges more valuable a higher status than the others. After a group has been working together for several hours, a trained observer can arrange a status ladder by watching the way the members talk and act. They talk directly and more often to the people they consider important. High-status people talk more to the entire group. The high-status people receive more consideration from the others. The others listen to what a high-status individual says; they often stop what they are doing to come to him; they stop talking to hear him, and they agree more and more emphatically with him. The group tends to ignore and cut off comments by low-status members.

Since rewards of much esteem and prestige are given to high-status members, several people usually compete for the top positions. In this competition they come into conflict; there are disagreements. The group's energy is directed to the question of who will win, and attention is drawn away from the work. In extreme cases the struggles become heated and the group gets bogged down. Every new group must go through a shakedown cruise during which the members test roles and find out who is top dog, who is best liked, and so forth. During the shakedown cruise, secondary tensions mount and people who are contending for leadership come into conflict.

Each contender for a high-status role is led to specialize through both his own efforts and the group's encouragement. The group agrees with him when he does what it wants him to and disagrees when he does not; it thus discourages him from a role it considers unnecessary or unacceptable. A given person does not have a monopoly on the role assigned him in this way, but he fulfills most of that role's functions in the group.

Group stability and communication increase side by side. When a group achieves a stable role structure and a high level of cohesiveness, an increase in feedback usually follows. A person who is strongly attracted to the group and wishes it well wants to maximize communication. He knows the group will do a better job if each member is thoroughly briefed. Therefore, if he does not know, he is likely to ask. In addition, if he has a stable place in the group, admitting his ignorance does not hurt his reputation. Sometimes bad habits that developed during role struggles carry over, and groups continue to function without adequate feedback. The group should make periodic evaluations of the feedback and make conscious plans to encourage it as needed.

Just as the need to appear more knowledgeable disappears with stable structure, so does the need to show off. A person can relax and be honest in a group with a high level of cohesiveness, and the change in attitude allows greater concentration on listening to the message. When roles stabilize, the members no longer feel the need to view each message in personal terms. They no longer think, "Does this message mean so-and-so is leadership material? that he likes me? that he doesn't like me?" Members can become more message-centered, which is the first step to improved listening. The members of an organization vary as to their skills in the art of communication. Some may have trouble holding long chains of argument in mind. Achieving effective communication takes considerable time and tension-producing effort. Communication is hard work. Groups should establish the rule that enough time will be allocated and spent (not wasted) to ensure that the proper level of understanding is reached during the meeting.

Formal status within a community or organization poses an almost insurmountable barrier to successful communication. The presence of a high-status person in a meeting immediately inhibits the free flow of communication and feedback. People wait for the high-status person to take the lead; they wait for cues from him about the proper tone of response. They tend to tell the high-status person only what they think he would like to hear. If a feeling of cohesiveness is generated within the work group, the dampening effect of the high-status person can be overcome to some extent. If the others discover he is sincerely interested in the good of the group, tolerates disagreements, and recognizes the necessity of sound communication, a productive meeting should follow.

Of all the roles that emerge in a work group, none has fascinated the philosophers, writers, social scientists, and man in the street more than the high-status, influential role of leadership.

In our country we are of two minds about leadership. If a member of a new group suggests that another person would be a good leader, that person's response typically is, "Oh, no! Not me.

Someone else could do a better job." Despite such protests, nearly every member of every group would like to lead. We would like right now to dispel that old saying that some people are born leaders and others born followers. This just is not so. All people would like to be leaders and usually are, if not in one group, in some other group. Some people have more skills in the leadership area and become leaders in more groups. But never underestimate the desire of every member of any group to take over the leadership role. Publicly, people sometimes do not admit this, but privately, they usually do.

Why this ambivalence? On the one hand, our democratic traditions suggest that all men are created equal and that nobody is better than anybody else. We maintain a belief in a classless society. Many groups in the 1960s made a strong commitment to not striving for leadership and tried hard to do away with the leadership concept in their group work because they found it distasteful. They preferred the idea of working in a commune or cooperative rather than in a corporation and tried to arrange their groups so there would be no "leaders."

Even the people dedicated to denying leadership because it meant power, and they viewed power as evil, discovered that their groups needed structure to survive and that structure implied leadership.

The most satisfactory explanation of leadership defines it as a result of the individual's traits (inherited characteristics plus training), the purposes of the group, the pressures put on the group from the outside, and the way the persons in the group talk, work, and relate with one another.

Such a contextual explanation provides a more complete view of leadership than other approaches. It includes the idea that leaders are to some extent "born," but it also suggests that potential leaders can achieve skills and improve talents. The contextual approach (the consideration of the total context, or all components, of each instance of "a group") explains why someone who emerges as leader in one group may fail to emerge as the leader of a second, apparently similar, group.

The members of a group spend time and energy on leadership because it is so important to the success of the group. We are touchy about the people who boss us around. We do not like to take orders. If we have to, we prefer a leader who gives wise orders in a way we can tolerate. The leader makes crucial suggestions and decisions about the way the work will be divided and the way the material resources of the group will be distributed. In the end, the group rejects potential leaders until they are left with the person who seems best able to lead *for the good of all.*

Sometimes the struggle for leadership is never resolved. Such groups become invalids. The members spend their time in backbiting and getting back at internal enemies. If after working together for some time a group is left with two or three potential leaders, each having substantial handicaps, the leadership may not be resolved.

CENTRAL PERSONS

Some people are so dominant in their verbal and nonverbal communications in a new work group that they fascinate the others. They may be positive or negative people; we shall call them *central* persons. A central person may be a *star.* He may be unusually capable and a potential asset to the group's productivity, or he may be exceptionally skillful at human relations and unusually charming. A central person who seems extremely hostile to the group and its purposes, who downgrades the work, or who makes it plain he feels the other members are incapable, is a potential threat to the group. A central person may even be someone who is unusually apathetic and uninvolved and simply refuses to take part in the group. All these people are central because they distract the group's attention from its tasks.

A common threatening central person is the *manipulator.* He comes to the group with the intention of exploiting it for his own ends. He intends to take it over and run it. Manipulators tend to be either *hard sell* or *soft sell.* The hard-sell manipulator usually comes on strong. He talks a great deal and takes charge immediately with a strong hand. "Let's get down to business. Now here's what we will do." When the group resists his leadership, he tries to argue and browbeat the others into line. When someone resists him, the others swing to support the contender, and the hard-sell manipulator then stands alone against the group, trying hard to talk everyone down. Sometimes, the hard-sell manipulator is not immediately challenged and is then certain he has succeeded in taking over. When he gives orders, however, they are not followed. People continually misunderstand or fail to follow through. He decides he has not been working hard enough at his leading, so he begins to give his orders slowly, carefully, in simple English as though he were talking to morons. This arouses even greater resentment and gold-bricking. He decides the group members are all lazy and irresponsible. Inevitably, another contender emerges and becomes leader. The manipulator is now extremely frustrated. His self-image is badly dented. He came into the group confident of his superiority and his ability to run the group his way, and the group has rejected him. He seldom examines where he has failed. Usually he turns on the group members; they are ignorant and stupid. If he remains in the group, he is often a troublemaker. Finding him an acceptable role takes ingenuity.

The soft-sell manipulator is often much more successful in his second phase. He often emerges for a time as the leader. He has many tricks and formulas of human relations at his command. He is friendly and congenial. He seems less bossy and more democratic. He sizes up the group to see who can be conned and who will be troublesome. He does more work outside the group's formal meetings, such as chatting with this or that member over coffee. He is a politician. After several weeks of working together, however, the others find him out. They discover that he is getting his way and that under his apparently congenial and democratic façade, he is using the group for his personal ends. When the soft-sell manipulator is found out, a challenger comes forward, and the group reshuffles roles until a new leader emerges.

CHANGING MEMBERSHIP

A change in group personnel is always unsettling. If a new person is added, this person brings with him certain skills and talents, and a role has to be found for him. All the roles have to be reshuffled to free enough duties to provide the new man with a job. When a member is removed, a role struggle again results. The remaining members must take on the tasks that the former member used to do. If he had important duties, the members who stand to gain by *climbing* upward on the status ladder may come into conflict. When a member is replaced, the new man does not simply take over his predecessor's role; reshuffling of all roles is necessary. The importance of realizing that any change in a group's personnel causes problems cannot be overstated. This knowledge will help you to help any group in which you are a member through the inevitable reshuffling of roles.

The effect of changing personnel by adding, removing, or replacing individuals is a repeat of the shakedown cruise. The typical result is a period of role instability and struggle that surprises and frustrates the members. People often do not understand what is going on and why it must go on. They respond by blaming the new member. "Everything was fine until he came." Or they bemoan the loss of a member. "Before John left, everything went along fine; we sure miss John."

FORMAL LEADERSHIP

Many of the groups to which we belong are neither one-time discussions nor *ad hoc* committees. Many groups are not composed altogether of peers and everyone does not start out equal. Many work groups function within a *formal* organization. The salesman works *under* a sales manager within a corporation. The teacher supervises a group within the framework of the class. The executive committee of the fraternity chapter functions within the larger organization. People come to such work groups with different status. Sometimes the status is internal to the organization, such as the dean meeting with a group of students. Sometimes the status is external to the group, such as a famous surgeon and a famous financier meeting on the same committee as student nurses and welfare mothers. Although status differences introduce complications, the basic process of group development can be adjusted to take these into account. In our consulting with many real-life organizations and businesses, we have found the principles transfer readily and facilitate understanding of the workings of so-called "structured" as well as unstructured groups. To illustrate the transfer, we will show how leadership is related to the management of organizational work groups. Using this application as a guide, you can make similar modifications of the principles to fit other situations.

The formal structure of an organization is static. The informal work groups that develop and change with a turnover in personnel and with fluctuating working conditions are dynamic. They constantly change, a little or a lot. Frequently the informal organization departs from the formal organization. The chart no longer fits the realities. You cannot figure out a man's power and esteem by finding out whether he is a supervisor, a vice-president, or an engineer. When formal leadership departs from natural leadership, trouble often follows. The real boss may not be the man with the title. What then?

The role struggle between a man with a formal position which can help him in his battle for control and a man with the esteem and power furnished by his standing with the members can

the key ideas

When people must work together, a social dimension resulting largely from communication is added to any work project.

When someone structures the group's work, the social and task dimensions come into conflict because giving and taking orders causes social tension.

Good work groups have good morale and get things done.

A highly cohesive group is one in which the members work for the good of the group.

The more cohesive the group, the better the communication, because cohesiveness encourages disagreements and questions.

At any given moment a person feels attracted to a group if it satisfies one or more of his basic needs.

People in new groups always feel some social tension because they are unsure how the others will react to them as people.

The person who seems bored and uninterested at a first meeting of a group is probably tense and most interested, particularly in how the others would view him if he spoke up.

Agreement is one of the basic social rewards in our society. Disagreements are socially punishing but absolutely necessary to good group work.

One important fact of group dynamics is that members tend to specialize in doing certain tasks over a period of time.

---

be long and bloody. Let us say that a person in a position of formal leadership leaves the organization and a new man takes his place. Assume that the replacement is a stranger to the members in the work group. The entire group is subjected to a shakedown cruise. In addition, the new manager must assume certain leadership functions for the work group because the formal position guide says he must. He is expected by top management and by the organization to lead his group immediately. He is not, however, accepted as the natural leader of the group without a period of

in chapter 12

When all members have a common expectation about how a person will behave, that individual has a *role* in the group.

A member's role is worked out jointly by the person and the group.

Members award a higher status to those roles they judge more valuable to the group.

Feedback is related to role stability and cohesiveness because a person can ask questions with less fear of losing status in a cohesive and stable group.

Formal status within a community or an organization poses a barrier to successful communication.

The leadership role is the one most fascinating to both the general public and the experts.

In our culture we both deplore leadership as an undesirable feature of a classless democracy and applaud the successful person who rises to a position of power.

The members of a group spend much time and energy on the leadership question because it is so important to the successful achievement of group goals.

A change in group personnel is always unsettling.

Many work groups function within a formal organization which, in turn, exercises a controlling influence on certain factors of communication.

When the informal organization departs from the formal structure, one can predict communication problems.

testing. He must find his role in the informal groups within his department according to the basic principles of group process. When he finally assumes his role, it is slightly different from that of the former manager, and the whole group experiences a re-shuffling of roles.

This same new manager does have certain standard levers furnished him by the organization to help him emerge as leader. These may include the right to increase salaries, give bonuses, promote, assign jobs and vacations, and punish tardiness, malingering, and poor work. You may think these levers give the new man an insurmountable advantage. Wisely used by a person who understands the dynamics of small groups, they may. Sometimes, however, the authority to punish and reward members turns out to be a a handicap rather than a help.

Here is how this might happen. The new manager, whoever he is, is a marked man! His boss is watching him closely to see how he will work out. He tries to do an exceptionally good job. The members of the group watch him more carefully. Will he turn out to be a man they can follow? If he begins with strong and decisive leadership moves, he can expect some resistance. He may also find he is misunderstood. Misunderstanding directions is a common way of resisting an order. To a man on trial, eager to prove his efficiency, such response may lead to frustration and anger. The new manager has now come to a crucial point. If he controls his anger and asks, "What have I done wrong?" he may be able to mend his fences and start to build a role of leadership within the group. If he understands the way people emerge as natural leaders, he may win the power and esteem that the authority and prestige of his job deserve, and without which he must remain ineffective and unsatisfied to some extent. If he lashes back and pulls the levers by which he can force members to obey, he will start a spiral that results in malingering, more crises, less production, and trouble with upper management. If he panics and decides he has not been firm enough, he may wildly put pressures on his men. He will lay down the law, read off the lazy workers, make sure his directions are crystal clear, and supervise the most minute details of the work.

The members of his unit will then reject him as their leader and someone else will emerge as the natural leader—the one to whom they all go with their gripes. Such groups disturb their members. Morale declines. Members have difficulty talking about anything but their troubles. They vent their spleen on "him" and on any members who have sold out to "him." They plot and plan ways to get back at "him."

Although our example applied the knowledge about the work group to a hypothetical business organization, the same principles apply to the newly elected club, sorority, or fraternity president, or to the Student Union Board members, the Black Student Union officers, the American Indian Movement, the YMCA board members, or any of the dozens of organizations, large or small, to which you belong now and to which you will belong in your lifetime.

SUGGESTED PROJECTS

1 / Divide the class into groups of five. For each group, have five common group roles printed on slips of paper that are folded up and picked blindly by the group members. No one discloses the role he has drawn. Discuss some perennial problem (for example, the need for more individual student–teacher time in most college courses) and stay in the role you have drawn throughout the discussion. After 5 minutes, stop the discussion and have each member write down the roles he thinks the *others* have taken. After this, compare notes and discuss roles in groups. If you drew a role very unusual for you, explain the difficulties you found trying to stay in character. Was there any feeling that, as you continued to play the assigned role, you began to feel more natural in it as time went on?

2 / Students are placed in leaderless groups of five or six. Each group is furnished with a tape recorder and spends one or two class meetings preparing a panel discussion program on some important public issue to present to the class. The group selects a moderator for the program and, after discussing the topic in front of the class for 30 minutes, throws the discussion open for audience participation. Each member of the group listens to one of the tapes taken during the planning meetings and writes a short paper evaluating the role emergence that takes place during the planning sessions and the actual presentation.

3 / Select a small group that you work with on a regular basis. This group could be part of an office or business organization, a committee of students working on a long-term project, a church or social action group, any task-oriented small group. Keep a journal of your experiences in the group. Describe the group's cohesiveness, role structure, and leadership. Where do you fit into the group's role structure?

SUGGESTED READINGS

Borden, George A., Richard B. Gregg, and Theodore G. Grove. *Speech Behavior and Human Interaction*. Englewood Cliffs, N.J.: Prentice-Hall, 1969.

Bormann, Ernest G. *Discussion and Group Methods*. New York: Harper & Row, 1969.

Bormann, Ernest G., and Nancy C. Bormann. *Effective Small Group Communication*. Minneapolis: Burgess, 1972.

Gulley, Halbert E. *Discussion, Conference, and Group Process*, 2nd ed. New York: Holt, Rinehart and Winston, 1968.

13 how to listen

Earlier in the book we described a model of the process of communication in which a source encoded a message and transmitted it through channels to a receiver. Our model includes the notion that the source has an objective or intent which causes him to start the conversation. When one person talks with another, the problem of whose objective will control the communication must be faced early in the interchange. If the target of the comment refuses to accept the speaker's objective or intent, he may encode messages with an objective of his own and try to assume the role of message source and force the other person into the role of listener (receiver). When the second person comments in a way designed to establish *himself* as a message source, what the second person says is not feedback. Feedback refers to that feature of the complete act of communication, as portrayed by our model, where the receiver provides verbal and nonverbal cues about how he interprets the speaker's messages.

Often people refer to the situation where nobody wants to be a receiver and everybody wants to be a message source as an instance of poor listening. The problem in such cases is not necessarily lack of listening skill, but unwillingness of the participants to assume the role of listeners.

The unwillingness to be the receiver of messages often stems from poor interpersonal relationships. The person who does not know the speaker personally may be ill at ease, tense, and unsure. He is unwilling to play the role of receiver until he knows the speaker better and can feel at ease in playing the part of the listener. The person who is suspicious, hostile, or antagonistic to the speaker often refuses to assume the role of listener because he feels that working to achieve any objective of the other person will be to his disadvantage. Listening is not a passive state that just happens; it is an active state of being, and a person has to agree to do it, be able to do it, and work at doing it.

Also common is the situation in which people do not assume the role of receiver when someone is giving a classroom lecture, a campaign speech, or a business presentation. The members of such audiences do not play the role of receiver because they are taking flight from the situation. There are a dozen other places they would rather be, and a dozen other things they would rather be doing. Playing the role of receiver is a time-consuming, tension-producing job. A person must often exert effort to keep his attention from wandering.

If we are at all creative, our attention can find materials more interesting than the speaker's comments. We have a colleague who claims that for years he has organized his next week's lectures every Sunday morning during the church sermon. Mental energy which could be used for listening is often spent in less constructive ways than organizing our week's work, however; perhaps the speaker has interesting mannerisms of speech or gesture, and we can count the number of times he says "y'know" or the number of times he twitches his eyelids, looks at the floor, or tries to put one hand in a nonexistent pocket in the back of his coat jacket. Perhaps a young man has spotted a great-looking girl sitting three rows in front of him in the audience and spends his time thinking how he will approach her after the lecture is over.

All too often, our minds drift away from, then back to, a speaker; we thus unthinkingly play the role of receiver for a while, then fail to do so, then find ourselves back in the role. It often happens that if we work at listening carefully to the people we least want to hear, we are amply rewarded by what we learn. In any case, we would be wise to make a conscious choice about whether we listen; we should think about whether we will be a receiver in such a listening situation and not leave the matter to chance.

Think through your own experiences and list some situations in which you were unwilling to play the part of message receiver. From time to time the decision not to listen is probably justified (as our colleague insists is the case for him when he sits in church), but the question of when you should be willing to take the role, and when not, is one that deserves more study than it usually receives.

For the remainder of the chapter we will concentrate our analysis on those situations in which you have decided that you *will* play the role of receiver. Even when you willingly take the part of a listener you will discover that the role requires some specific skills which need to be understood and practiced in order to increase listening competence.

LISTENING CAN BE LEARNED

One of the major misunderstandings in regard to listening is that once we explain the importance of it, a person will say, "You're right. I never thought much about it, but listening *is* important. From now on I will pay attention. I will listen." Like most communication skills, however, listening is not much improved by merely *trying* to listen better. Speaking and listening are learned in much the same manner as are reading and writing. The major difference is that we all learn to speak and to listen at an early age, before starting formal schooling, but most of us do not learn to read and write until we begin school. Many people, over the years, have thus come to the mistaken conclusion that we need not *study* how to speak and how to listen in school because we all already knew how to do both before coming there. Listening, like running, is learned at an early age, and just as a person with a talent for running the dashes can profit from expert coaching and diligent practice with guidance, so can anyone learn to listen more efficiently with practice under guidance from an expert in listening.

Actually, the process of hearing speech and decoding denotative meanings, interpreting attitudes, and responding with feelings and emotions to verbal messages is every bit as difficult as scanning the writing on a page and reading its meanings. For instance, when listening to a spoken message, the receiver must decipher the sounds, which may be hard to hear because of noise, faulty articulation, or too-rapid presentation. Of course the listener may ask the speaker either to repeat the message or to slow down, at least in an informal interaction, but in general, the listener has much less control of the rate of transmission of the message than has the reader, who can easily control his own reading rate.

HOW TO LISTEN MORE EFFECTIVELY

A runner may tire at the midway point in a race but force himself to continue running despite his pain and fatigue. A person listening to a speaker can do much the same thing by forcing his attention to stay on what is being said. Concentrated effort to focus on the message and understand it can overcome listening fatigue and the natural tendency of our attention to wander.

A little practice can help a person become aware of those moments when his attention begins to waver. As you listen, you need to keep part of your mind on how well you are listening; you can learn to pull yourself back to the message when you catch yourself losing interest. If the speaker is developing an idea that seems dull, trite, or uninteresting, or if he is going too slowly so that we find ourselves thinking ahead of him, we may be tempted to relax and indulge in daydreaming.

One way to keep from drifting away from a dull speaker's slow-moving train of ideas is to anticipate what point he will make next. By guessing where he will go, we arouse our interest in checking to see if, indeed, we were correct. And if we guess right, we have then thought about the idea twice and are more likely to remember it than if we had not made the prediction. If we guess incorrectly, we still may wonder why the speaker took the turn he did instead of the one we thought he would take, and in either case, we have tricked ourselves into attending to what he said.

Another tactic that can help combat the boredom of listening to a slow speaker is to take out 10 or 20 seconds from time to time to review quickly what the speaker has just said. You will find that summarizing from time to time helps you recall the important ideas later.

We have to focus our attention on any message before we can begin to interpret it. You will no doubt recall the old story about the farmer who told his neighbor he was going to teach his mule how to drag a log by a chain. After announcing his intention, the first thing the farmer did was pick up a big board and hit the mule over the head with it. "What'd you do that for?" the startled neighbor asked. "I thought you were going to teach him how to drag logs!" "Yup," the farmer nodded in agreement, "but first I have to get his attention."

Assuming that we now know how to force our attention on the message, we can learn further techniques of effective listening. We should focus on the structure of the message. People who listen for factual details tend to have trouble recalling the main ideas and seldom remember many of the facts, either. They thus end up with a vague idea about a mass of undigested material. All of us tend to remember patterns more easily than isolated details. Whole systems of memory improvement depend upon connecting the things to be remembered with something we know well. For example, when we meet a number of people at a party and wish to remember their names, if we can connect each person and each name with a house on a street that we know well, we can often recall the names of the persons later. Simply trying to remember a series of names without associations is difficult.

If you practice listening for the main outline or structure of a message, you will find your understanding increasing. You will know that you are a professional listener when you can hear a badly organized message and refit its parts into your own organizational pattern. You may, indeed, be able to recall more of what a message source said during a conversation than the speaker himself can if you organize the material more effectively than he did.

Finally, an important key to misunderstanding, even when a person is playing the role of receiver and is seeking actively to listen, is related to the third aspect of language discussed in Chapter 3. Certain words arouse our emotions. A speaker's dialect may cause us to respond with anger, suspicion, or fear. The power of words to cause emotional responses is a factor in poor listening. A person is an emotional state is generally upset and acts to some extent as though he were in shock. He loses his ability to think clearly, just as he loses his ability to make small, isolated, subtle physical movements. Someone who has become highly emotional also tends to strike out verbally, perhaps even physically, at people and objects not directly related to the cause of emotional condition. Angry people may kick an inanimate object or yell at an innocent bystander.

Even when we want to listen, we may respond emotionally to a word or phrase and lose some of our listening abilities. Just as we lose our ability to make fine adjustments with our fingers when we are nervous and upset, we begin to mishear.

Of course a certain amount of excitement can improve our ability to listen, just as stage fright can be used to help us give a better public performance. Excitement, under control, makes us function better. People can experience a considerable level of excitement and high feeling and be keyed up to more efficient use of skills and talents. Students giving speeches before a class often exhibit both the crippling effects and the positive use of excitement. One may become so emotional he goes into a sort of shock reaction, is unable to think clearly, and makes many random physical gestures. (We are glad to report that in this day of family picture-taking, making reports to classes at the elementary-school level, and excellent high-school courses in speech, we rarely encounter this degree of nervousness in a college student of public speaking.) Most students find that the excitement of giving a speech can be used to make their minds work more efficiently. Coaches of athletic teams are well aware of the fine line between working the team up for the game and getting the players wound so tightly they do far less than their best.

In listening, as in speaking before an audience and in participating in athletic events, the trick is to be genuinely involved, interested, and efficient. Remember that when you find yourself getting boiling mad, you are also losing your ability to listen well.

After we have learned the techniques of keeping our attention on a message, or structuring the message as we hear it, and of controlling our emotional responses to language, we can listen with *understanding*. When we listen to a communication with the aim of understanding, we *comprehend* the message.

Much of the difficulty we experience in working with one another we attribute to communication problems. Marriages are often said to fail because of a breakdown in communication. A colleague of ours argues, in an ironic way, that if it were not for misunderstandings, we would have a world with much more conflict and violence than we do have. His point is worth making if only as an antidote to the popular assumption that communication problems are the basic causes of all conflicts. Our colleague further argues that most people filter their incoming communications in such a way that they protect their self-image. Thus they often rearrange what others say so that it fits in with their own comfortable preconceptions, biases, and prejudices. If we always had a clear understanding of what other people were trying to say, he argues, we would come in conflict with them much more often!

Nonetheless, interpreting a message to mean something other than what the source intended can cause difficulty, and most occasions require that we at least comprehend what the other person is saying before the conversation can proceed to either agreement or disagreement.

Many times we need to do more than just understand what denotative meanings a speaker wishes to convey to us. We must also critically evaluate the message. We need to examine the speaker's assertions to see if they accurately describe the purported facts. If we can personally check what is said by observation, we can discover whether the message is true or false. Once we discover a message is false, we may go on to infer a motive or intent on the speaker's part to account for the falsehood. We may decide that the speaker deliberately misled us, in which case we may say he lied about the matter. We may decide that the source intended to tell us the truth, but he made an error. In either case, of course, although we understand what the source is saying, we do not accept the statement as an accurate depiction of events.

We may also listen critically to the form of the message and decide that it is an unsatisfactory message on formal grounds. In Chapter 10 we discussed the nature of reasoning and how the form of a message can often reveal whether it is logical. When a message says both that something is the case and that the same thing is not the case, the message contains a contradiction. We discount the contradictory message as illogical and cannot tell anything about the facts from it. The contradiction is a matter of the form of the message, the second aspect of language. Often a speaker asserts that several assumptions about the world are true and if we conclude that they are true, then we can conclude that some other statements he makes are also true. Unless the message is shaped into a logical form, the concluding statement may not follow even from true premises. For instance, if we know it is true that John has 3 apples and it is also true that Mary has 5 apples, we may still reason to a false conclusion if we decide that together they have 9 apples. In this case, the assumptions are true, but the form or logic of the message is wrong. The proper form for the sentence is $3 + 5 = 8$. When we use an improper form, such as $3 + 5 = 9$, we have made an error in the form of the argument. We do not need to check the world to see if there are 3 and 5 apples that will combine to total 9 apples; we can tell that $3 + 5 = 9$ is wrong simply by looking at the form of the statement.

Finally, we must listen carefully and criticize messages reflecting rumor, propaganda, and persuasion. People encounter rumors frequently and usually listen to them with interest. Rumors are messages in general circulation which cannot be factually confirmed, such as gossip, unofficial messages based upon guesses, or incomplete hints. Many times the rumor relates to official organizational secrets that are of considerable importance to the people in the organization. Rumors in the form of gossip often relate to matters that are socially unacceptable, and thus the concerned parties will keep them secret if possible. Gossip may relate to such things as the boss's wife becoming an alcoholic, the know-it-all neighbor's daughter's illegitimate baby, the professor who passed out drunk at the president's party—you could add to an endless list. Most people enjoy listening to gossip.

People often start a rumor in response to an unclear but important situation in an attempt to make some sense out of it. Rumors are usually in the form of speech communication, and they are passed on from person to person with some rapidity. Common sense, however, tells us that rumor is, at best, poor evidence for denotative meanings about the world of facts. Even as we admit this, we acknowledge that rumors are attractive because they seem to put us in the know about behind-the-scenes events.

Of course, rumors are not always false. Often they are unclear, confusing, or too simple, but sometimes the information passed on from an eyewitness to another person is important to us. When listening critically to any rumor, we should remember the three basic things that tend to happen to a story when it is passed on from person to person:

1 / Persons who pass a story on from one to another, tend to shorten the message, drop out details, and make it easier for the listener to understand. They arrange the remaining details into a structured and dramatic story.

2 / If some feature of the rumor is unusual, people tend to repeat and sometimes exaggerate that detail. If the story tells of an incident involving a man who is very tall, in subsequent versions the man may become huge or gigantic.

3 / The details that are repeated are often fitted into the biases of the individuals who pass on the story.

If a rumor is the best source of information about something of importance to us, we should try to figure out what the facts are as best we can, remembering how things get distorted as they are passed on by word of mouth.

Even after a person is sure he understands a message, he should critically evaluate the propaganda elements within it. In Chapter 9 we examined in detail the techniques of suggestion. A critical listener should evaluate the words a speaker picks to name things and people and to refer to properties and relations. Does the speaker always choose a word with a bad connotation to name certain people? Does he use words to slant his message in favor of some people and some programs and against other people and other courses of action? (The authors often catch their children sending out such loaded messages; two school acquaintances are always spoken of, for instance, as Dumb-Bill and Icky-Elizabeth.)

You should also consider the dramas in the message. Who are the heroes and who are the villains? What values are suggested by the dramatic actions? What are the reality links for the dramas? A critical listener should look at the motives attributed to various actors in the dramas. (Also remember that social scientists who try to study human behavior are often disillusioned about research that attributes motives to people. Attempts to study motives scientifically tend to break down in disturbing ways.)

LEVELS OF LISTENING

Earlier we used the analogy of the track star who is a dash man and the person who is an expert listener. Just as the runner sometimes trots, sometimes lopes, sometimes runs hard but easily, and on important occasions, runs with great effort and determination, so an expert listener sometimes listens for understanding, sometimes listens critically, and sometimes listens with all-out effort and every resource at his command.

Often we meet others in a casual communication situation in which the messages we send back and forth are rudimentary and fulfill certain cultural expectations about social interaction, manners, or convention. We meet an acquaintance on campus and say, "Hello; how are you?" and the other person responds, "Hi, fine; how are you?" The two of us go into the coffee shop and request, "Cuppa coffee." The waiter asks, "Cream?" We answer, "Yes, please." This sort of communication is a simple action-reaction affair in which we send and receive messages that require little listening ability. To be sure, we may misunderstand something even at the action-reaction level, but for the most part, we get along with simple listening skills at this level.

On other occasions, we are more involved in the communication event. In these instances we wish to listen, to understand, and to evaluate the messages. We then try to provide feedback; we attend carefully to what is said; we try to decipher denotative meanings; we evaluate the messages critically; and the whole process is essentially a classic expression of the basic model of communication presented in Chapter 2. The speaker willingly plays the role of message source, searches constantly for feedback, and keeps encoding new messages to achieve a level of understanding satisfactory for all parties to the communication. The listener willingly assumes the role of message receiver, asks questions, rephrases ideas to check with the source about how well he understands the ideas, and gives nonverbal cues to agreement, disagreement, understanding, confusion, and doubt.

The last communication situation is less common than the others but extremely important. On some occasions, much as a runner feels when running in an important race, the listener finds himself deeply involved in a significant and important communication event. One person encodes a message, and the listener not only comprehends and evaluates the message, but also discovers meanings in the message that had not occurred to the speaker himself. Much as a creative reader can discover more in a book than the author intended, a creative listener can make a comment that adds new meaning to the message. When the listener feeds the idea back into the communication event, the speaker sees the significance and importance of the new contribution as he reads still more into the messages that are now flowing rapidly, causing increasing excitement.

In discussions and conferences, people sometimes find themselves caught up in a chain of fantasies similar to the creative moments individuals experience when they daydream about a creative project or an important problem. Someone suggests a drama such as those we discussed in detail in Chapter 9 regarding the persuasive power of suggestion. The idea is picked up by another participant, then by another, and soon a number of people are deeply involved in the discussion and excitedly adding their reactions and ideas to it. Under the suggestive power of the group fantasy the constraints that normally hold people back are released, and people feel free to experiment with ideas, to play with concepts and wild suggestions and imaginative notions. This sort of idea interplay can also happen between two people who have reached a high level of supportive interpersonal communication.

The total involvement of the listener in a communication transaction creates a situation where the flow of meaning is no longer from source to receiver, as is the case when a programmer works with a computer, but where all participants are adding to a common reservoir of meaning until the result is greater than any one person could have managed by himself. The final growth and insight and learning in such a communication event take place in the person who originally played the role of source, as well as in the individual who began the transaction as listener. The creative involvement of all participants requires all the communication skills, including the highest levels of listening ability. Interpersonal trust, a positive social climate, skill in expressing ideas, sensitivity to dialect and suggestion, ability at nonverbal communication—all these components are important to the deep and important communication event.

An athlete does not spend all his time running important races at top speed; so, too, we should not hold up the pattern of deep significant communication as the formula for all communication. But when the time is right, and the people are in tune with

the key ideas

Often what we think of as poor listening is not so much a lack of skill as an unwillingness to play the role of receiver.

Poor interpersonal relationships among the people involved often account for their unwillingness to listen to one another.

A listener often must exert effort to keep his attention from wandering.

We should make a conscious choice about whether we will listen to a speaker; we should not leave the matter to chance.

Even a person who wants very much to listen may fail because he is unskilled in the art.

Trying to listen is not enough; practice in listening techniques with guidance is also necessary.

Listening is as difficult as reading.

We have to force our attention on a message before we can interpret and criticize it.

one another, the deep and significant communication transactions in which we participate are among our most exciting and rewarding experiences. A creative listener is as highly skilled a participant in interpersonal communication events as is a polished, fascinating speaker. Good listening requires effort within the framework of a dynamic exchange of personalities and ideas. You have to stay tuned in to someone else when you listen.

SUGGESTED PROJECTS

1 / Make a list of words that tend to make you respond in such a way that you can hardly listen to what comes next.

2 / Think back to the experiences in communication you have had in the past week. Select three situations and decide which level of listening would have been most appropriate for each. Write a short

in chapter 13

People who listened for factual details have more trouble remembering what a speaker said than people who listened for the main ideas.

If we respond emotionally to a speaker's language, we lose some of our ability to listen.

We need to understand what the other person is saying before we can intelligently agree or disagree.

When we listen critically, we need to ask if the denotative meanings are true to the facts.

A simple level of communication is the action-reaction sort of comments we make to pass the time of day or make simple requests.

The highest level of communication requires creative listening that adds meanings and insights to a message that go beyond the speaker's intentions.

A high level of communication finds the listener joining in the creation of new meanings.

A creative listener is as highly trained and skilled as is a polished and fascinating speaker.

---

paper analyzing your experience as a listener in each of the three situations. Was your listening level the most appropriate one in each instance? If not, as you look back upon the situation, can you figure out why not?

3 / Select a group that is important to you, such as your family, your fellow workers, or your close friends. Analyze the listening skill of several other people in the group, and then analyze your own listening in that group. Can you suggest ways to improve the others' listening ability as well as your own?

SUGGESTED READINGS

Barker, Larry L. *Listening Behavior*. Englewood Cliffs, N.J.: Prentice-Hall, 1971.

Bormann, Ernest G., William S. Howell, Ralph G. Nichols, and

George L. Shapiro. *Interpersonal Communication in the Modern Organization*. Englewood Cliffs, N.J.: Prentice-Hall, 1969. "Listening to the Spoken Word," pp. 167–177; "Getting the Message," pp. 183–199; "Evaluating the Message," pp. 203–212.

Huseman, Richard, C., Cal M. Logue, and Dwight L. Freshley. *Readings in Interpersonal and Organization Communication*. Boston: Holbrook Press, 1969. "Communication through Listening," pp. 457–496.

Lewis, Thomas, and Ralph G. Nichols. *Speaking and Listening: A Guide to Effective Oral-Aural Communication*. Dubuque, Iowa: William C. Brown, 1965.

Nichols, Ralph G., and Leonard Stevens. *Are you Listening?* New York: McGraw-Hill, 1957.

14 how to analyze the audience for a public speech

For much of the book we have discussed the principles of inter-personal communication as they are applied to the casual, informal conversations of our day-to-day living. We come now to specific consideration of that less frequent but extremely important form of communication—the speech one person gives to an audience.

The public speech is a formal, careful communication event—a showcase where the speaker becomes the center of atten-tion and has a chance to star or to fail in the eyes of a number of people. We thus approach public-speaking situations with more care than we do our casual, daily interpersonal conversations. We plan the public speech more carefully, we worry more about how it will go and about how the audience will respond to us and to our ideas.

Some of the time a person spends in preparing for a pub-lic speech will be devoted to questions of self. What will happen to me? Will the audience like me? Will I forget what I want to say and make a fool of myself? Will I be nervous? What should I wear? Should I try to be funny? What am I interested in? We are all interested in ourselves and will have no difficulty spending enough planning time on matters related to ourselves, how we feel, how we will benefit or be punished by the situation. Indeed, teachers of speech communication often spend a good deal of in-structional effort to pry students away from considerations of self so they can turn their attention to other facets of speech planning.

Some of the time a person spends in preparing for a public speech will be devoted to matters relating to the message itself. What would be a good topic? How can I find information related to the topic? How can I organize the speech? Usually students need to spend a good deal of time on the message in order to do well in a public speech. Some students, on the other hand, and possibly a good many faculty members, become overly concerned with the message and worry about it as though it were an entity divorced from the circumstances that surround it. You should consider yourself and your message as you prepare a public speech to be sure, but still another consideration is of equal importance.

A substantial portion of your planning time for any public speech should be given to an analysis of the audience and the situation. A good public speaker is not self-centered or message-centered, but *audience-centered.*

The audience-centered speaker makes all his final planning decisions in terms of his analysis of the listeners. Indeed, the art of interpersonal communication as well as the art of public speaking is the adaptation of ideas, world view, information, and arguments to a listener, to several listeners (a small group), or to many listeners (an audience). Let us say that three speakers have essentially the same information to present to an audience. Consider the three ways they might go about preparing the speech. One might be mostly speaker-centered and give a lecture in which his nonverbal cues indicate that he is worried about how he looks, how his voice sounds, how his gestures are affecting the audience, and seems concerned that his fingernails are clean. His verbal expressions might indicate he is sure of his own intelligence and superiority and feels he has worked up the material of the speech brilliantly, has accomplished many things, knows many great people personally, and is most important indeed. (Doesn't he sound charming?)

A second speaker might be mostly message-centered and give an obviously laboriously prepared lecture filled with difficult-to-follow statistical information and references to events and people unknown to the audience, all put together in language more suitable for a scholarly journal than a busy college audience.

A third speaker (our knight in shining armor, obviously), might be audience-centered; he delivers essentially the same information as the other two, but uses language that is clear to the audience, supports his ideas with examples that tie into the audience's experience, and holds his hearers' attention by showing how what he is saying relates to their wants, hopes, dreams, heroes, and villains. The essential difference between the first two and the the last of our hypothetical lecturers is that the last is skillful in the art of communication.

The audience-centered speaker understands that information has to be adapted to the listener and that the techniques discussed throughout this book are tools to use in adapting ideas to people. He knows about hypothetical examples and how he can use them to arouse the listener's interests. He knows what the selection of names for people and things means in terms of suggestion, and he chooses his words carefully with the audience in mind. He knows about dialect's relation to classes of society, geography, race, and ethnic backgrounds, and he understands how his own dialect and his own use of standard and nonstandard grammar will affect the people in his audience. He understands the importance of public dramas in which the members of his audience are most likely to participate; he thinks about their probable heroes and villains and adapts his remarks to all these things. He considers every element of his speech in terms of the people who will be hearing it and the occasion when they will be hearing it. In the parlance of advertising, the audience-centered speaker thinks always in terms of what it (the audience) will or will not *buy*.

GENERAL FEATURES
OF AN AUDIENCE FOR A PUBLIC SPEECH

The public speech is a cultural event with some rather clearly understood rules of procedure in most societies. Within the general set of conventions that govern the public speech are a number of common situations that tend to arouse in the people attending the occasion a similar set of expectations. People who attend a political rally have not only the general expectations of all people who come to a public-speaking occasion, but have, in addition, some more restricted notions about what will happen and what will be an appropriate response from them as audience members. People who go to a revival meeting, to a funeral, to an after-dinner speech, to a lecture, or to a keynote address at a political convention, all have some general common mental and emotional set toward the public speech, but also have some more specific expectations aroused by their stereotyped notion about, say, what a funeral eulogy should be or how a good lecture should be given.

For many public speeches the audience anticipates that one individual will deliver an extended message. The audience comes to hear a certain person speak on an advertised subject or title. The public speech has a definite format that often includes a time at which the audience is to gather and the speech is supposed to begin, and quite often, a time when the speech is to close. Americans are time-conscious and pay a great deal of attention to the length of a speech. If the speech draws out longer than they have anticipated, audience members often grow restless.

For many public speeches the audience expects and appreciates an event in which the speech itself is preceded by suitable activities that set the stage for the speaker. A simple format for a speech could be to have a local dignitary call the meeting to order and introduce the speaker by identifying his background and experience. The speaker then delivers his message, and the dignitary who introduced him thanks the speaker and closes the meeting. The basic format is often elaborated so that the speaker is preceded by music, group singing, or performances by lesser personalities to increase the audience's susceptibility to the main speaker. Big revival meetings, for instance, often have prayers, announcements, songs, and introductions before the evangelist delivers the main message of the evening. Political rallies generally have music, introductions, and some enthusiastic partisan comments before the main speaker comes to the podium.

After the speech, the audience may participate in questioning the speaker or in making comments. The occasion may call for more music or some additional comments by other people.

Generally, the people planning the public speech arrange things so the audience has some place to sit or stand, so distractions are minimized, and so the speaker is provided with a public-address system in good working order and everyone present can hear him.

The variety of specific expectations aroused by such situations as the after-dinner speech, the revival speech, the agitator's speech at a political demonstration, and the funeral eulogy would include questions such as: Does the audience expect and enjoy humor? Does the audience listen quietly to the speaker? Does the audience interrupt and heckle? Does the audience interrupt to reinforce the speaker with shouts such as "Hallelujah! Praise the Lord!" or "Right on!" "You tell 'em, George!" Does the audience expect the speaker to read a carefully prepared message? Does the audience expect the speaker to deliver an extemporaneous speech with high feeling and vigorous nonverbal communication? To some extent, of course, expectations of audiences are culture-bound; more than likely a black rural southern congregation will expect a different funeral eulogy than will a small-town Scandinavian Lutheran congregation in Minnesota.

An adept speaker may sometimes break one or two of the

expected conventions that relate to a certain speech occasion and even benefit from the novelty of the violation—people usually enjoy a mild surprise—but if he violates a number of the conventions surrounding a public speech, the audience will often be confused, indignant, bored, or even angry. If a minister, for example, introduces some humor into an ordinarily serious religious meeting, most of the audience will respond as the speaker hopes. If the minister violates other expectations, in addition—for example, in the way he is dressed, his style of language, his dialect, his use of profanity, his use of bald humor, and if he appears drunk while delivering the sermon, the audience's expectations will be seriously disturbed.

All the general and specific expectations of an audience attending a public speech put some pressure on the speaker to adapt his ideas to the form of the occasion.

People gathered in a large group to hear a public speech respond differently than they would in two-person conversations or even small discussion groups. Because one person is the center of attention and the primary source of messages, and because a large group of people play the role of receiver, the dynamics of the situation are changed in several important ways.

You will remember that in Chapter 9 we talked about the tendency of people to conform to the behavior of those around them, calling this *aping behavior*. The social pressure of 4 or 5 people is strong, but the power of 50 or 100 is much greater, and when thousands of assembled people stand up or shout, the influence of the crowd upon any individual is immense. Have you ever been part of a large audience at a football game, a student demonstration, a religious revival, when the crowd began to groan or shout or chant, and felt yourself the emotional impact of thousands of voices moved by a common feeling or emotion?

If the audience comes to a public-speaking situation expecting to hear a fire-breathing politician, a hellfire-and-damnation revival preacher, or a violent revolutionary, the members are often predisposed to respond with high feeling. The planners of the meeting, trying to fulfill these expectations, may precede the main speaker with music and warm-up speeches, as we mentioned earlier. By the time the speaker begins, the audience is quite excited, and if he is skillful, the orator will soon have focused the attention of the listeners upon his speech.

If the audience is warmed up and the speaker delivers a particularly good line, some audience members may begin to clap, yell, and shout encouragement. The response of the audience stimulates the speaker. He loses his preoccupation with self. Encouraged by a positive audience response, he is stimulated to proceed along the lines that strike a reaction. He is now more effective, and the audience responds more strongly. Not only does the audience stimulate the speaker, and the speaker in turn stimulate the audience, but the audience members stimulate each other. Excitment and emotions are contagious in a large crowd, and a person is hard put to keep quiet or remain calm in the midst of an audience caught up in the emotional response of the moment.

We have, admittedly, taken the above examples from that group of public-speaking situations which conventionally arouse expectations of emotional excitement. The same principles of audience behavior, however, apply to other situations. The audience attending a lecture by a Nobel Prize winner, for instance, places equally strong pressures to conform on individual members. If the speaker is wearing a tuxedo, if the ushers whisper as though loud and boisterous talk were out of order, if the audience sits upright and with great dignity, the pressure is strong on all audience members to do likewise. If members of the audience begin to cough, grow restless, look at their watches, all these behaviors put pressure on the speaker and other audience members alike.

The audience responds to various details of communication in a fashion that differs in some regards from the more casual and informal interpersonal speech communication situations. The larger the audience, the more likely it is to expect an elevated style of language from the speaker. The keynote speaker at a political convention generally uses a more careful and formal speech style (and is expected to do so by the audience) than the same politician uses when he is talking over a strategy move with five of his staff members in his hotel room.

The larger the audience, the more it expects and demands that the speaker appeal to the so-called "higher" motives of mankind. The new president of the United States giving an inaugural address is expected to appeal to the better nature and the more unselfish motives of the American people. The late President John F. Kennedy said in his inaugural address, ". . . ask not what your country can do for you—ask what you can do for your country." His statement was in line with the expectations for the occasion as well as for the vast size of the television audience. If the president were to express similar sentiments in the same lofty style in a meeting with an assistant and three leaders of the antipoverty movement lobbying for legislation to guarantee an annual income for everybody, he might well get, and deserve, a scornful laugh.

On the other hand, the speaker at a high-school commencement would receive an outraged reaction from much of his audience if he said he knew the seniors were not interested in a lot of pious baloney from him, that all they wanted was to get out of the auditorium, out of their robes, and into their cars to head for the nearest pot party or beer bust to get stoned out of their heads in celebration of the end of their four miserable years in high school, and that he, for one, thought they had the right idea.

The larger audience enjoys a rosy picture of the world and mankind, whereas the same message in a group of one or two people in a casual setting causes embarrassment or laughter. By the same token, the tough-headed recognition of basic desires which is appropriate to small groups of people sounds crude and disgusting in large assemblies.

One of the reasons we predict the continued importance of public speeches to large groups is that such speeches provide one of the few places in our culture where people expect and get fantasy themes composed of heroes with high motives and where they are appealed to on the basis of their better nature. No matter how shoddy the community or how crude the general mode of conduct, people require some sense of worth and significance. The appeal to the better nature of the audience is a high form of flattery and is a source of pride and significance. Aside from the speech to a large audience, the only other major source of mass communication is television, and it does not provide many rosy depictions of life and of the community. The predominant style of the fantasy themes of the newscast and the television documentary, with few exceptions, is the style of the inside dopester (a person who has all the inside information). Television newsmen tend to cut all public figures down to size and point out that important people are not larger than life, but ordinary people just like the rest of us, maybe even a little worse in some regards. The general tone of the story presented on television is factual, and what the tone presents as fact is tinged with skepticism about high motivations; the reporters appear to be continually searching for shoddy or unethical behavior. Saints are not dramatic; sinners, on the other hand, make good news copy.

ANALYZING AN AUDIENCE

While the audiences of public speeches share many similarities, each audience is also unique. The first question a skilled public speaker asks about a given audience is: How much alike are the audience members in terms of background, experience, interests, and attitudes? In Chapter 10 we discussed the statistical measures of typicality and the idea of the range within a group of statistics. If all the audience members at least resemble the typical member on important features related to the speaker, the topic of the speech, and the occasion, the problem for the speaker is clear and can be handled directly. If the audience members are greatly diverse, the problem becomes much more difficult, and the speaker may have to seek some broad and abstract common ground or some overriding goal that can in some way unite such a varied group.

A speaker may start by finding out the composition of the audience in terms of such obvious, but often important, qualities as age, sex, socioeconomic class, race, ethnic background, religion, and occupation. Not all factors are always important. For many speeches, the audience's age may be irrelevant, but for other situations, it may be crucial. We noted in Chapter 3 that dialects reflect social structure, and so a speaker planning to adapt language and grammar to his audience would need to know if the members were primarily from the working class in an inner city or from an upper-middle-class suburb, if they were predominately Mexican-American, or black, or Indian, or white.

A speaker often adapts to an audience by selecting an appropriate example or analogy to clarify a point, and if the audience is composed of farmers and their families, he selects different examples than he would if the listeners are members of the American Medical Association.

More important, often, than the general information about age, sex, and social economic background, are the audience's attitudes and interests. A person planning a persuasive speech in behalf of more state-supported junior colleges would like to know if the audience is generally in agreement that junior colleges ought to be supported, or hostile to paying more taxes for junior colleges, or interested but undecided, or apathetic to the whole question. Likewise, he would benefit from knowing how many of the audience members hold attitudes toward his position that are friendly, hostile, undecided, or apathetic.

A speaker making a thorough analysis of his audience finds that specific details are vital; the general features of the audience provide only hints that help when making a more complete study. The speaker with the time and opportunity to study the audience and the occasion would do well to apply to his analysis much of the material relating to persuasion presented in Chapters 8–10. Questions such as the following should be explored: What sort of person will these people more likely trust and believe? What can I say to get their confidence? What are the public dramas that excite and move these people? Who are the heroes of their group fantasies and public dreams? Who are their villains? What dramatic actions do they use to build a sense of community and purpose? What attitude do they take toward these lines of action? For example, if all the audience members participate in a public drama which casts the president of the United States into a heroic role, then the speaker who says that the president, whoever he is at the time, is a man of low morals, insincerity, and bad motives will find himself in trouble with that audience. On the other hand, if all the audience members participate in a common drama in which the president is cast as villain, a negative statement about him may draw a strong, positive response from the listeners. If the audience members are strongly divided in terms of their political fantasies so that some see the president as a sympathetic figure fighting villainous forces, and others see him as a dark and evil personality, the speaker may well decide not to mention the president at all!

GATHERING INFORMATION
ABOUT THE AUDIENCE

Often the experienced speaker knows what sort of information about the audience would be useful to him, but does not have the resources to collect it. In those long-range and important campaigns of persuasion where the success or failure of a new product, the election of a candidate to major office, or the organization, recruitment, and administration of a social or political movement is at stake, the campaign planners generally have sufficient resources for elaborate formal surveys of their potential audiences.

Experts in persuasion have brought scientific marketing and polling techniques to a high state of perfection and proved usefulness. Most public-relations firms, advertising agencies, professional fund-raising companies, and experts in political campaigning and revolutionary organization know how to sample the audience, administer attitude tests or questionnaires relating to opinion, and discover what a target audience thinks about a product or an issue or a particular personality. Some of the public-opinion polls publish their results in newspapers, and even speakers with little time or money can find out how various age groups with various educational backgrounds are currently responding to such general questions as: How well do you think the President has been doing? When money is available, pressure groups often take their own polls to discover audience attitudes.

Sometimes the main themes of a persuasion campaign are pretested by showing samples of the persuasive material to people, who indicate their reactions by pressing buttons on special monitoring machines or answering questionnaires.

We mention these elaborate and expensive techniques of audience analysis mostly to show how far the art has been developed beyond the mere collection of information about age, sex, and geographic origin. Most of us do not have the resources needed to use these sophisticated audience-survey techniques; yet we can often acquire useful information quickly and cheaply. While the following example is hypothetical and exaggerated, it contains elements that resemble the speech situations in which you might find yourself.

Professor Gilbert Johnson, our example, teaches at State University. He has been a life-long student of the process of eutrophication (too much plant food in a lake causing a lush growth of water plants which, in turn, decay in the late summer sucking the oxygen out of the water). When ecology became an important issue in the 1960s and 1970s, Johnson suddenly found his specialty popular with the general public. He won several awards and then attracted national notice on a television program. Soon he found himself in great demand as a speaker around the country.

Unfortunately, Professor Johnson's previous speaking experience had been in lecturing to classes of students who were already, at least to some degree, interested in the subject and willing to listen to a detailed, solid presentation. He found his public audiences growing restless, coughing, even dozing off. Gradually, over a period of months, and with the help of a fellow faculty member knowledgeable in speech communication, Johnson discovered that his problem was one of audience adaptation. He began to change his approach and in a while was getting standing ovations and receiving more invitations to speak than he could comfortably accept. (And here the authors indulge in some fantasizing about the value of their field, their careers, and this book!)

Back to Professor Johnson. He has just accepted an invitation to give a speech entitled "Eutrophication and What We Can Do About It," for the Sandy Hill City Commercial Club's bimonthly luncheon. He immediately sends his secretary to the campus library. She brings back a pad of notes about Sandy Hill City and its surrounding county, Goodwin. The secretary found that the main industry includes the gravel pits and stone quarries south of town; a cement factory has the second most important town payroll. Sandy Hill City is one of the oldest settlements in the state and is the site of the Goodwin County Historical Society Museum, which contains, among other things, the personal effects of the town's most famous son, Brigadier General Allan Snyder, World War I ace of aces and leading proponent of the development of air power prior to World War II. Armed with this information and various devices he has learned about audience adaptation, Johnson begins his speech to the Commercial Club as follows:

"Eutrophication and What We Can Do About It." (He smiles.) I guess the first thing we can do about it is define it. (Audience chuckles.) I will define it in a minute, but first I'd like to share some of my thoughts with you as I was flying here over the lush farmlands of the central part of the state. I think far too often those of us living in cities forget the contribution the farmers of counties like Goodwin and the thriving towns like Sandy Hill City make to our economy and our quality of life. The countryside was beautiful, fertile, tilled—productive. I could see this as we landed. And as we taxied up to the Goodwin County airport terminal (which is, I was surprised to discover, a remarkably handsome facility, the newest in the five-county area I'm told), I was impressed by the thriving bustle at the airport. The growth and power of this nation is made up of the dozens of cities such as Sandy Hill City.

When my taxi drove north toward the downtown area from the airport, I was struck by the immense size of the Terrara gravel pits. I asked the driver to pull in so I could get out and look at them. Producing, as they do, 35 percent of the gravel and crushed rock used in this state, the Terrara gravel pits make a real contribution to the entire state's economy and progress and really put Sandy Hill City on the map.

When we started driving toward town again, we had no sooner gotten under way than we came upon the imposing buildings of the Snyder Cement Works, and I suddenly recalled the name of Allan Snyder, World War I flying ace and far-seeing statesman in the air force—a native son. I had a little time left before I was due at the hotel, so I asked the driver to take me by the Goodwin County Museum . . .

In the real world, most audiences would consider this much overdone, still it demonstrates that our professor could find out a great deal about his Commercial Club audience in a short period of time; he combed the public sources of information (libraries,

the key ideas

A good public speaker is audience-centered.

The public speech is a clearly understood cultural event in most societies.

A skillful speaker may successfully break a few of the cultural norms for a given type of speech, but only a poor speaker would violate a number of them and expect a good audience response.

The small group's pressure for conformity is much less than that of a large audience.

If a speaker gets an audience response, he is stimulated to greater effort; this, in turn, further affects the audience.

Excitement and emotional responses are contagious in a large crowd; the audience response affects the individual listener.

---

newspapers, and the like) and he allowed some time in the area to talk to the natives themselves before he was to speak.

Often when we are asked to give a speech we can learn about the audience we will address simply by interviewing the person who contacts us to make the talk. This person will probably be able to tell us about the room or auditorium where we will speak, about who will attend and what they will expect. As a person gains experience speaking to various sorts of audiences, he develops an awareness of what is expected from him in various speaking situations. A PTA meeting in a large urban school presents one kind of audience; a PTA meeting in a suburb presents another kind of audience—similar in many ways, different in some others. The luncheon meeting of a businessmen's service club is a different audience than a social-business dinner of the same group.

Our best advice, therefore, is to remember that there are many sources of information about audiences and you should collect as much information as you can. Further, you should give public speeches whenever and wherever you can if you want to develop skill in audience analysis and adaptation; by so doing you will gain a personal knowledge about varied audiences, how they respond to

in chapter 14

The larger the audience, the more it appreciates an elevated style of speaking plus appeals to its higher motives.

Public speeches fill our need for fantasy themes composed of heroes with high motives.

Television, with its emphasis on shoddy and unethical behavior, is a poor medium for building community-sustaining myths.

An important question for a speaker is: How diverse is the audience in its attitudes toward my position?

When preparing a public speech we often have less complete and less accurate information about our listeners than we do when we plan an interview or a committee meeting.

A public speaker can use broad strokes and get the desired response from a large audience.

---

you, and how you adjust to control their response. If you have the chance to give a speech to your class, set aside enough time to study your classmates as members of an audience. If you focus on them as potential members of an audience, you will find that you know a lot about them simply from interaction with them as you go to and from the classroom, from class participation, and from discussions. Think of them as individuals in a real audience rather than as "just our speech-communication class." Try to think through their response to you, quite objectively, and plan and rehearse your speech keeping your specific audience in mind. Adapt your examples, analogies, evidence, and positive and negative suggestions to these people—these individuals collected at a particular time to hear you.

When giving a public speech you will often have to work with less complete and precise information about the listeners than you can have when you are speaking in an interview or small group situation. As a public speaker, you seldom get as much feedback from the audience about how well your messages are comprehended and how they are evaluated as you can get in less formal communication situations. At the same time, however, you do not need as much specific feedback from larger audiences because the public speaker can use broader strokes and get the desired response with less carefully adjusted messages. A member of a large audience adjusts his listening to react to someone talking to us rather than just to me. He thus does not expect the same person-to-person adjustment he would demand if you were engaged in a conversation.

While we live in an age of electronic communication, a time in which intimate and informal conversation is prized and common, we also live in a culture which uses the formal public speech for many important occasions and purposes. The complete communicator, in the present age of increased need for quality interpersonal communication, also needs to know about audiences for public speeches and about how to adapt his ideas to them.

SUGGESTED PROJECTS

1 / Assume that a visiting speaker asks you to brief him about his probable audience. Analyze students at you school. Identify their heroes, villains, and dreams, as well as their general interests and attitudes.

2 / Pick some city or town within 100 miles of your school and analyze its Chamber of Commerce as an audience for a speech, to be made by a student, concerning student attitudes today towards business as a career. What sources would you use in informing yourself about this audience?

3 / Select a topic for a persuasive message. Using the same topic, pick two different audiences and prepare two short messages adapted to each of the audiences. Explain your audience analysis in each instance and explain your objectives in tailoring each of the messages as you do.

SUGGESTED READINGS

Clevenger, Theodore, Jr. *Audience Analysis*. Indianapolis: Bobbs-Merrill, 1966.

Eisenson, Jon, J. Jeffery Auer, and John V. Irwin. *The Psychology of Communication*. New York: Appleton-Century-Crofts, 1963.

Jeffrey, Robert C., and Owen Peterson. *Speech: A Text with Adapted Readings*. New York: Harper & Row, 1971. "Analyzing the Audience and the Occasion," pp. 78–94.

15 how to communicate with a large group

Some speech courses stress public speaking to such an extent that much of the material on interpersonal communication which forms the core of this book is neglected. We have tried to put the two-person talks, small group discussions, and conferences, interviews, and mass-media persuasion back into the center of the communication picture. Having stressed the relevance of improved daily communication in all our lives, however, we do not want to go to the opposite extreme and deny the importance of public speaking and presentations in the United States today. (We also realize that many principles of communication can be taught most effectively by having students carefully prepare messages and deliver them to large groups of people in a formal setting.)

Every culture needs to have the right spokesman say some formal words at important periods in the life of the family, institution, community, or nation. At times of beginning or ending—at the start of a new public building or civic enterprise, at the end of a project or large program, at birth, at marriage, at death—we feel the need for words to recall the past, to celebrate the present, and to dream of the future. We need to add perspective to the everyday hustle and bustle that occupies most of our time. The speech to celebrate community, family, or individual is firmly embedded in most cultures, and ours is one which has historically prized public statements at such times.

In the United States, the value of public discussion and debate is widely accepted. Every state, as well as the national government and most local and county governments, has a policy-making group of elected officials who debate important issues before settling the matter by taking a vote.

Few countries in history have been as involved in adult education and social uplift on as large a scale as has the United. States. An early and important expression of the adult-education movement was the lyceum, a group of people who formed an educational club and hired a series of lecturers to talk on various educational topics. As these clubs grew in popularity, they were tied together by state and national associations and were able to establish routes or circuits so that nationally prominent speakers could tour the country, assuring that even lyceums in remote towns could hear famous speakers. You should recall that this was happening in the days before the development of the mass media. A visiting speaker was a big occasion in towns and cities all across the land. Supplementing the lyceum was the chautauqua movement, which provided the public with lecturers in an outdoor setting much like the religious camp meeting.

Today we continue the traditions of the lyceum and chautauqua. Most every high school has a series of assembly lectures; every college campus has a number of similar speeches on varied topics by different speakers. At larger schools a student can usually attend one or two special lectures a week if he wishes.

Every business, educational, governmental, or religious organization uses a form of communication called the *presentation*. The presentation is a carefully prepared message officially ordered and sanctioned by the organization. To be sure, the members of the modern organization do use many written messages, but in the United States, the preference for oral communication is strong, and many important topics are discussed in meetings that begin with a well-prepared, carefully rehearsed multimedia presentation.

All the principles we have discussed earlier in the book in relation to interpersonal communication can be adapted, with some modification, to the public speech and the presentation.

As we noted in Chapter 14, a public speech arouses culture-bound expectations from the people who take part in the event. Scholars of speech have studied the cultural norms governing public speaking in the United States and have found some basic patterns that describe the appropriate message form and content and the expected audience behavior for many given occasions.

In this chapter, we will indicate the main types of speeches and presentations important to contemporary society and provide some guidelines for adapting knowledge and skill about interpersonal communication to these more public speaking occasions.

THE PERSUASIVE SPEECH

The participants in one common communication event in our culture come with the general expectation that the speaker will deliver a persuasive message. The audience expects a persuasive message when a speaker known to take a definite stand is scheduled to talk on a controversial subject. Our discussion of the persuasive speech will concentrate on the culturally expected features of the message.

Like persuasion in interpersonal communication, the persuasive speech tends to influence the listener's choices and to narrow audience response to the one the speaker prefers. Notice that the message source designs the persuasive speech to arouse a specific response or change of attitude from the listener. We noted in Chapter 14 that the good communicator must be audience-centered; when you are preparing a persuasive speech, the importance of studying the specific audience for your speech and of learning its hopes, dreams, hobbies, interests, loves, and hates cannot be overemphasized.

The concept of *motive,* properly defined, can be used not only as a tool to criticize persuasive speaking but also to help the person preparing a speech. We have examined in detail in Chapter 9 how persuasive messages use the device of saying that a person has such-and-such a motive in order to build him up or cut him down. Our concern here is with the idea of motive as descriptive of what, in fact, drives members of the audience to act the way they do. Many people talk of motivating other people. When a salesman says he must motivate the customer to buy the product and a teacher says he must motivate the student to study for a test, they seem to be saying that they can install within the customer or the student a motor which will impel the customer to buy and the student to study. We must realize that whatever basic motives the listeners possess are in them already, and as persuasive speakers, we have to adapt to the motives present in the audience. We cannot install motives in people because motives develop in a complex way, usually over a period of time. A person's motives are influenced by his heredity, his upbringing, and the people after whom he has decided to model himself.

A person may develop further wants, motives, and goals while caught up in a chaining fantasy in a small group meeting or while having a series of deep conversations with another person, but when a person goes to hear a persuasive speech, his motive structure is largely formed. The speaker has little hope of changing that structure. When we manage to persuade a member of an audience, we do so largely by attaching our suggestions to the motives he already has. Only by hooking into previously held motives can we make individuals in an audience want to do or believe what we are trying to persuade them to do or believe.

People tend to do what they want even though, upon careful study of the facts, what they want at the moment may not always be the best thing in the long run. A good automobile salesman tries to make the customer *want* the car first; then he suggests logical reasons why the person should buy it. The salesman often suggests, "Why don't you get in and drive it around awhile?" He hopes that when the customer gets behind the wheel and drives the car, he will come to want to have the car for his own. The persuasive speaker should carefully evaluate the wants of his audience and then present his ideas in such a way that he makes the audience *want* to do what he suggests.

We all perform much of our daily routine out of habit. When you first started senior high school, or later, college, your old habits and patterns were torn up; you had to develop new ones. Usually such periods of our lives are troublesome for us. We do not know where to go next, what to do. We often feel homesick for the good old days, or really for the good old ways. When you analyze the audience for your persuasive speech, remember that if you can show that by following your advice the members of the audience can continue in the same comfortable ways, they will often choose your suggestion. On the other hand, if you want to change things, you will have to shake up your listeners and make them believe that their present habits cause serious trouble and that they must change their ways. If a person is in the habit of smoking cigarettes, before you can persuade him to change his habit, you have to prove to him that he may be in for serious trouble if he does not stop smoking. You must remember that your persuasive message may "cost" the listener a comfortable habit; you have to be ready to meet the challenge of his resistance to change.

Persuasive speeches arise in two main situations. First, a number of people have grown increasingly restless with the way something is being done. They are unsatisfied in some basic part of their lives. These people begin to think up new and, to them, better ways to do something about it. They are now ready to attempt to persuade other people to support their drive for a change. Once a substantial number of people begin to argue and persuade the community to change things, the second situation arises: Another group becomes disturbed because it feels the present situation is satisfactory, and fears the proponents of change will succeed. This group begins to take steps to persuade the community to reject the proposals for new programs. Persuasive speeches are given either (1) to get the audience to work for, vote for, or in some way help adopt a new law, program, or way of doing things, or (2) to get the audience to work against, vote against, or in some way prevent the adoption of a new law, program, or way of doing things.

If you are disturbed or upset by the way things are going and wish to advocate change, you should develop a speech outline that has three main parts. The first point in a persuasive speech for change is, "Things are in a mess." Take the topic of the draft for military service. Someone who wishes to change it should begin with the point, "The present draft system is a mess," and then use the basic building blocks of communication (a point to be proved and the evidence, examples, statistics, and testimony of experts that support the point) to build his case against the draft. The second point in a persuasive speech for change is, "Here is my program to solve the problem." Under this point, the speaker for change explains his recommendations. He probably describes not only his recommended changes in the draft, but also his proposed changes in the law. He also urges the audience to take some positive action to help get the changes made. He may say, "My program for solving this mess is to abolish the draft entirely. You can help in this regard by signing the petition I have here in my hand." The third point in a persuasive speech for change is, "If you do as I say, here is what is in it for you." The speaker then describes in graphic detail the benefits that will accrue if the listeners follow his advice and support his proposal.

Let us see how the entire outline looks:

PERSUASIVE SPEECH TO CHANGE THINGS

I. Things are in a mess
   A. Point to be proved
      (statistics, testimony, examples)
   B. Point to be proved
      (statistics, testimony, examples)
II. Here is my program to solve the problem
   A. Point to be made clear
      (examples, analogies, narrations)
   B. Point to be made clear
      (examples, analogies, narrations)
III. Here is what is in it *for you* if you adopt my program

Of course, you will not find many occasions when the exact phrases, "things are in a mess," and "here is my program to solve the problem," can be used in your speech. You will need to phrase the points differently for each specific occasion.

The proof of the case tends to come in the first point, where the speaker describes the present conditions and explains the nature of the problem. The persuasive impact tends to come in the third point, where the speaker describes how the wants of the audience will be satisfied by the new program. Here, in shorthand form, is a quick, persuasive speech:

> Your present car is a mess. The paint is scratched, the tires are shot, the motor needs overhauling. The repairs will soon cost more than new-car payments and in the meantime you can't count on your transportation. Here's my program for you. Let me put you into this neat little Rattlesnake four-cylinder convertible. You not only get dependable transportation but you get a whole new outlook on life. The girls who won't date you now will begin to flock around you. You'll get a new sense of the zest for life as you tool down the freeway in this sweet little sports car.

The speaker who wishes to persuade an audience *not* to adopt a new proposal has several different options in planning his speech. Essentially, the basic outline consists of three points that take issue with the three main points of the speech advocating the change. Thus the first point is "Things are going along just fine"; the second point is, "The proposal would not work"; and the third point is, "The proposal would make things a lot rougher on you." The speaker need not use all three points, however. For some arguments, he may select only one and argue simply that things are just fine and submit two or three major reasons for believing change is unnecessary. He may pick several points and argue, for example, that there is no need for a proposal as drastic as the one under consideration, and even if there were a need, this plan would not help matters any.

Let us see how the entire outline works:

PERSUASIVE SPEECH AGAINST CHANGING THINGS

I. Things are going along just fine
   A. Point to be proved (evidence)
   B. Point to be proved (evidence)

II. The proposal would not work
   A. Point to be proved (evidence)
   B. Point to be proved (evidence)

III. The proposal would make things a lot rougher on you
   A. Point to be proved (evidence)
   B. Point to be proved (evidence)

The persuasive part of the speech against a proposal can come in the first point if the speaker describes the desirable aspects of the way things are and makes the audience appreciate and want to keep the good things they have. Of course, the speaker can also be persuasive in the third point by presenting the dangers in vivid and graphic terms so that the audience is repelled by the results of the new plan as the opponent presents them.

THE LECTURE

Another common communication event in the culture of the United States is one in which a speaker has important information or know-how to give to an audience. The audience comes to learn from the expert. The speech form expected under the above circumstances is the *lecture* (sometimes referred to as a *speech to inform.*)

In our culture, we expect a lecture to be an objective and many-sided view of the material. The lecturer does not intend to narrow the choices of the listener; rather, he aims to open up new horizons and give the listeners new perspectives for viewing the topic. Of course, few of the real-life lectures we attend are just what we expect them to be. Every lecturer has some biases, and often he is not as objective as the model suggests. Still, though we tolerate some departure from the ideal cultural norm, if a speaker advertised as a lecturer gives, instead, a powerful persuasive pitch for his pet legal project, we are disturbed by this violation of a cultural norm.

The material in Chapter 7 on "How to Inform" illustrates the general tone and expectations about content that people in the United States have for a lecture. The lecturer is supposed to encourage feedback and strive to achieve understanding by answering questions in a complete and open way. We expect the lecturer's language to be a clear and careful reporting of denotative meanings and descriptions of factual information. While we anticipate that the persuasive speaker will select language to slant his speech in favor of his bias, we expect the lecturer to use language in a way that represents various positions and arguments fairly; his tone is, "These are the facts, and these are the various ways people look at the subject, and you can draw your own conclusions after I have given you all the information."

THE PRESENTATION

The presentation is a speech form that has emerged within the last few decades to meet the needs of our highly developed urban culture. Most of us now work in organizations, institutions, or corporations. Representatives from various groups within the company, the church, the governmental agency, or the school need to give and get information in formal communication settings officially approved by the organization involved. Because these official speeches are so important, the people preparing them have called upon the latest communication technology to aid in their preparation. Recent developments in film, audiotape recording, television or videotape, photography, and graphic arts, stimulated by the use of commercial advertising on television, are used in preparing a presentation. The result is that the new speech form, the presentation, is essentially a multimedia communication. The speaker uses every trick in the book and even tries to invent new gimmicks to make his message effective and persuasive.

Supervisors or employees with the power to do so usually authorize a given presentation, assign the people to work on it, and decide who will actually give it. The person who gives the presentation is often not a professional speaker because the organizational position and status of the message source are important parts of the presentation. Thus, even though the vice-president in charge of personnel is not a particularly able speaker, he may have to give a presentation because the content of the message is such that someone in a position of authority in personnel has to deliver the speech. All of us who come to work in business and industry, in governmental, educational, or religious institutions, may well expect to deliver presentations at certain key times in our careers.

How you give a presentation on the job can be crucial; when you present yourself and your ideas about your particular specialty to your peers and your superiors, they will make judgments about your skill, understanding, and competence on the job. Also, many of the highest-level decisions are influenced by presentations. Lower-management people often work up proposals and make a presentation of their recommendations to the higher levels within the organization, who make a final decision.

Sometimes presentations are given repeatedly, especially for purposes of public relations. A company representative might give a presentation to visitors touring a plant. Another representative might go out to groups and schools in the community and give a presentation about the organization. The most common situation, however, and the more critical or important occasion, is the instance in which a presentation is prepared with a definite persuasive purpose, with a specific audience in mind. The audience for a presentation may be one or two people only, as was the case not long ago when a salesman for combination doors and windows gave us an elaborate presentation in our living room. He had models of various windows, a series of brochures, and slides of installations, and he demonstrated the way the various models of the windows worked as he gave his sales pitch. (We did buy five windows, but not before he had spent an extra hour telling us about his presentational speech training within the company!) More usually, of course, presentations are given to groups of people ranging in size from five to twenty, or even, occasionally, hundreds.

Presentations are the most carefully prepared, rehearsed, and tested messages given by members of organizations. Quite often the organization's top management and best specialists review a presentation before it is given. The dry-run rehearsal is the rule rather than the exception in presentational speaking.

One effective way to make a presentation is to have the audience directly experience the material in the message. In order to do this, the audience could go to the event in a field trip, or the speaker could bring the event to the audience. Suppose the person is making a presentation about the teaching of reading to children in an inner-city school. He might take the audience to the school and have them observe the teaching as it is going on. He could, on the other hand, have a teacher and some pupils from the school come before the audience to demonstrate the teaching there.

Another way to make the audience participate in the presentation is to allow it to take part in a simulation or model of a process you are speaking about. For example, members of the audience might go to a planetarium and see, projected overhead, a simulation of the heavens, or they might operate an automobile simulator while the speaker adds verbal information about highway safety.

A number of multimedia aids are useful even though they do not furnish the audience with the active participation that often yields the highest interest and understanding; there is the *demonstration* which allows the audience to be present while the speaker participates, as when a speaker mixes and bakes a cake while talking about the merits of a new cake mix and rapid-baking oven.

Exhibits are displays which resemble a demonstration without as much direct intervention from the speaker. The presentation associated with an exhibit usually involves the speaker's taking the audience on a guided tour of the exhibit. The speaker may pause at certain stations along the tour and demonstrate a process or recreate a historical event. Exhibits consist of an almost unlimited variety of materials including posters, models, mock-ups, objects, chalkboards, recorded sounds, videotape playbacks, and still or motion pictures.

Closed-circuit television and audiotape-recording equipment are extremely useful aids to the presentation. The speaker can produce one reel of videotape, for instance, which has on it photographs, diagrams, graphs, charts, filmstrips, slides, clips from motion pictures, models, mock-ups, scenes recorded on location, posters, cartoons, interviews, excerpts from speeches, and his own narration or comments. The speaker may also give his presentation and incorporate segments of videotape as he proceeds. A speaker may use audiotape in much the same way to supplement a demonstration or exhibit or to illustrate a point in a presentation.

Motion pictures provide excellent aids for a presentational speaker but at a considerably greater expense than videotape. A person making a presentation may be able to find segments of commercially prepared film available which are suitable for incorporation in his speech. The expense of shooting and editing film for a given presentation is so high that only extremely important presentations use specially prepared film segments.

Still pictures, graphs, charts, line drawings, and cartoons are dependable and useful techniques for communicating messages. Carefully developed and integrated into a well-prepared presentation, these aids are often used in our modern organizations.

Speakers continue to use the old reliable aids to presentation such as the chalkboard (blackboard), and anyone studying presentational speaking should learn to use it well. Large cards with information on them can be placed on an easel beside a speaker so that all members of the audience can read whatever diagrams, charts, illustrations, or photographs the speaker wishes to use. A flip chart is a good aid in giving presentations; this consists of a pad of newsprint-sized paper, mounted on an easel and designed to be flipped back and forth to show various charts or diagrams as needed. The speaker can have blank flip cards on which he writes with a heavy marking pen whatever he wishes to use as visual aids to his verbal message.

The flannel board is a large board covered with fabric; the speaker can prepare display items backed with the same material so they will stick to the cloth on the board. The speaker can build up his visual aid by placing illustrations, figures, and so forth, on the board as he speaks.

Speakers often supplement their presentations by using slides or film strips projected on a screen. Still pictures may show people, events, fossils, geologic features of the earth—whatever would be useful. Graphs, charts, diagrams, maps, and other graphics are easy to see when projected on a screen with a slide projector, and they are easy to store and carry. One of the most useful devices is the overhead projector which throws an image of whatever is drawn on a transparent surface upon a screen in front of the audience. The speaker can prepare drawings and diagrams on the transparencies in advance, or he can write upon a transparent sheet while he speaks, much as he would use a pad of paper, and the writing will be projected onto a screen in front of the audience.

More and more evidence is accumulating that the presentation is the public speech of the future in our culture. The brief persuasive commercial messages on television have become a popular art form and the style-setting edge of communication in our society. Children who start watching television at an early age are often so intrigued by the commercials that some of their first words and songs are those they learn from television advertising. As a spin-off from the large investment of money and talent in television commercials, we have now a well-developed multimedia technology of persuasive and effective communication. More and more organizations are drawing upon the multimedia knowledge for aid in the development of important presentations. The implications of the presentational techniques developed in business for the whole field of education are enormous. The truly gifted lecturer is probably as rare and difficult to find as a gifted golfer or chef, but with the wealth of presentational aids available many more people can give highly effective messages which will both instruct and impress listeners.

SPEECHES ABOUT PEOPLE

Persuasion is often concerned with the human personality. We have stressed the importance of interpersonal trust, liking, and respect. People are interested in personalities. We come under the spell of striking and dramatic people, and we grow to love or hate individuals until they dominate our thoughts and dreams. Our chapters on persuasion have given detailed descriptions of the techniques of suggestion speakers can use to project an image of a person to an audience. On some occasions in our culture the audience expects that almost the entire speech will be devoted to biographic information, praising or blaming that individual's life and character.

The technical name for a speech devoted entirely to praise of a person is a *eulogy*. When someone dies, often a speaker gives a funeral eulogy describing the deceased's life and interpreting its meaning in a favorable way. Usually speeches about people present them in a favorable light. Sometimes, however, a speaker devotes an entire speech to damning a person, and the name for a speech that cuts down a person in this manner is a *dyslogy*. Few dyslogies are given in the United States, although in many political campaigns there is a large element of personal attack against the opposition by the partisans.

On some occasions people gather to hear a speech celebrating their history, heritage, culture, or community. Often the speech to build group cohesion consists largely of praising heroes and attacking villains. Certain key persons, such as the founders of an organization, club, fraternity, company, state, or nation, become the focus of attention, and the speaker praises these people for values the community wishes to celebrate and recall. The typical nineteenth-century Fourth of July address in the United States was such a speech form. The speaker would praise the "Founders of the Constitution," and the "Signers of the Declaration of Independence." Many Fourth of July orations included eulogies of George Washington.

Although relatively few people find themselves called on to give eulogies, many of us are called on to give short speeches in praise of a person; we refer to the duty that often falls to an officer of a club or organization, the job of introducing a featured speaker at a meeting. The speech of introduction is another culturally developed message form.

The audience expects a *speech of introduction* to be brief, but it also expects certain things to be taken care of in this speech.

The listeners expect the introduction to tell them enough about the main speaker to enable them to evaluate his expertness and to make them more eager to hear his speech. Usually the audience expects the person giving the introductory remarks to say only favorable or complimentary things about the speaker. A good speech of introduction, however, should be more than a simple listing of accomplishments ("he has written 14 articles and 3 books, holds 8 degrees, and has won 12 honors and 7 national awards"); it should recognize the uniqueness of the audience and occasion and humanize the speaker by revealing some part of his personality that warms the audience to the individual.

The good speech of introduction, in our culture, avoids too much praise of the speaker. Whereas, in general, an audience does not object to overstatement or flattery from the speaker himself, most audiences tend to become embarrassed when one person overdoes the praise of another person who is also on the speaker's platform. (The exception to this cultural norm is the political convention or rally. We expect and tolerate outrageous flattery in partisan political meetings. There are also ethnic groups in our culture that practice more public personal praise. In considering this matter if you are to make an introduction, you must rely on an analysis of your particular audience.) Experienced speakers live in fear of the inexperienced person who gives them a glowing introduction no one could live up to! More than one speaker has had to use some stock retort to acknowledge an overblown introduction without publicly embarrassing the person who gave it. One such retort we heard was, "Thank you for that great introduction. I was wondering where you heard all those things, and then I remembered my mother knew I was speaking here tonight."

If possible, the best procedure is for a person making an introduction to check with the speaker ahead of time to find out what material the speaker himself would particularly like to have included in the introduction. In this way the introduction can tie in with what the speaker plans to say and help set the tone the speaker plans to use. Moreover, once you meet the speaker, even briefly, you have a better idea of what remarks he will prefer and what remarks he might find embarrassing. If you have an introduction written out in advance, he can check it out for himself.

At times in our culture a meeting or a conference has an opening session which features a speech of welcome to all the delegates. A *speech of welcome* is expected to deal with the person or organization sponsoring the meeting and giving the welcome (for example, "On behalf of the college . . ."), with the people receiving the welcome ("I am particularly pleased to talk with students dedicated to ending pollution"), or with the occasion ("We are most pleased to be the site for this vitally important workshop in changing attitudes toward the human environment"). Generally we expect the speech of welcome to praise the hosts, guests, and occasion. The speaker aims to make the guests feel they are important and the event is significant. Like a speech of introduction, the welcoming speech should be brief.

Both the introduction and the welcoming speech serve a primarily ritualistic function. You will recall that a ritual is a set way of doing something which has long been the habit of a group, an organization, or a culture. Both speaker and audience will be satisfied with a brief, routine comment. All of us, however, appreciate a touch of originality and artistry in our ritual speeches, and we appreciate a speech of welcome that both fulfills the needs of the occasion and goes on to do more. An assistant to the Mayor of New Orleans managed this recently when he gave a welcoming speech on behalf of the city to the members of the national Speech Communication Association convention. The speaker was a black man who began in the expected way by praising New Orleans much in the style of a tourist advertisement. He praised the tourist attractions, the charm and history of the city. Then, with a quick transition, he caught the audience by surprise and began describing the seamy side of New Orleans. He talked about the poverty, racial injustice, and crime. Many audience members found themselves sitting forward in their chairs at this unexpected turn in his remarks. The speaker then concluded with an optimistic note that the citizens of New Orleans were working on all these problems, and that a new day would dawn. His skillful blend of the expected plus the unexpected aroused the admiration of the teachers of public speaking who heard him; he had definitely made a routine speech of welcome into a much more memorable, though brief, message.

A final sort of speech about persons is one of praise which is usually given when an individual wins an award or is honored for past achievements. Again, the speaker making the award or noting the occasion is primarily praising good motives, honorable actions, good character, and effective work.

PRINCIPLES OF ORGANIZATION

The principles of organization relating to public speeches and presentations tend to be the same no matter what the occasion.

The speaker preparing a message for an audience has to do three main things in order to organize his speech for maximum effect: He must *select* the material to include, he must *arrange* the items in some order, and he must *proportion* the items by deciding how much time to give to each point.

In beginning his preparation, a good speaker collects the best information and supporting material he can. Then, after analyzing his audience, he selects from the available material that most suited to his audience. Now he must analyze the remaining material and discover a good clear central idea for his speech. The central idea for a persuasive speech should be worded as a positive suggestion: "Buy this Bearcat now!" "Picket City Hall Tomorrow!" The central idea for a lecture or an informational presentation should be a simple declarative sentence. A central idea for a lecture might be: "I will explain a good basic model of interpersonal communication."

Vaguely worded central ideas such as, "I will tell you something about interpersonal communication," are poor guides to use in organizing a speech. Complex sentences which contain several ideas, such as, "I will explain a basic model of interpersonal communication and discuss the nature of communication theory," are likewise troublesome because they require a speaker to keep *two* main ideas before the audience.

Once the speaker has picked a specific and clear central idea for his speech, he can select material which is appropriate for his audience and which fits logically under his central idea.

The next task in organizing a speech is to arrange the material in some order. In the case of the persuasive message, we have already provided the basic outlines for speeches in favor of and against a new program. If a speaker is preparing a lecture, he might arrange his ideas around a logical progression of main ideas growing out of the information. For instance, a person lecturing on the process of communication might use three points: (1) the nature of process, (2) the parts of the communication process, and (3) how the parts function together.

Speakers often arrange the points in a lecture in a time sequence, according to spatial relationships (that is, where things are located in relation to one another), or according to complexity (starting with simple concepts and ending with the more complex ideas). The time order is a good one for explaining a process in terms of what happens first in time, what second, and so on. Lecturers talking about history often use a time sequence. The space order is useful for subjects such as architecture or geography.

Lectures in mathematics or the natural sciences often move from the simple concepts to the more complex applications. A speaker needs to think through his material and decide which kind of arrangement would best suit it, as well as his audience, and as a rule, he should stick to the one kind of arrangement only.

Deciding how much time to give to each point is a matter of judgment, depending on the total amount of time allotted to the speech and on the audience's attitude and knowledge. The speaker has to think carefully about his arguments, deciding which is the most important, what material is familiar to the audience, and what is unfamiliar and must be more fully developed.

A good speech has a beginning, a middle, and an end. The beginning is called an *introduction*, the middle is called the *body* of the speech, and the end is called the *conclusion*.

A good introduction catches the audience's attention, arouses and holds its interest, and lets it know what the speech is to be about. Because a speech is different from a theme or essay in that the speaker is talking directly to people sitting in front of him, he must spend some time at the beginning of his remarks just getting everybody's attention. The listeners need a chance to size up the speaker as a person, to get acquainted with him.

The body of the speech contains the main points that make up the message proper. If, instead of speaking, you were writing an article about the same material, the bulk of the article would be similar to the information contained in the body of a speech.

The conclusion of a speech is a brief comment that rounds off the message and gives the audience a feeling that you have finished. A conclusion tends to be a summary of the main ideas in a speech, an appeal for action or reaction, or a summary plus an appeal.

When a speaker constructs a good unified speech from the basic building blocks of communication (a point to be proved plus its supporting material), he not only needs to arrange the blocks into a satisfying structure, but he must provide some connecting links among them. Thus the final important skill in organizing a speech is the ability to provide transitions. *Transitions* are brief comments composed of statements or questions or both that lead the hearer from the point just finished to the next point in the speech. Transitions tie the various points of a speech together.

Inexperienced speakers feel the need for transitions but have a tendency to use one or two words over and over again. Novice speakers say "and another thing" and "another point," or "next" and "next," or "also" and "also." The good speaker has to learn to use varied transitions that summarize the point just made, forecast the point coming next, or better yet, both summarize and forecast. He might say, for example, moving from his first point to his second, "Now that we have seen how present marijuana laws encourage drug abuse among the young, what can we do about it? The answer is to pass a law legalizing but restricting the use of marijuana similar to laws we now have for the use of tobacco." Subsequently he goes on to develop the point about passing a new law.

We are going to conclude this chapter, and this book, with a general sample speech outline which indicates one good way to plan a speech or presentation. Any speech you give is bound to have individual requirements that you will have to work out for yourself. This outline includes a wide column (to the left) in which you can comment about the communication techniques you plan to use to achieve your purposes. This method has proved useful to our public-speaking students over the years. It helps develop some objectivity about why and for what effect you put the speech together in a particular way, and it helps you develop a sense of control over your material. Many beginning public speakers can dig out much material on a subject for a speech and can make a fair prediction about the probable response of their audience (the other members of the class), but when it comes to deciding what material to use, what to leave out, and how to order the material once they have decided to include it, they are lost without a model outline to follow.

The outline on the following pages is for a persuasive speech, but the same sort of outline can be used for all other forms of public speaking if you modify the content according to the kind of speech.

No one way to organize a speech guarantees its effectiveness. Everything that you have learned in this course—about language usage and structure, audience-centered messages and utilizing feedback, the many factors involved in persuasion—are vital factors in public speaking as well as interpersonal communication. Outlines can aid structure, but the individual art, the creativity, the fun of speechmaking comes when you make the *choices* of what will go into the outline.

To use the outline, start with the left-hand column. Write out what you plan to do. Put in some detail. Then in the right-hand column write a comprehensive outline of the content of your speech.

I am starting with a striking example to catch the attention of the audience and also to reveal that my speech will be about abortion laws.

I will begin with an example of a girl who was raped, became pregnant, sought an abortion, was turned down, and became mentally ill.

This is my central idea.

Urge your representative and senator to support the current legislation in the state legislature.

BODY

Point 1

I. Our current laws regarding abortion pose a major problem for the citizens of this state, for

Supporting material

A. Our current laws encourage lawbreaking, for
1. Statistics
2. Examples

B. Our current laws cause much human misery, for

1. Statistics
2. Examples

This is my transition from point 1 to point 2.

Clearly our present abortion laws are intolerable. What is the answer? The best solution is abortion on demand.

Point 2

II. Abortion on demand is a good law, for

A. Abortion on demand works simply, for—Example of the way new law would work.

B. Abortion on demand is humane, for—Literal analogy of current situation compared with abortion by demand.

This is my transition from point 2 to point 3.

Abortion on demand is a simple and workable solution to our present abortion mess. What differences does a change in the law make to you? How do you stand to gain from change?

Point 3

III. Abortion on demand will be beneficial to you, for

    A. It will eliminate lawbreaking, thus

        1. Society will save money on law enforcement and penal systems.

        2. Society will no longer punish innocent victims unjustly.

    B. It will reduce the misery associated with all unwanted pregnancies.

CONCLUSION

I will summarize the main points of my speech and make an appeal referring back to my example in the introduction of the misery suffered by the girl who was raped, whose whole life will now be scarred by the resulting mental problems triggered when she was refused an abortion.

the key ideas

At times of beginning or ending, we feel the need for formal words recalling the past, celebrating the present, and dreaming of the future.

In the United States all forms of public speaking are prized, cultivated, and practiced.

The persuasive speech is a common and important communication event in our culture.

A public speech seldom changes the basic motive structure of a listener.

We cannot install motives in people; we must attach our suggestions to the listener's motives.

People tend to do what they want to in the short run even if the evidence indicates it will be bad for them in the long run.

The speaker who wishes to change the audience's habitual routine has the burden of proving the change is necessary.

People tend to give persuasive speeches (1) when they wish to change things or (2) when they are worried that the advocates of some change they do not want will succeed.

In our culture we expect a lecturer to give us an objective, many-sided view of his topic.

SUGGESTED PROJECTS

1 / Select a topic of concern to you and, taking a controversial stand on the matter, develop a 5–8-minute persuasive speech on the topic. Prepare a carefully planned speech outline to turn in to the instructor prior to giving your speech, as directed in this chapter or modified by your instructor.

2 / Select a topic of some complexity that will require careful explanation for the audience to understand. Develop a multimedia presentation using a range of visual and audio aids to help you clarify your ideas for your audience.

3 / During one of the rounds of speeches or presentations suggested above, your instructor will assign you the task of giving a brief introduction to a classmate's speech.

in chapter 15

We expect the language of a persuasive message to be slanted, but we want the lecture to be phrased in a more denotative and objective style.

A new speech form that evolved to meet the needs of an urban culture is the multimedia presentation.

Presentations are the most carefully prepared, rehearsed, and tested messages given as official organizational communication.

As a spin-off from expensive television commercials, we now have a well-developed multimedia technology for communication.

The speech of introduction is a special speech form in our culture.

An inexperienced person may give a speaker a too-glowing introduction that no one could live up to.

Many speeches in praise of individuals primarily serve a ritualistic function.

Because many of them are too often routine and dull, audiences appreciate touches of originality and artistry in ritualistic speeches.

The principles of organization of material apply equally well to almost all forms of public speaking.

The process of organization consists of selecting, arranging, and ordering the material for the message.

---

4 / Select a person, living or dead, whom you admire or dislike and prepare a 5-minute speech either praising or attacking that person.

SUGGESTED READINGS

Dickens, Milton. *Speech: Dynamic Communication*, 2nd ed. New York: Harcourt, Brace & World, 1963.

Jeffrey, Robert C., and Owen Peterson. *Speech: A Text With Adapted Readings.* New York: Harper & Row, 1971.

Linkugel, Wil A., and David M. Berg. *A Time to Speak.* Belmont, Calif.: Wadsworth, 1970.

index

Hitler, Adolf, 155, 160, 166
Homeostatis, 104
Human potential movement, 11
Human relations, 111
Humanistic psychology, 109
Humor, 151–152, 244

Identification, 147
Images, 107, 144, 146–149
Information, 119
Informative speaking, 261–262
International phonetic alphabet, 66
Interview
    job, 4–5
    pause in, 73
Intimate space, 85, 92
Introductions, 266–267, 270

Jackson, Jesse, 167
Johnson, Lyndon, 44

Kennedy, John F., 167, 246
Kinesics, 88
King, Martin Luther, Jr., 143

Labov, William, 50
Leadership
    contextual explanation of, 220
    formal, 223–226
    of one-time meetings, 200–203
    small groups, 219–221
Lecture, 261–262
Listening, 28
    attention, 230–231
    creatively, 236–237
    emotion, 232
    interpersonal relationships, 228
    levels of, 236–238
    persuasion, 141
    rumors, 234–235
    structure, 231–232
Logic
    defined, 189
    interview and conference, 189–190
    listening critically to, 234
Long, Huey P., 8
Loudness, and emphasis, 71–72
Lyceum, 256

McCarthy, Eugene, 148

McCarthy, Joseph, 164
McLuhan, Marshall, 1
Manipulator, 221–222
Manson, Charles, 184
Mass media communication, 169–170
Meaning, 101–102
Mehrabian, Albert, 62
Message, 18, 29, 39, 42
Message-centered communication, 106, 241–242
Message units, 177
    basic point in, 132–133
    patterns of, 135–136
    supporting material for, 132–133
Misarticulation, 48
Motives, 257
    defined, 163
    large audiences, 246–247

Nadar, Ralph, 164
Name-calling, 163
Narratives, 133
    defined, 131–132
    explanation use, 124
    personal experience, 132
National Training Laboratory, 11
Natural pitch level, 76
1984, 10, 157
Nonverbal communication, 33, 62
    emphasis, 63–64
    importance of, 62
    persuasion, 142

One-time discussion group, 211
    defined, 198
    leadership, 199
    leading the meeting, 201–202
    participating in, 203–204
    planning the meeting, 200–201
    stereotyping, 199–200
Organization of public speeches, 268–272
Orwell, George, 10
Outlining, for public speeches, 271–273

Paralanguage, 83
Paralinguistics, 62
Pauses, 33, 63, 72–73

808.5
B735s

95902

Bormann, Ernest G
Speech communication